The Psych

Why You Believe V

~~~~ ~~~

Noah Halberg

Noah Halberg

Dedication

This book is dedicated to the hapless individuals, some unusually brave and original, who challenged the crowd and lost.

Contents

Acknowledgements

I suppose I should thank my dad for providing room and board while I worked on my book. My work would have been harder and it would have taken longer if I hadn't been free to devote all of my time and attention to it. Aside from what I owe to the writers discussed in this book, my college professors John Malone and Neil Greenberg were important influences. Dr. Malone helped me appreciate the value of studying psychology from a historical perspective and I owe Professor Greenberg for much of my understanding of the physiology of needs. His encouragement of cross-disciplinary approaches to research was also helpful.

Preface

The issues I discuss in this book first came to my attention as a teenager, though I couldn't quite articulate them back then. I liked to argue on message boards where there were a lot of smart people, which made my thinking more rigorous, but which did not change many minds, at least as far as I could tell. There were some formidable debaters at some message boards, particularly the ones devoted to science and rationality. Creationists visited those boards all the time and tried to refute the evolutionists there, but they were always soundly defeated. And yet they kept using the same arguments over and over again, and they never changed their minds, unless they did it without telling anybody. I was outraged by this. I thought that if you lost an argument you should think carefully about your position and either alter it or abandon it. The creationists did not see things that way. One of the more sophisticated ones, upon losing a debate with an evolutionist, said that although the evolutionist may be right by human reason, God's reason was superior to human reason, and so he would stick to his position. In my own debates, when I was able to corner someone, I noticed that they, too, would not relent. They acted as if something important to them was at stake—if not some treasured belief, then their self-respect. I was different, though to be honest I didn't always announce when I had changed my mind. I remember that when I was 14 and a complete novice at debate that I said something stupid and had my arguments shot down with little effort; and yet I didn't stick to my foolish beliefs but exchanged them for more sensible ones. I noticed that other people did this too, but it was only a small minority. I think the people who did change their minds were overrepresented out of all proportion to their numbers in the general population at the scientific and rationalist message boards. My experiences with people outside of that circle has been that they are more like the creationists than the scientific rationalists, sticking firmly with whatever ideas are important in their circles. I didn't seek to explain why there were some people who changed their minds when refuted and others who did not; I just assumed that the people who didn't change their minds were stubborn, dishonest, or at the mercy of their strange beliefs. But, in truth, the scientific rationalists had their own dogmas and their own patriotic zeal, and I bought into it just as everyone else did.

When I changed my mind, at the same time I changed which group I belonged to. That wasn't my intention, but it did turn out that way. If you initially support extensive regulations on the right to own and carry guns, for example, and then you change your mind so that you think that most regulations on gun ownership should be abolished, you are not merely changing your mind; you are changing the group which you belong to. It works the same way if you change your mind in the other direction. But who belongs to your group? Quite likely, your friends, family, and associates. If you changed your mind on such a divisive issue you would alienate those people, at least if they cared at all about politics. Could you live with their disapproval? Most people can't and do what they can to avoid it. It is far easier and in most cases far more beneficial to just go along with what the group believes. You can abandon one group for another but for most people that's difficult. They lose all of the time and effort that went into cultivating their social networks, without which it is difficult for most of us to thrive. We rely on our family, friends, and associates to help us in times of need, and for companionship, and very often for advancing our careers or businesses. Man is, as Aristotle said long ago, a social animal.

I have had unusual experiences. I moved around a lot when I was young. On average I moved every year or two, and altogether I moved more than ten times before I went to college. This meant that it was difficult for me to consider myself as belonging to any one group. I was the new guy a lot of the time, and always conscious of being an outsider at first. I was always aware that I would soon be moving on. I never knew exactly when, but I knew that it was always possible that I would only be staying for a year. So it made little sense for me to become overly attached to the groups I was in. I got in the habit of seeing myself as more of a guest than a real member of any group. I think this has helped me retain and develop my independence of thought, but it has also, I think, made life more complicated for me in some respects.

The further I departed from what other people around me believed the more I felt myself becoming a stranger to them. I became hesitant to speak openly about all the radical ideas I had been exposed to on the Internet. And while it felt okay to debate online, where you could quit a message board at any time, it was harder to do it in person, where you had to see the same people everyday for school or something. The average person finds argumentative people to be disruptive or domineering. But I found that there are some people who enjoy debate because they, too, want to improve their thinking. When I found people like that I discussed my wild ideas with them and I argued with them.

The first college I went to had much more conservative students than other colleges do. By that I mean they didn't budge from convention and were intolerant of deviance in others. I had grown my hair out longer back then because I thought it would be neat to have long hair like Kenshin from the Rurouni Kenshin anime series. I was treated rudely and decided that it was better to fit in in appearance even if my thoughts were radically different from theirs. But even then I was keenly aware of the difference in my thinking, and in my behavior. Everyone else seemed to want to join in in group activities while I preferred to be alone, thinking about things and cultivating myself. I remember going to a pep rally or something during freshman orientation and feeling very much out of place. Everyone else that I could see was cheering for the home team, everyone in unison. I, on the other hand, didn't see what the big deal was. For them, football was one of the major reasons why they went to college; for me, football was a just a game, and not something to get overly excited about. I was urged to join in. I continued to stand there with a blank look on my face. Later on in the school year, during a home game, I was walking back to my dorm room when I passed by a student chanting the team's slogans like, I thought, a madman. I just kept on walking with a blank look on my face, saying nothing. He called me a rude name and I felt an urge to hit him, but I restrained myself. I thought a little later on about what would have happened if I did hit him. I think nearly everyone else would have supported him against me. He was a member in good standing of the crowd and I was being recalcitrant. I think you can get your car keyed if you show up at a football game at certain Southern universities with the wrong team's bumper stickers. Being the unsociable person that I was, my view was that college was for learning and not for football and if the football team wanted to play they could go do that somewhere else. That was, of course, not a very popular opinion. Anyway, I transferred after the first year.

At the second university I went to the groupishness was not so intense, though a lot of people were still wound-up around game day. I was polite with them, but I still felt uncomfortable. From my own observations and from my private reading I became aware of how even academics and self-designated liberals were stubbornly groupish, only they believed different things and behaved in different ways. While they accepted some things that the self-designated conservatives did not, they did not accept some of the things that the conservatives did accept. While at my first university I read Howard Zinn's socialist history, and while at my second university I read all sorts of conservative literature, things like Russell Kirk's *the Conservative Mind* and James Burnham's *the Machiavellians*. I also read a lot of controversial things, not despite the fact that they were controversial but because they were controversial. Other people are shocked whenever a taboo is violated, but I enjoyed violating taboos, at least privately. I attended a few meetings both of the College Democrats and of the College Republicans, but I didn't commit to either. I couldn't decide which to join. They both seemed to want only good party people and I wasn't a good party person. It can't be the case that one party is right all the time and the other party is always wrong, and yet being a member in good standing of a party seems to require always being partisan.

But people don't join parties and other groups to discover the dispassionate truth about the world. They're doing it because they want to associate with likeminded people. From the point-of-view of both the sincere Republicans and sincere Democrats my opinions would probably have seemed perverse—but I didn't venture to find out for sure; I kept my thoughts to myself, mostly, which seemed to me to be the most prudent course. I wasn't being timid; I didn't have any strong convictions because I wasn't really sure what to think.

I was becoming more and more aware over the course of my college career of just how much the individual was at the mercy of the group. I didn't want to join any of the groups with which I came into contact because they all seemed to demand a renunciation of independent thought and behavior as the price of admission. They never say this, but the assumption will make itself felt to you if you deviate too much. And yet, don't we all need to become independent adults eventually? At least if we are not to be a burden on our family or society? But if you want to earn a decent living you must network. You have to be able to mix comfortably with people not just in order to get a job but in order to keep one, because you have to deal with customers and coworkers and bosses. If you have a job you can't deviate too much from what is expected of you there, and there are norms at work just as there are everywhere else. If you want to succeed professionally in academia, for example, you have to be sponsored by established professors and grant-making institutions, and these will only sponsor you if you assent to their norms. You can't just go against those if you want to succeed professionally. And I think you'll find that these observations hold almost no matter what you do. People seem to have more freedom to deviate in some areas than others; for example, an artist can deviate more from established norms than a soldier; however, there are always limits. My observation is that deviant members are sometimes tolerated as long as they don't deviate *too* far from the norm, but they are never permitted to enter the inner circle of the group. An otherwise outstanding person may be passed over for promotion because of his deviance. I know of some concrete cases in ostensibly very different fields where this has happened.

Anyway, as these facts made themselves more and more apparent to me, and as it became apparent to me that I had to make up my mind soon what to do with my life if I didn't want to renounce certain opportunities forever, I felt like I was in state of crisis. I had, I am fairly sure, a nervous breakdown in college. I used to think everyone else was crazy and I was the rational one, and now, foreseeing that stubbornly maintaining my independence of thought was going to make it difficult for me to live life as a normal, independent adult, I thought maybe there was something wrong with me. There didn't seem to be any place for someone like me in the world. I read a lot about mental illness in my senior year of college. I really enjoyed the psychologist Kay Jamison's books. I thought maybe I was bipolar, since I was often depressed and at other times I was, I thought, highly energetic and creative. I don't think I'm bipolar now, but I was trying to understand just what was going on, and no one around me could relate or really help me. Bipolar disorder seemed like the best explanation at the time.

I changed majors repeatedly during my junior and senior years. I was trying to figure out a career path that would allow me to think for myself and do what I wanted to do, within reasonable limits, and not martyr myself. I deferred graduation for another year but left before that year was up. The reason for staying was that I wanted to change majors again and I needed more time to make up my mind. But things couldn't go on like that. I didn't see any future for me in academia judging from my experiences and my reading, and academia was one of the things I was considering. I left college abruptly. Technically I did graduate and I received my diploma, but my case was peculiar.

After college I left for Alaska. I felt like I would have more freedom there. When I thought about Alaska, I thought about wide open spaces and a lack of crowds. I thought about manly independence, the way Americans used to be. But I didn't have a very good plan for what to do when I got there. I drove to Alaska, despite the hazards of driving there in winter. I stayed in a hotel there for a couple days, maybe, and then I left. My car didn't make it back, though. It was totaled and I took the Greyhound buses back. I sent my belongings back by mail. I felt simultaneously guilty and resentful about my continued dependence on my dad, but I didn't know what else to do. I didn't want it to be that way.

After I returned home I thought about how I was going to make a living in the short run. I thought that maybe joining the military was a good idea. That could be my day job and I could read and write and think when I was off-duty. I'd be able to see the world and have a wide variety of experiences. I would get the G.I. Bill and would be able to use it to go to graduate school if I wanted another degree. I would have college courses paid for by the military if I took them while I was active duty. I came from a military family so it wasn't too strange a choice. I knew that if there was one organization known for groupthink that it was the military, but I chose to ignore the fact. I didn't have a better plan, and I felt like I needed to do something other than hang around at my dad's expense.

I had some time to do some reading and writing and thinking before I joined the military; I signed up when I was 23, I think, and was in when I was 24. I think this downtime is when I first read the works of the crowd psychologists of the late nineteenth and early twentieth centuries. When I was in college I read the works of Walter Lippmann and Edward Bernays, who did propaganda work for the United States during World War I. Their books confirmed my suspicions about human nature. Lippmann said that people do not see the world as it really is but through the lenses of their cognitive biases and partisan passions. They were, for the most part, ignorant of the world beyond their reach. Lippmann was convinced that only dispassionate experts were in a position to make well-informed decisions on public policy. Edward Bernays talks in his books about how groupish people are, and how susceptible they are to leadership. He talks about how crowd psychology was well-understood by certain experts (like him) at the time who were capable of manipulating it to their advantage. During World War I he and the other propagandists influenced as many opinion leaders to as possible to support the war in a propaganda campaign of unprecedented scope. If people, with few exceptions, took their opinions from their opinion leaders, and the opinion leaders could be brought around to support the war, then so would everyone under their sway. It worked. A country which had, up until that point, stayed neutral in European disputes entered the war on the side of the Allied Powers. Bernays's experiences in the war gave him the knowledge and skills to co-found (with Ivy Lee) the field of public relations, which is today a vast enterprise.

I looked into some of the books that Lippmann and Bernays cited. The authors were people like Wilfred Trotter, Gustave Le Bon, and Gabriel Tarde. These were the classical crowd psychologists. They provided the theory which the propagandists of the Great War applied. It seemed to me that a theory with such remarkable practical successes must have a strong basis in fact. That's the case in the other sciences, so why not psychology and sociology as well? But more importantly the crowd psychologists provided me with some answers for the predicament I was in.

Wilfred Trotter's book *the Instincts of the Herd in Peace and War* left a strong impression on me. Trotter explained exactly why I was having the problems that I was. Trotter said there are two reasons why people believe things: because of herd suggestion—that is, because we are imitating those around us—and because of sense experience. Sometimes these conflict. Some people accept herd suggestion over experience and others accept experience over herd suggestion. Those who accept herd suggestion tend to get along better with their group, and they tend to have better psychological health. Those who accept experience have more realistic understandings of their environments but it costs them in terms of their relationships with the group and in terms of their psychological health. Trotter says that people are herd animals and herd animals can't stand to be apart from the herd. This is the reason for the rational person's distress. Anyway, Trotter thought that the more suggestible sort of people tended to live more successful lives.

After a long wait I joined the Navy. I was in the nuclear program. The people there were among the smartest in the service, but still, I got the impression that their training made their thinking rigid. Whatever they learned they learned by rote. The important thing was not becoming a creative genius but learning not to make any mistakes, ever. That's reasonable enough, I guess. People get anxious when you start making unauthorized innovations with nuclear reactors.

Boot camp was actually a lot like you see in the movies. You send your belongings, including your old clothes, back home, you have your hair shaved off, and you all dress and do everything alike. Everyone is crowded together in tight quarters. You have no time to yourself. If you want to go to the bathroom you have to wait until the group goes, and then you all have, if you're lucky, 10 minutes to get in, use the bathroom, and get out. Aside from writing and receiving letters on Sunday mornings, influences from the outside world are cut off. The people in charge of you have absolute power. You are drilled and drilled. Everything has to be done a certain way; nothing is left to chance; your socks and underwear must be folded a certain way, your clothes and toiletries and other belongings must be put away in the appropriate compartments, your bed has to be made in a certain way and in a hurry, and so on. If you mess up you do pushups. If the group messes up the group does pushups. Sometimes if an individual messes up the group does pushups and people resent the guy, which is probably the point. Sometimes the chief or petty officers will ask you if you think you're an individual, and you're supposed to say "no." If you said "yes"—I didn't hear anyone say it—you'd probably be doing pushups for a long time. No, you are not an individual. You're an interchangeable unit of the group just like everybody else.

I was in the Navy for 7 months or so. The military and I were a bad match for each other so I was discharged. I stayed long enough to finish boot camp and the first part of my training at nuke school. As I said before, all the learning there is by rote. Also, the volume of work is enormous compared to what civilian students are accustomed to. Mandatory homework time can become considerably long for people who are struggling. By the time I left I was compelled to do homework for 25 hours a week (the maximum is 30). By "compelled to do homework" I mean that you have to stay in the building the whole time, and they keep track of where you've been and for how long. This is in addition to a full day of classroom instruction and labs and things, as well as physical fitness training. When you weren't doing anything else you were usually required to clean something. People were always cleaning things, even when they were already clean. I think the military actually tries to eliminate any discretionary time that anyone might have, at least while they are being trained, on the principle that the devil finds work for idle hands. Maybe it's meant to keep people from being exposed to conflicting influences. Maybe it's meant to do both things. Anyway, thought requires leisure and it was no place for any kind of thinker.

After I left the military I thought about becoming a writer. This seemed like it might be the best option available to me, though I remained open to other possibilities, like entrepreneurship. In any event I didn't think I could work for anybody else. I just didn't have the temperament to be a subordinate in a bureaucracy.

I did a lot of reading on the art of writing, but I also read hundreds of books on all sorts of other subjects: psychology, sociology, philosophy, history, political science, economics, biology, the classics, military strategy, journalism, propaganda, technology, popular fiction, great literature, poetry, art, architecture, and just about anything else I could think of. When I read most aggressively I was finishing a book every day or two. This is easier than it sounds if you listen to the books with the Kindle's text-to-speech feature, as I did with most of the books. I took notes while I was reading so I was still paying close attention. I know a lot about some of these subjects and very little about others (like art and architecture), but it was important to me that I not be completely ignorant about some aspect of the human experience.

I read more about crowd psychology during this time and about how organizations work, and I felt as if I had really understood now what my experiences meant. Some of the crowd psychologists are more understanding of crowds, more inclined to see the brighter side of them. But most of them, like Sir Martin Conway, Gustave Le Bon, and Everett Dean Martin, are not at all inclined to view them positively. For Conway the crowd is an absolute menace to individual liberty, and it's utterly stupid compared to the free individual. For Gustave Le Bon the crowd is an unthinking mass of brutes guided by an authoritarian leader, and with the collapse of the traditional authorities crowds were becoming more and more powerful. Everett Dean Martin laments the collapse of civilized discourse and its replacement by a never-ending ream of bawdy publicity.

Other crowd psychologists wrote more dispassionately about their subject. Gabriel Tarde talks about how ideas and behaviors travel by means of the subconscious, and about how they are originally formed by individuals by the association of ideas (and passions) and are spread from social superiors to social inferiors. He also talks about how there are always two major parties in a society— the party of fashion which is receptive to new ideas and behaviors, and the party of custom which prefers the old ones. Boris Sidis talks about how, when the conscious mind becomes disaggregated from the subconscious mind under the appropriate conditions, a crowd can become a mob. Sidis says that the indirect influence of a crowd leader is greater than his direct influence, since not only does the leader influence each member of the crowd but each member also influences every other member in turn. The suggestive power of an initial impression can thereby be magnified to a staggering extent. Wilfred Bion talks about how the leaders chosen by the group are often paranoid or are downright madmen. They are not chosen despite the fact that they have these qualities but because they do have them. Bion is completely imperturbable while he says these things, like he's describing the behaviors of some other species.

Another thing that has long concerned me is the nature of

authority, since this is another restraint on the freedom of the individual. The crowd psychologists talk about it, but the Italian elitists prove, I think conclusively, that hierarchies cannot practically be escaped. That doesn't mean that the individual will never be free but that it's more complicated than most people imagine to secure it. I will talk about this also in my book, as well as ways to survive and hopefully thrive as an individual among crowd men and oligarchs.

Another thing which has been a strong influence on me, and which informs my work, is E.O. Wilson's scheme of consilience, or the uniting of the natural sciences, social sciences, and humanities under a single intellectual framework. I cross disciplines freely in this book and combine them where I can. The reader can judge for himself whether I've succeeded in building a coherent intellectual framework that is consistent with the facts.

Even the educated reader will probably not be familiar with many of the ideas in this book. Many of the ideas are old or come from outside academia or from the margins of it. But I don't think they are any less true on that account. They were helpful to me and if they were helpful to me I think they will be helpful to others as well.

Introduction

My goal with this book is to give the reader a solid understanding of the nature of crowds, and of what the individual's capabilities are relative to the group. Another goal of mine, which I don't intend to accomplish with just one book, is to create an intellectual framework that integrates the natural sciences, social sciences, and humanities; but crowd psychology is only one piece of the puzzle, although I think it is one of the most important ones. I'll talk about the subjects on the borders of crowd psychology which I hope to integrate with it, but I will deal with them only in a general way. Elite theory is generally considered to be a separate subject from crowd psychology, but I treat it as a sub-discipline. However democratic simple groups may be, when they develop a sophisticated division of labor—or become organized in other words—a class of leaders is always formed, which we may call elites. The elites monopolize power and influence as much as they can, and although they rule, they can rarely act with impunity. There is no danger of the masses ever becoming free of masters, short of a return to savagery, but the masses can shift their allegiances to different leaders among the ruling class or, if a revolutionary group exists, they can shift their allegiances to that.

In the first part I'll be talking about the psychological mechanisms that create and move crowds, about the relationship between the crowd and the individual, about the different kinds of crowds, about the different kinds of crowd leaders, and about how crowd psychology has been manipulated in the past and is being manipulated in the present by shrewd people (in, for example, propaganda and public relations). I'll talk about how crowd psychology is one of the pillars of civilization, allowing laws and customs to exist which restrain what otherwise might be a Hobbesian war of all against all. Something as ordinary as waiting in line rather than shoving everyone aside to get to the front is a product of crowd psychology. Stopping at stop signs and obeying traffic lights are products of crowd psychology. Customs like religions and holidays are products of crowd psychology. But lynch mobs and economic bubbles and bank runs and wars are also products of crowd psychology.

I suppose I should explain exactly what I mean by "crowds" and "crowd psychology," and how these things are different from related phenomena. If you selected people at random from the world population and had them enter an auditorium, when they first arrived they would not be a crowd no matter how many of them there were. Suppose in one corner of the room you had a Swahili, a Russian, a Mongolian, a Chinese person, an Indian, a Frenchman, a Bolivian, an Australian aborigine, an American, and an Arab. Their backgrounds would almost certainly have little in common. They almost certainly will have never met. They may not all speak the same language, so they might not be able to communicate except through hand and facial gestures, which vary somewhat across cultures. If they tried to coordinate their activities they would have a difficult time with it.

So a crowd is something different from a mere collection of individuals. What we would have in the auditorium when everyone first arrived is a bunch of individuals. If a crowd leader showed up at the podium I imagine that it would be extremely challenging to try to make a crowd out of them on the spot. To what common sentiments would he appeal? Crowd leaders have to appeal to common sentiments in order to move a crowd. I don't think it would be impossible to make these people a crowd, but they would have to have some shared sentiments and experiences first. If you put the group through something like boot camp, they might be able to be made into a proper crowd. But then you would have the problem that not everyone spoke the same language. So perhaps they could be made into a crowd if they all learned to speak the same language first. But even then their differences could be the source of schisms if undo attention were paid to them. Also, they would most likely have to be young, since our habits tend to become fixed by the time we reach middle age.

So a crowd is a group of people with shared sentiments and experiences. They also have shared opinions. Some of the crowd psychologists use different terms for what is basically the same thing. Wilfred Trotter, for example, prefers the term "herd." Wilfred Bion prefers the term "group." They are all referring to the same thing, though. "Mob" is sometimes used as a pejorative for a crowd, but in this book I will be using it in a different way; I will be reserving its use, as Boris Sidis does, for crowds in which the conscious mind has been completely disaggregated from the subconscious mind so that there is nothing to check the impressionable, violent, cowardly sub-waking self. A mob has a mind of its own; it is the aggregation of the sub-waking selves of every member of a crowd in which the conscious mind has been disaggregated from the sub-waking self. I will be using the term "the public" to refer to the crowd of crowds that makes up a society. I will be using the term "the masses" as a synonym for this. A crowd of crowds is more general in its sentiments and experiences than individual crowds are. So the crowd of Republicans and the crowd of Democrats are parts of the same crowd of crowds, the public of the United States. Republicans and Democrats have many differences in their sentiments and experiences, but they have many in common as a result of living in the same country, making them subunits of a larger crowd. Classes are another example of subunits which make up a crowd of crowds.

I suppose I should explain just who the crowd psychologists were. Most of the writers I cite wrote their books in the late nineteenth and early twentieth centuries. They didn't form a school, but they all read from similar sources and observed the same things going on around them. The nineteenth century was a time of unprecedented change in the political, economic, and social life of Western civilization. At the beginning of the nineteenth century, the French Revolution and the Napoleonic Wars unsettled the old order, and although Napoleon was defeated and the revolution was contained, Europe would never be the same again. The

Industrial Revolution also drove the changes of that century. We can safely say that over the course of the nineteenth century, the power of free individuals (monarchs, aristocrats, and other notables) to make decisions about the fates of their societies declined dramatically, while the power of the crowd to decide the fate of their societies, including the fates of free individuals, of whatever sort, increased dramatically. This is something that Sir Martin Conway talks about in detail in his book *the Crowd in Peace and War*. Gustave Le Bon was also alarmed by the increasing power of the crowd, and he said so in his famous book, *the Crowd*. Le Bon said that the collapse of old institutions meant that the power of the crowd was the only source of authority still standing, and so naturally it filled the power vacuum. Le Bon's book is perhaps the single most influential treatise on crowd psychology that was written back then, and it inspired many others to document their own observations and develop their own theories.

Wilfred Trotter was also one of the most influential of the crowd psychologists— almost on par with Le Bon. Le Bon and Trotter are consistently cited in later texts. In my section on Trotter I emphasize certain things in his work which other writers did not. Trotter provides what is actually, I think, an excellent framework for understanding group behavior in terms of evolutionary biology. It provides what could be a sensible resolution for the current controversy between the kin selection and group selection theorists. It also provides an excellent framework for understanding how ideas and behaviors spread from person to person in a group, which is another popular topic among students of human behavior. It is somewhat similar to the meme theory, but it doesn't make quite the same assumptions.

Gabriel Tarde also had a fair amount of influence. Other crowd psychologists included Everett Dean Martin, Boris Sidis, Edward Ross, and Sir Martin Conway. There were others besides these but the ones I talk about were particularly influential or insightful. I also talk about Charles Mackay's *Memoirs of Extraordinary Popular Delusions and the Madness of Crowds*, although Mackay wrote more than half a century before the others. The World War I propagandists Walter Lippmann and Edward Bernays were influenced by the crowd psychologists and had practical experience applying the theories. So these two wrote, not from the positions of mere spectators and theorists, but as practical men. So their work should be carefully considered. Wilfred Bion was a psychoanalytic theorist from the same tradition who wrote his important works in the middle of the twentieth century. I include him to show how crowd psychology had evolved, and to offer a fresh perspective.

I also talk about *the Wisdom of Crowds* by James Surowiecki, which was written about a decade ago, and which takes a lot of the current thinking about group behavior and puts an optimistic spin on it. The author cites the work of Le Bon and Mackay and denies their thesis that people generally behave foolishly in crowds, and he proposes instead to prove that crowds can behave more wisely than individuals if certain conditions are met. He doesn't deny that crowds behave foolishly sometimes, as in the cases of stock bubbles and riots, but he seems to view these as aberrations.

Surowiecki's discussion of coordination problems is consistent with the work of Ross, and I find it to be reasonable. But when it comes to determining what the facts are and acting intelligently upon those facts, I think his work is misleading. He's arguing past Le Bon and Mackay most of the time because he defines crowds in a different way than they do, and in a different way from which most people define crowds. Surowiecki thinks that the aggregation of individual opinions constitutes a crowd, but the crowd psychologists explicitly deny this. Surowiecki's first two conditions for intelligent crowd behavior are a diversity of opinions and the freedom of each individual to determine his own opinions, but if either of these two conditions is met the aggregate ceases to be a crowd. A crowd by definition cannot have a diversity of opinions; crowds are by definition uniform in opinion. If a deviant appears it will punish him. The pressures to conform are powerful, and Surowiecki admits them. But he still isn't talking about crowds for much of the book but something completely different. The Iron Law of Oligarchy, which I will talk about later, makes it difficult for him to meet his third and final condition for intelligent group behavior, which is decentralization, or in other words the absence of hierarchical organization. Sometimes it can be met, though, as in the cases of markets and bee hives, where it works well, but in other cases, like militaries, corporations, government bureaucracies, and political parties, it probably can't work.

I agree with Le Bon and the others that crowds had become much more powerful over the course of the nineteenth century, and they seem to me to have remained very powerful up until the present day, and may actually be more powerful now. My view on why crowds became so powerful is that more and more people became concentrated in urban areas, as industry required, but this had unintended consequences. People are more suggestible when large numbers of them are concentrated in small areas. The great increase in population probably contributed to this. I strongly suspect that the increased division of labor made people more suggestible as well. Specialization narrows a person's mind, and makes him accountable to leaders instead of being responsible for his own welfare as an independent craftsman would be. Peasants are content to follow the ways of their fathers and mothers before them, and are not as susceptible as workers to the suggestions of socialists and nationalists. The workers at big industrial concerns, on the other hand, are natural fodder for mass movements. Workers could be and were organized into socialist and nationalist cadres. Also, it was much easier for democratic politicians to organize workers into voters and activists than it would have been for them to organize peasants. Also, peasants used to be dependent on the land for their subsistence, hence they were dependent on the landlords, the old aristocrats—hence on the old regime. The uprooting of the peasants weakened the old regime even as it strengthened the new social forces.

A common theme in the works of the crowd psychologists is that ideas, emotions, and behaviors are contagious. But why is this?

Gabriel Tarde had an elegant explanation for it, one that I think is true in its broad outlines. Tarde says in his book, *the Laws of Imitation*, that ideas are formed by the combination of beliefs with other beliefs, the combination of beliefs with passions, and the combination of passions with other passions, and they are spread by the laws of imitation. Ideas travel through the medium of the subconscious mind and they spread in a wave motion, with one person influencing a number of individuals, who each influence a number of other individuals, and so on; so Tarde imagined waves of ideas to move the way waves of sounds do.

Tarde's conception of how new ideas and behaviors are formed sounds to me a lot like associationist psychology, but he has a heterodox version of it. The associationist school of psychology believed that complex ideas were made up of simpler ideas, and that simple ideas were combined into more complex ones according to at least three basic laws—similarity, contrast, and contiguity. Actually, there was a lot of debate over exactly how many laws there were, and whether some were reducible to others, but that gets us into a messy debate, so I will make that caveat and continue by giving a commonly accepted version of the laws. The law of similarity states that things that are perceived to be similar to one another tend to be associated together in the mind. The law of contrast states that ideas that are perceived to be different tend to be associated together in the mind. The law of contiguity states that things or events that occur together in space or time tend to be associated together in the mind. So by the means of these laws simple ideas are combined into complex ones, and then, if Tarde is right, they spread through the medium of the subconscious mind from one individual to other individuals, and from there to still other individuals, so that the ideas of a single person can spread to an entire population unless checked by other ideas or by the unwillingness of a group to imitate others. In my book I am adopting William James's version of the laws of association, which is both elegant and comprehensive, rather than Tarde's version. Tarde's version sounds plausible to me, but James's is better supported and easier for me to work with. I will talk about it in detail later in the book.

Tarde has more to say on the ways in which ideas are spread. He says that ideas tend to spread from social superiors to social inferiors. This is an important point to keep in mind; I will refer to it frequently later on.

A prominent theme in the work of the crowd psychologists is the conflict between the individual and the group. This theme is especially prominent in the works of Trotter and Conway. Trotter thought that the individual's departure from the thinking of his group was a source of profound psychological distress. He says that people, as herd animals, have evolved so that we cannot live without other people. In the wild, herd animals that depart from the group starve or get eaten. Selective pressures have ensured that only the most suggestible have survived.

Conway talks about how the crowd is totally intolerant of deviance within its ranks, as any individual could potentially form a new crowd which exists not only apart from, but necessarily in opposition to, the old crowd. From where would the recalcitrant individual draw his recruits? They have to come from somewhere. Most likely they would come from his old crowd, at least in large part. But a gain for the new crowd is a loss for the old crowd. At some point the new crowd might overtake the old crowd and threaten its existence as a crowd. Conway says that from the crowd's point-of-view, it is better that a member should die than that he should leave the group, not only owing to the fact that apostasy increases the numbers of rivals, but because martyrs are good for morale. Martyrs were great for the early Christians, after all. Conway talks about how these observations apply equally to bees, who kill stranger bees, and to Amazonian tribes, who kill people from other tribes if they come across them. And it's not just strangers who they kill. They kill members who have been absent for too long. Bees kill their own if a member has returned after being gone for a few days, while Amazonian tribesmen kill their members if they've been gone for six months. Conway says that rubber companies took advantage of this fact by capturing them and holding them for at least six months; after that point, the tribesmen were theirs for life.

Crowds are not only intolerant of deviants within their own ranks, but of other crowds as well. Everett Dean Martin puts a particular emphasis on this. He says that crowds are creatures of hate. They hate deviants the most, but they also hate other crowds. When they can, they lord it over other groups. They use victories over others to feel self-important, and they are always chauvinistic.

Another prevalent theme of the work of the crowd psychologists is how susceptible crowds are to leadership. They won't obey just any leader, though. As Gustave Le Bon emphasizes especially, they respond best to authoritative leaders. They like leaders who are totally self-confident. They despise leaders who show weakness or uncertainty. They prefer leaders who make simplistic emotional appeals, not ones who give them high-brow lectures. An intellectual may scoff at a crowd leader's shallow sloganeering; the crowd rejoices in it.

There are different kinds of crowd leaders. The two best attempts I've seen to classify them are Sir Martin Conway's and Wilfred Bion's; the rest seem to assume a uniform type of leader, or they just don't examine the subject very closely. Conway says there are three types of crowd leaders: the crowd-compeller, the crowd-exponent, and the crowd-representative. Crowd-compellers are perhaps most easily recognized. These leaders move crowds but are themselves unmoved by them. They develop their own ideas which they compel their crowds to act upon. Crowd-exponents usually don't have ideas of their own but are creatures of the groups they lead. They act as mouthpieces and delegates. Crowd-representatives act as symbols of the group. They may believe and do whatever they please in private, but in public they must conform to their designated role. The best examples of this type are the constitutional monarchs in many European countries.

Bion's conception of group leaders is significantly different from Conway's. (I will be speaking of "groups" here instead of "crowds," as that is the term Bion prefers.) Bion starts with the assumption that there are fundamentally different kinds of groups.

Groups differ in their character depending on their purpose for coming into existence. The character of the group determines what sort of leader it has; a good leader in one type of group might be a bad leader in another type. Bion says in his book *Experiences in Groups* that there are three kinds of groups, and each forms to provide for some basic need which people have. One is the fight-flight group, and these form, as the name suggests, either to fight or flee an enemy. A common example is an army. Bion says that if a leader does not either direct the group to fight an enemy or flee one that he will be abandoned as a leader in favor of someone who will. Bion says in complete seriousness that the group prefers someone paranoid, because if it is not obvious to the group who the enemy is it will be obvious to a paranoid person. A second type of group is the dependence group. In this group, everyone is dependent on the leader, who is assumed to have some kind of supernatural powers. Bion says, again in complete seriousness, that the group prefers an actual madman to be in charge. Magical and religious cults are common examples of this type of group. The third type of group, which I found to be more nebulous than the other two, is the pairing group. Pairing groups have to do with mating or with the arrival of some long-awaited person or thing. Aristocracies and messianic cults both belong to this category. The leader is the couple or the unborn genius or the coming messiah. In Bion's conception, it is possible for the leader of a group to be a supernatural entity or someone who is otherwise not present with the group.

Bion talks about a fourth kind of group, but this one is not at all like the others, but exists in each of them and has a special role to play. The first three types are assumption groups. They are concerned with maintaining the existence of the group, and indeed, they believe that the groups exist for their own sake and not for any kind of purpose. The special fourth kind of group is the work group. This group makes sure that the group performs the tasks for which it was formed. Most of the members of the group, including the assumption group leader, are beholden to the beliefs and customs of the group even if they hamper the group's ability to achieve its goals. The work group, on the other hand, has a strong grasp of reality, and it has the know-how to accomplish group goals. But it is always, by necessity, a small group. Bion says this is because the majority of people reject the demands of personal development. That is the far easier course, so most people take it.

Another common theme in the works of the crowd psychologists is how the judgment of crowds is usually poor. Le Bon, Conway, and Lippmann put a particular emphasis on this. Le Bon says that the crowd is capable only of the most rudimentary form of reasoning and is moved almost wholly by emotional appeals. Conway says that all nations are natural born fools and have no choice but to rely, for better or worse, on the ideas given to them by their crowd-compellers. For Conway, it is free individuals who possess intelligence, never groups. Lippmann was a journalist and one of his main interests was in how the public got the information that formed their opinions, and how they acted upon that information. People don't know what is going on outside of their immediate surroundings but must rely on the reports of others. In other words, on reporters and experts. But he says that most people don't keep up with currents events and don't bother much about educating themselves. Outside of their immediate environments and particular specialties, people are hopelessly ignorant. And then there is the matter of what people do with the information that they do get. Lippmann talks about all the cognitive biases people have, about how people are swayed by partisan passions. This is the sorry state of the public mind, the public opinion upon which government officials are chosen and public policy is decided. Lippmann was convinced that only impartial experts could make sensible decisions on public policy, and that decision-making should be left in their hands, and that the public should be persuaded to go along with expert decisions. So if, in a democratic government, public policy must equal public opinion, it seemed sensible to Lippmann to change public opinion to fit public policy, and not to change public policy to fit public opinion, as it was then the custom to advocate.

In my book I'll also be talking about the practical applications of crowd psychology. As I talked about in my preface, Edward Bernays, Walter Lippmann, and others used their knowledge of crowd psychology to muster support for America's intervention in World War I on the side of the Allied powers. Bernays co-founded the field of public relations with his knowledge of crowd psychology and his experience of applying it in World War I. Some of the examples Bernays gives of applied crowd psychology in his book *Propaganda* are remarkable. In one case, a struggling industry was not only saved but made into a booming industry entirely by the use of propaganda. Recall that people tend to imitate others, especially if they are perceived to be socially superior. The agents of the velvet industry in Bernays's day knew this, and so they got in contact with some distinguished French noble ladies and convinced them to wear velvet. They did. French clothing designers and manufacturers responded by making more velvet. Businesses in the United States followed suit. Large stores started selling more velvet and the small ones did too, following the example of the large stores. So the top opinion leaders in fashion were the distinguished French noble ladies, and the others formed layers of an opinion hierarchy, each imitating the opinion leaders above it. At the bottom was the ordinary American woman who wanted to be fashionable. Yet ordinary consumers had no idea why they bought the things they did. As I said in the preface, the same sort of thing was done in World War I: the propagandists influenced as many opinion leaders as possible to support the war, and then all the people under their sway supported it too.

One last thing I will talk about on this subject is how crowd psychology is pertinent to current events. It's incredibly important for understanding the world we live in today. We've been seeing classic crowd behavior in the Middle East since the 2011 revolts. Other governments are also under pressure. Modern electronic communications have changed the ways in which crowds are formed, and have, on balance, increased their power. It is now possible to create a crowd of people who don't live anywhere near each other; all their communications can take place through

Facebook, email, Skype, cell phones, and the rest. The Internet has proven incredibly difficult for the authorities to control, which means that while governments could stop people from forming and coordinating crowds in the past, now crowds can organize on the Internet. I think this is why the Arab revolts happened in 2011 and not in 2001. The technology just was not sophisticated enough yet, and not widely available enough to pull it off.

The second part of my book is about elite theory. Elite theory is the subfield of sociology concerned with how elites are formed, how they rule, and how they are replaced. Notwithstanding the democratic slogans of our day, all societies are ruled by elites— by a small minority who control most of the wealth, honors, important positions, weapons, expertise, and other instruments of power and influence. The most important theorists on this subject were the Italian elitist school who wrote their works about a century ago. These were Gaetano Mosca, Vilfredo Pareto, and Robert Michels. I will also be discussing the work of a neglected English writer named W.H. Mallock who had similar ideas. I'll also be discussing the work of Joseph Lopreato and Timothy Crippen, two Darwinian sociologists of our day who have attempted to explain sociology in terms of evolutionary theory and behavioral science. The Italian elitists were important influences on Lopreato and Crippen, and as you will see they are definitely on to something. The Italian elitists aren't just consistent with the ethological studies of dominance hierarchies but are consistent with biology on the topics of deception and self-deception as well. A common theme in the work of the Italian elitists is that rising elites claim to be working on behalf of the whole society, but when they finally obtain power they always become the new elites; the masses have only effected a change in masters. According to Michels's Iron Law of Oligarchy, whenever a group becomes organized a bureaucracy is formed, but whenever a bureaucracy is formed the rank-and-file surrender their power to the people who control it. He gives exhaustive proof of this in his book, *Political Parties*.

I've covered Mallock's work in order to show that real democracy is not possible in economic life, just as the Italian elitists show that it is not possible in political life—I mean, outside of small, primitive, self-contained communities. It's true that there are no central planners in a free market economy, but it's also true that large corporations—oligarchies—dominate it. The socialists argued that the capitalists were just skimming profits from the laboring classes and were not doing any real work. It followed that the capitalists could be eliminated without compromising industrial efficiency. The workers could govern themselves. However, as Mallock demonstrates, with actual examples of utopian socialist communities, workers cannot organize themselves efficiently without masters. It's not just the capital that they need from capitalists; they also need their brains and initiative, as well as the firm hand to organize them properly and keep them doing what they are supposed to be doing. When everyone is capable of vetoing all collective action, and leaders can be replaced on a whim, productivity collapses and the group lives at the margins of subsistence.

There is another reason why socialism fails, Mallock says, and that's because people will not do their best work without hope of personal gain. They don't care for their tools and they don't care about their own property or the property of others. The reason why the socialists were opposed to private property was because they thought, with reason, that political democracy was a sham if private property were permitted. A small elite would always take control over the instruments of production and would control most of the community's wealth, and they would use their economic might to obtain political power over everyone else. Mallock concedes this point but says that nevertheless, the alternative is far worse. Whenever socialism has been tried, the community has either collapsed or else it has reverted to allowing private property. Mallock bases his conclusions on hard evidence, not on ideology, and his arguments are rigorous. His conclusion is that hierarchy is indispensable in civilized life.

At first sight it would appear that the ideas of the Italian elitists and Mallock are inconsistent with Bion's theory. Bion argues that it is the group that has the power and the leader must play his proper role in order to continue in his position. The Italian elitists and Mallock, on the other hand, argue that it is the leaders who have the power and the masses are nearly powerless without leadership. I think these two positions can be reconciled, however. I think Bion is right about small groups that lack a sophisticated division of labor. However, the larger a group becomes and the more sophisticated its division of labor gets, the larger its bureaucracy grows, and the more indispensable the bureaucracy becomes. The rank-and-file lose power to the leaders as a result.

There is another apparent difficulty to be resolved. It's important to distinguish between the crowd leader and the bureaucracy, because they behave in different ways. As William H. Whyte argues in *the Organization Man*, managers adhere closely to convention and are always skeptical of innovation, whether it comes from below or above or from the outside. They resent attempts by the CEO to direct them against their will. The CEO is more skeptical of the organization than the middle managers are, and wishes it to become a pliant instrument in his hands. So I was thinking that in well-organized groups, there are three basic parts: the crowd leader or top boss, the oligarchy or bureaucracy, and the masses or workers. Each of these has its own interests and sometimes these interests come into conflict. In a group like this, the only serious contenders for power are the top boss and the bureaucracy. In a small group with a limited division of labor, there may be nothing that resembles an oligarchy or bureaucracy, so that there is only the crowd leader and the masses. The masses are not dependent upon a bureaucracy but can replace the leader directly if he tramples on or disregards their sensibilities. So the masses have the most power in this arrangement.

But that brings up another apparent difficulty. Vilfredo Pareto says that an oligarchy may be either innovative or conservative. I think this is true. But that would suggest that identifying oligarchies with bureaucracies is a bit of a stretch. Is there such a thing as an innovative bureaucracy? Maybe. I am using the word "bureaucracy" to refer to a subgroup of people who manage the conduct of specialized workers in a group with a sophisticated division of labor. This definition fits both middle managers and ruling bands of financiers and industrialists. A ruling band of financiers and industrialists will tend to be more innovative than a ruling band of soldiers, landlords, and priests. Can a corporate bureaucracy be innovative? I think that perhaps it can be. The technology companies of our day are a lot more innovative than more traditional industries. Private sector bureaucracies are almost certainly more innovative than public sector bureaucracies. This is because the profit motive exists in the private sector and so companies and individuals have incentives to take calculated risks, although they might choose not to take them. In the public sector, there are very few incentives for risk-taking; for nearly all bureaucrats nearly all of the time, there are no incentives at all for taking risks. Government bureaucrats manage the property of others; they don't manage their own property while at work. Also, they stand to lose their jobs if they don't follow an elaborate list of rules. So they are by nature risk-averse.

In the third part of my book I elaborate on the theories I discuss in the first two parts. By then the reader will have a good idea of how ideas and behaviors are spread but perhaps not how they are originally formed. In Part Three I explain how ideas and behaviors are formed. They are formed by the laws of association, which are derived ultimately from the Law of Habit, which is the backbone of William James's psychology. I explain how the laws of association form categories of ideas, and how these categories actually influence what we see with our eyes; most of what we see is not raw sensation. If you had a different set of mental categories, you would literally see the world in different ways. If you saw it in different ways you would think about it differently and react to it differently. Some sets of categories correspond better to the world outside our heads than other sets do. So in the absence of social pressure it would pay an individual to constantly revise his categories and their contents in order to think about and react more effectively to his environment. But note the caveat. Social pressures compel us to accept the customary categories, which might serve an individual reasonably well but are probably not the best since they must be simple enough and palatable enough for the least capable of the group to adopt. A person who innovates with mental categories will find himself out-of-synch with the other members of his group, and they might even turn against him for spreading what they consider to be dangerous ideas. I think this is what happened to Socrates, who of course was killed by the mob, and I think that Plato's doctrine of forms is really about forming better mental categories. I will argue that Thomas Kuhn's theory of scientific revolutions is really about the same thing. I will show that the military strategist John Boyd had very similar ideas.

In this section I talk about how Kay Jamison's work on the relationship between creativity and mental illness. An extraordinary number of famous artists, poets, writers, and composers displayed symptoms of bipolar or unipolar depression and many committed suicide. I think this may be explained partially by Trotter's work. Developing new ways of thinking about things may provide a person with considerable advantages, but it separates him mentally from the rest of the group. This causes psychological distress. This could help explain why the genes for such debilitating illnesses have not been selected out.

In my final chapter I'll reveal my plan so far for a complete theory of human nature. It combines what I have talked about in this book up until then with some ideas from other fields which complement them. In that chapter I'll talk about how our ideas and our behaviors are ultimately determined by our physiological needs. I define "physiological needs" broadly. A narrow definition would include the needs pertaining to basic life processes, needs which, if not fulfilled, would result in bodily damage or death—so things like food and water, and an environment which is not too hot or too cold. My definition includes these things along with the needs identified by Abraham Maslow in his hierarchy of needs. These include, in addition to basic physiological needs, the need for safety, the need for love and belonging, the need for esteem, and the need for self-actualization. In James's version of the laws of association, which I accept, interest acts as a filter to what ultimately enters our minds; only the simple ideas that pass through the filter of interest are combined to form complex ideas. The mental categories I referred to previously are formed in this way. But what determines what is "interesting"? I argue that it is our physiological needs, broadly defined. If this is true, then it means that our needs determine our mental representations of the world, the only ones we will ever know. We'll never see the world as it really is, independently of our senses and brain processes. This is consistent with the *Umwelt* theory of the evolutionary biologist Jakob von Uexküll.

The theory I'm developing here has implications for crowd psychology. As I will talk about later, Bernays relied on the psychologist William McDougall's list of basic instincts in appealing to the masses. Among these were the desire for food, the desire for sex, and the desire for shelter. I was thinking that Bernays's theory could be reframed in terms of Maslow's hierarchy of needs. So a propagandist would appeal to at least one of the needs in the hierarchy in persuading people to do things. There are good reasons for reframing the theory this way. One is that economic theory can also be reframed in terms of human needs. It already has been, actually. Carl Menger, one of the pioneers of the Marginal Revolution that established the modern theory of value, framed his theory in terms of needs. A thing was a good and had value if and only if it satisfied some human need. Another pioneer of the Marginal Revolution, William Stanley Jevons, says in his *Theory of Political Economy* that economic science obeys the laws of human physiology. He claims that he was inspired by an obscure book that sought to establish this point.

But it isn't just ideas that pass through the sieve of physiological needs. Behavior does too. This was one of the most important ideas of the behaviorist Clark Hull. It was called drive theory. The idea was that what causes people to behave one way rather than another is their physiological needs. People and other animals act so as to satisfy their needs; if they don't they won't survive or thrive. If an animal is hungry it will act so as to obtain food. If it is successful it will continue to behave in the future in the way that allowed it to satisfy its hunger. If its efforts failed, it will behave in those ways less often in the future. It will try something else, and if that works it will repeat *that* behavior. The same idea holds for obtaining water or mates or, I am willing to bet, anything else in Maslow's hierarchy of needs.

So this is how ideas and behaviors which are not strictly instinctive are formed. And by the final chapter the reader will have a good idea of how they spread to others in a group. I argue in the final chapter that Tarde's law that social inferiors imitate social superiors is a special case of a more general law: people imitate those who have the same immediate needs that they do and who have been successful in meeting them. So if you're trying to become an actor (one way of meeting the need for esteem) then you'll tend to imitate successful actors. If you're trying to get rich you'll imitate those who have made a lot of money. If you're trying to lose weight you'll imitate people who have successfully lost weight or who claim to know how best to do so. Note that people don't always know how best to satisfy their needs. So people are "rational" in the sense that they always act so as to satisfy their physiological needs, but they are "irrational" in the sense that they don't always know how best to do that. That's why people get ruined buying into scams or economic bubbles. So we could frame this as a basic law of crowd psychology: the ideas and behaviors that tend to spread in a population are those which are perceived to satisfy human needs. "Perceived" is a critical qualifying word.

In the final chapter I also have a section on the arts. I rely heavily upon the theory developed by the mythologist Joseph Campbell in his first volume of *the Masks of God*. I should note that Campbell's work, particularly *the Hero with a Thousand Faces*, is popular among artists, and is used by screenwriters for example when writing their scripts. *Star Wars* and the *Lion King* were heavily influenced by Campbell's work.

Anyway, Campbell's argument is that mythology (a term which includes religion) is the mother of the other arts and that a functioning mythology is a system of culturally-conditioned sign stimuli. Sign stimuli play a central role in the instinctive behavior of all species, not just our own. Campbell says that these are images which exist in the subconscious minds of each species. Every human shares a set with every other human. These trigger instinctive behaviors when we encounter stimuli in our environments that match them closely enough. Newborn chicks run for cover when they see something that resembles a hawk, even if it is a man-made object. But they won't run when they see a pigeon or some other bird which is not a natural enemy of the species. Even if hawks were to disappear from the world, the images would still exist in the subconscious minds of the chicks, ready to be activated by art like the man-made object in his example. We are the same way. We have images in our subconscious minds that correspond to the stimuli in our ancestral environments, but which we might not encounter in day-to-day life in a modern civilization. Nevertheless, these images can provoke responses from us if we find them in a work of art.

Campbell talks about super-normal stimuli and how these are used in art. Super-normal stimuli are exaggerated versions of the stimuli that an animal normally responds to, and it will actually prefer artificial stimuli with exaggerated features to the real thing if presented with both. So the males in one species of butterflies prefer darker females to lighter ones, and they will choose an extremely dark man-made object that looks like one of its species over a real female, if presented with both. Campbell thinks we are the same way. The gods themselves are super-normal stimuli. We also make use of them in all sorts of rites and rituals. Human females have used make-up to improve their appearances for thousands of years, and Campbell thinks this is another example of super-normal sign stimuli.

Campbell explains our propensity to create super-normal stimuli for ourselves with the ethology of play. He says that we are immature apes, so we retain the ability to play well into adulthood.

Campbell says that there are two kinds of sign stimuli—a very specific stereotyped kind, and a more general open kind. Our species doesn't have any stereotyped sign stimuli, he says; ours are all the open kind. What that means is that we only inherit general patterns; the specific forms which we respond to are determined by cultural conditioning. These are unique to each cultural group. So Westerners, Indians, Japanese, and Native Americans respond to sign stimuli which have much in common but which are each expressed in distinct forms. I argue in this section that crowd psychology accounts for the cultural part of our systems of sign stimuli, our mythologies.

I talk a bit about the mental processes of artists. I think they're combining ideas by the laws of association just like other creative people do, but they combine fiction with fact in creating models of the world, whereas a scientist or engineer would ideally combine only facts in their models of the world. These models are fictions to the extent that they are simplified accounts of the facts, but the goal is always consistency with the facts. Artists are often deviants, and seem to others to be unsociable, and I think this is due to the fact that, owing to the nature of the work they do, they must have different ideas than the crowd does. But they pay the price in terms of their mental stability, as Trotter would have predicted. Again, as Jamison shows, rates of mental illness and suicide among artists are high compared to the rest of the population.

Finally, I present Boyd's theory of war. It's actually a theory of how to win in any competitive situation. I've said already that it's a theory of learning; I should note that it is also a theory of management. Anyway, the ability to develop new ideas and behaviors in response to changing conditions is one of the greatest advantages that an individual enjoys over the group. Boyd doesn't say that, but it's important to me to point that out. So Boyd's theory provides a way for individuals to compete successfully in a world dominated by crowds. It's also consistent with the ideas presented up until then. So I've done everything I can to make everything in this book consistent with everything else. Hopefully it should all appear seamless.

Chapter 1: The Mental Mechanisms of the Crowd

Mass Hypnosis

When I was in my senior year of high school I went to see a hypnotist's performance. By that point I had already acquired a skeptical habit of mind, so I wasn't expecting very much from it. I figured it would be like a magician's show, where there was always some unexciting explanation for the apparently impossible. But no: hypnotism was actually, to all appearances, a real and a quite astounding phenomenon. The hypnotist called volunteers from the audience, who I am fairly certain were not secretly aides of his. There was too much spontaneity about it all. The hypnotist sent a lot of the people he called up back because, I think, they could not be hypnotized. But a lot of them could be and were. He had them close their eyes and relax, and he told them in repeated, monotonous, but soothing tones that they were falling into a deep sleep, deeper and deeper, deeper and deeper, deeper and deeper, deeper and deeper. When the hypnotizable subjects were hypnotized he went to work with his suggestions.

The hypnotist got people to do all sorts of bizarre things. He told one guy he was a Russian ballerina. The guy believed it and played the part. And, what was totally stunning to me, he was actually really good. He spun around in midair like he had been practicing for years. I wondered if it had been some elaborate set-up, but again, everything seemed too spontaneous. One person was told that he was driving down a road and was being chased by ninjas. He believed it. He was going hundreds, or maybe it was thousands, of miles per hour down that road but those ninjas were fast and they were catching up to him. The ninjas were running, not driving. The audience was laughing at everything that was going on, so the hypnotist made one girl the laughter police. Her job was to write tickets for people who were laughing, and she performed her duty conscientiously. But so many people were laughing that the poor girl couldn't catch them all. The exasperated girl pleaded with the audience to stop laughing, but this only made things worse.

What do psychologists have to say about hypnosis? Actually, modern psychologists, at least the more visible ones, don't talk about it much if they talk about it at all. Is it a real phenomenon then, or did my eyes deceive me? According to William James, the founder of American psychology, hypnosis is indeed a real phenomenon. While under hypnosis people can indeed be gotten to believe anything. Post-hypnotic suggestions can indeed be instilled by a hypnotist, and subjects really will carry them out. But as James's student Boris Sidis says, sometimes hypnotists encounter resistance from the conscious mind. Some of the things James has to say about hypnosis in *the Principles of Psychology* are astonishing. Even bodily processes over which we ordinarily have no control, like sneezing, the beating of the heart, and the temperature of the body can be manipulated. A chair may become a lion in the mind of the subject or a broomstick may become a beautiful woman. One subject may believe that she is married to her hypnotizer, and another one might act out a crime suggested to him. But James does not think people are mere puppets in the hands of their hypnotizers; they know at some level that it is all an act, and they resist if they are asked to do something which they would ordinarily strongly oppose. I'm going to quote James at length:

> First of all comes amnesia. In the earlier stages of hypnotism the patient remembers what has happened, but with successive sittings he sinks into a deeper condition, which is commonly followed by complete loss of memory. He may have been led through the liveliest hallucinations and dramatic performances, and have exhibited the intensest apparent emotion, but on waking he can recall nothing at all. The same thing happens on waking from sleep in the midst of a dream— it quickly eludes recall. But just as we may be reminded of it, or of parts of it, by meeting persons or objects which figured therein, so on being adroitly prompted, the hypnotic patient

will often remember what happened in his trance. One cause of the forgetfulness seems to be the disconnection of the trance performances with the system of waking ideas. Memory requires a continuous train of association. M. Delboeuf, reasoning in this way, woke his subjects in the midst of an action begun during trance (washing the hands, e.g.), and found that they then remembered the trance. The act in question bridged over the two states. But one can often make them remember by merely telling them during the trance that they shall remember. Acts of one trance, moreover, are usually recalled, either spontaneously or at command, during another trance, provided that the contents of the two trances be not mutually incompatible.

Suggestibility. The patient believes everything which his hypnotizer tells him, and does everything which the latter commands. Even results over which the will has normally no control, such as sneezing, secretion, reddening and growing pale, alterations of temperature and heart-beat, menstruation, action of the bowels, etc., may take place in consequence of the operator's firm assertions during the hypnotic trance, and the resulting conviction on the part of the subject, that the effects will occur. Since almost all the phenomena yet to be described are effects of this heightened suggestibility, I will say no more under the general head, but proceed to illustrate the peculiarity in detail.

Effects on the voluntary muscles seem to be those most easily got; and the ordinary routine of hypnotizing consists in provoking them first. Tell the patient that he cannot open his eyes or his mouth, cannot unclasp his hands or lower his raised arm, cannot rise from his seat, or pickup a certain object from the floor, and he will be immediately smitten with absolute impotence in these regards. The effect here is generally due to the involuntary contraction of antagonizing muscles. But one can equally well suggest paralysis, of an arm for example, in which case it will hang perfectly placid by the subject's side. Cataleptic and tetanic rigidity are easily produced by suggestion, aided by handling the parts. One of the favorite shows at public exhibitions is that of a subject stretched stiff as a board with his head on one chair and his heels on another. The cataleptic retention of impressed attitudes differs from voluntary assumption of the same attitude. An arm voluntarily held out straight will drop from fatigue after a quarter of an hour at the at most, and before it falls the agent's distress will be made manifest by oscillations in the arm, disturbances in the breathing, etc. But Charcot has shown that an arm held out in hypnotic catalepsy, though it may as soon descend, yet does so slowly and with no accompanying vibration, whilst the breathing remains entirely calm. He rightly points out that this shows a profound physiological change, and is proof positive against simulation, as far as this symptom is concerned. A cataleptic attitude, moreover, may be held for many hours. – Sometimes an expressive attitude, clinching of the fist, contraction of the brows, will gradually set up a sympathetic action of the other muscles of the body, so that at last a tableau vivant of fear, anger, disdain, prayer, or other emotional condition, is produced with rare perfection. This effect would seem to be due to the suggestion of the mental state by the first contraction. Stammering, aphasia, or inability to utter certain words, pronounce certain letters, are readily producible by suggestion.

Hallucinations of all the senses and delusions of every conceivable kind can be easily suggested to good subjects. The emotional effects are then often so lively, and the pantomimic display so expressive, that it is hard not to believe in a certain 'psychic hyper-excitability,' as one of the concomitants of the hypnotic condition. You can make the subject think that he is freezing or burning, itching or covered with dirt, or wet; you can make him eat a potato for a peach, or drink a cup of vinegar for a glass of champagne; [5] ammonia will smell to him like cologne water; a chair will be a lion, a broom-stick a beautiful woman, a noise in the street will be an orchestral music, etc., etc., with no limit except your powers of invention and the patience of the lookers on. [6] Illusions and hallucinations form the pieces de résistance at public exhibitions. The comic effect is at its climax when it is successfully suggested to the subject that his personality is changed into that of a baby, of a street boy, of a young lady dressing for a party, of a stump orator, or of Napoleon the Great. He may even be transformed into a beast, or an inanimate thing like a chair or a carpet, and in every case will act out all the details of the part with a sincerity and intensity seldom seen at the theatre. The excellence of the performance is in these cases the best reply to the suspicion that the subject may be shamming -- so skilful a shammer must long since have found his true function in life upon the stage. Hallucinations and histrionic delusions generally go with a certain depth of the trance, and are followed by complete forgetfulness. The subject awakens from them at the command of the operator with a sudden start of surprise, and may seem for a while a little dazed.

Subjects in this condition will receive and execute suggestions of crime, and act out a theft, forgery, arson, or murder. A girl will believe that she is married to her hypnotizer, etc. It is unfair, however, to say that in these cases the subject is a pure puppet with no spontaneity. His spontaneity is certainly not in abeyance so far as things go which are harmoniously associated with the suggestion given him. He takes the text from his operator; but he may amplify and develop it enormously as he acts it out. His spontaneity is lost only for those systems of ideas which *conflict* with the suggested delusion, The latter is thus 'systematized'; the rest of consciousness is shutoff, excluded, dissociated from it. In extreme cases the rest of the mind would seem to be actually abolished and the hypnotic subject to be literally a changed personality, a being in one of those 'second' states which we studied in Chapter X. But the reign of the delusion is often not as absolute as this. If the thing suggested be too intimately repugnant, the subject may strenuously resist and get nervously excited in consequence, even to the point of having an hysterical attack. The conflicting ideas slumber in the background and merely permit those in the foreground to have their way until a real emergency arises; then they assert their rights. As M. Delboeuf says, the subject surrenders himself good-naturedly to the performance, stabs with the pasteboard dagger you give him because he knows what it is, and fires off the pistol because he knows it has no ball; but for a real murder he would not be your man. It is undoubtedly true that subjects are often well aware that they are acting a part. They know that what they do is absurd. They know that the hallucination which they see, describe, and act upon, is not really there. They may laugh at themselves; and they always recognize the abnormality of their state when asked about it, and call it 'sleep.' One often notices a sort of mocking smile upon them, as if they mere playing a comedy, and they may even say on 'coming to' that they were shamming all the while. These facts have misled ultra-skeptical people so far as to make them doubt the genuineness of any hypnotic phenomena at all. But, save the consciousness of 'sleep,' they do not occur in the deeper conditions; and when they do occur they are only a natural consequence of the fact that the 'monoideism' is incomplete. The background-thoughts still exist, and have the power of comment on the suggestions, but no power to inhibit their motor and associative effects. A similar condition is frequent enough in the waking state, when an impulse carries us away and our 'will' looks on wonderingly like an impotent spectator. These 'shammers' continue to sham in just the same way, every new time you hypnotize them, until at last they are forced to admit that if shamming there be, it is something very different from the free voluntary shamming of waking hours. (p. 602-606)

So what does hypnosis have to do with crowd psychology? This is a question which James's student and colleague Boris Sidis (1898) was concerned with in his book, *the Psychology of Suggestion*. Sidis said that in order to hypnotize someone certain conditions must be met, and these are the fixation of the attention, the distraction of attention, monotony, the limitation of voluntary movements, the limitation of the field of consciousness, inhibition, and immediate execution. It seemed to Sidis that these conditions could be more easily met in crowds than in other environments, and that the orators and ringleaders who moved them were in fact acting as hypnotists. So crowd psychology is mass hypnosis and crowd leaders are the hypnotists of the masses.

I'll quote Sidis on the conditions necessary to hypnotize a subject. He says that an indispensable condition in getting a subject to accept a suggestion is to fix his attention on some spot, and to have him hold it there for no longer than five seconds:

> In all my experiments the one indispensable condition was to fix the attention on some spot and thus prepare the subject for the acceptance of the suggestion. I asked the subject to look on some particular point chosen by me, the time of fixation usually varying from two to five seconds. In my experiments with letters and figures the attention of the subject was fixed on the white surface of the screen for about two seconds before the first character of the series appeared; then, again, between each figure or letter and the next following there was an interval of two or three seconds during which the subject had to look fixedly at the uniformly white screen. In my experiments with coloured squares, or on choice suggestion, the condition of fixation of attention was scrupulously observed; the subject had to fix his attention on a particular point for five seconds. The same condition was observed in my experiments on suggestion of movements and of acts. The fixation of attention, as I said, was usually not continued longer the five seconds. Thus, out of 4,487 experiments made on suggestion, only 500 experiments (those dealing, with suggestion of movements) had a fixation time higher than five seconds. (p. 44)

If the subject's attention isn't fixed, the suggestion will not take hold. Distraction of the attention is the next condition for normal suggestibility. What that means is that the subject has to fix his attention on a spot or object that has nothing to do with the suggestion he is being given. If this isn't done, the experiment fails:

> The next condition of normal suggestibility is *distraction of the attention*. The subject had to fix his attention on some irrelevant point, spot, thing that had no connection with the material of the experiments, no resemblance to the object employed for suggestion. Usually I asked my subjects to fix their attention on some minute dot, because a large spot or a big object might have interfered with the suggestion, on account of form, size, etc. The attention had to be diverted from the objects of the experiments. I found that when this condition of distraction of attention was absent the experiments, as a rule, failed. (p. 46)

It's also important to prevent the subject from being exposed to extraneous impressions, like noises coming from adjoining rooms, or new people coming into the room after the experiment has begun. The subjects have to become accustomed to the objects in the room, and any change in their environment, however slight, interferes with the experiment; strong impressions can bring the experiment to a halt. This third condition Sidis calls *monotony*:

> In all the experiments I had to guard against a variety of impressions. Slight noises coming from the adjoining rooms in the laboratory, a new man coming into the room where the experiments were being carried on, a book dropping, an Italian playing on the street organ, and many other kindred impressions, were distinctly unfavourable to the experiments, and had to be avoided as much as possible. The subjects had to accustom themselves to the conditions and objects in the room, and any new impressions strongly interfered with the success of the suggestion. A fresh, new impression, however slight, proved always a disturbance. When the impression was a strong one, or when many impressions came together, the

experiments were interrupted and the whole work came to a standstill. The experiments could be carried on only in a monotonous environment, otherwise they failed. Thus we find that *monotony* is an indispensable condition of normal suggestibility. (p. 46-47)

The fourth condition is that the subject be as quiet and as still as possible. This condition Sidis calls *a limitation of voluntary movements. Limitation of the field of consciousness* is arguably also a condition, he says, but it is a result of satisfying the previous four conditions. When the conditions of fixation of attention, monotony, and limitation of voluntary movements are all satisfied, "the field of consciousness of the subject is contracted, closed to new incoming impressions, limited only to a certain set of sensations, fixed, riveted to only a certain point." Sidis says that contraction of consciousness can be achieved in other ways, however, such as when the subject is exposed to a sudden, violent impression:

> A sudden, violent impression may instantly effect an enormous shrinkage of the field of consciousness, and then the other conditions will naturally follow, or rather coexist; for consciousness will reverberate with this one violent sense impression and will thus attend to only the latter. There will also be monotony, since this one sudden and violent sense impression tolerates few neighbors and drives out fresh incomers. Voluntary movements will then certainly be limited, since the stream of consciousness is narrowed, and along with it its ideomotor side. The fact that limitation of contraction of the field of consciousness may occur by itself without having been preceded by the conditions mentioned above led me to consider it a separate condition of normal suggestibility. (p. 48)

It's important for the subject to banish all ideas from his mind not related to the experiment, to make his mind perfectly blank. This is called *inhibition*; without it, the experiment fails:

The experiments, again, could not be carried on without the condition of *inhibition*. I asked the subject that, when he concentrated his attention and fixed a particular dot pointed out to him, he should try as much as it was in his power to banish all ideas—images that had no connection with the experiments in hand; that had no connection with the experiments themselves; in short, that he should make his mind a *perfect blank*, and voluntarily *inhibit* ideas, associations that might arise before his mind's eye and claim attention. Of course, this condition was rather a hard task to comply with, still it was observed as far as it was possible. When this condition was neglected by the subject the experiments invariably failed. *Inhibition*, then, is a necessary condition of normal suggestibility. (p. 48)

The last condition, and the most important one according to Sidis, was *immediate execution*. As soon as the subject perceived the signal he was to immediately write, act, or choose.

Sidis noticed, however, that hypnotic subjects would not always act upon suggestions, and he hypothesized that this was because the conscious mind was filtering unwanted suggestions out before they reached the subconscious mind. So this is what keeps people, in ordinary times, from acting upon everything that a crowd leader says. But, says Sidis, the conscious mind can be disaggregated from the subconscious mind under the appropriate conditions, and then suggestions from the outside will more readily take hold. When the people in a crowd have their conscious minds disaggregated from the subconscious mind, a mob forms. Then it will commit almost any kind of barbarity.

According to Sidis, the subwaking self is extremely credulous and will believe that two and two make five if told with sufficient emphasis. It is is cowardly and servile, and will yield readily to authoritative commands, but if you show any hesitation it will show fight. It is devoid of all morality. It "dresses to fashion, gossips in company, runs riot in business panics, revels in the crowd, storms in the mob, and prays in the camp meeting." It has acute senses, but no sense. Association by contiguity is the only mental mechanism it possesses. It lacks all personality and individuality. It is unable to maintain its integrity against outside suggestions. Only the waking, conscious self can have any kind of moral ideals or any kind of will, and only it can live up to its ideals:

> The subwaking self is extremely credulous; it lacks all sense of the true and rational. "Two and two make five." "Yes." Anything is accepted if sufficiently emphasized by the hypnotizer. The suggestibility and imitativeness of the subwaking self was discussed by me at great length. What I should like to point out here is the extreme servility and cowardliness of that self. Show hesitation, and it will show fight; command authoritatively, and it will obey slavishly.

> The subwaking self is devoid of all morality; it will steal without the least scruple; it will poison; it will stab; it will assassinate its best friends without the least scruple. When completely cut off from the waking person it is precluded from conscience.

> The subwaking self dresses to fashion, gossips in company, runs riot in business panics, revels in the crowd, storms in the mob, and prays in the camp meeting. Its senses are acute, but its sense is nil. Association by contiguity, the mental mechanism of the brute, is the only one that it possesses.

> The subwaking self lacks all personality and individuality; it is absolutely servile; it works according to no maxims; it has no moral law, no law at all. To be a law unto one's self, the chief and essential characteristic of personality, is just the very trait the subwaking self so glaringly lacks. The subwaking self has no will; it is blown hither and thither by all sorts of incoming suggestions. It is essentially a brutal self.

The primary self alone possesses true personality, will, and self-control. The primary self alone is a law unto itself—a person having the power to investigate his own nature, to discover faults, to create ideals, to strive after them, to struggle for them, and by continuous, strenuous efforts of will to attain higher and higher stages of personality. (p. 295-296)

Sidis says that the suggestions given by the leader of a crowd reverberate from individual to individual in a mob; each person both influences and is influenced by others; and so a mob behaves like an avalanche, becoming more suggestible as it becomes more suggestible, and becoming more dangerous to the degree that it is taken with the leader's suggestions:

The suggestion given to the entranced crowd by the "master" spreads like wildfire. The given suggestion reverberates from individual to individual, gathers strength, and becomes so overwhelming as to drive the crowd into a fury of activity, into a frenzy of excitement. As the suggestions are taken by the mob and executed the wave of excitement rises higher and higher. Each fulfilled suggestion increases the emotion of the mob in volume and intensity. Each new attack is followed by a more violent paroxysm of furious demoniac frenzy. The mob is like an avalanche: the more it rolls the more menacing and dangerous it grows. The suggestion given by the hero, by the ringleader, by the master of the moment, is taken up by the crowd and is reflected and reverberated from man to man, until every soul is dizzied and every person is stunned. In the entranced crowd, in the mob, everyone influences and is influenced in his turn; every one suggests and is suggested to, and the surging billow of suggestion swells and rises until it reaches a formidable height. (p. 303)

Sidis attempts to quantify the energy of the suggestions from each actor in a crowd, the total amount of energy produced through their interactions, and the speed at which the total energy grows. If his back-of-the-envelope calculations are even remotely accurate, then the suggestive energy of crowds is extraordinary, even if the leader's influence is initially small relative to the total amount:

> Suppose that the number of individuals in the crowd is 1,000, that the energy of the suggested idea in the "master" himself be represented by 50, and that only one half of it can be awakened in others; then the hero awakens an energy of 25 in every individual, who again in his or her turn awakens in everyone an energy of 12.5. The total energy aroused by the hero is equal to 25 X 1,000 = 25,000. The total energy of suggestion awakened by each individual in the crowd is equal to 12.5 X 1,000, or 12,500 (the hero being included, as he is, after all, but a part of the crowd). Since the number of individuals in the crowd is 1,000, we have the energy rising to as much as 12,500 X 1,000; adding to it the 25,000 produced by the ringleader, we have the total energy of suggestion amounting to 12,525,000! (p. 303-304)

Sidis says that mob energy grows faster than the increase of numbers, and that a mob has a personality of its own, created by assimilating the disaggregated personalities of the individuals who make it up:

> The mob energy grows faster than the increase of numbers. The mob spirit grows and expands with each fresh human increment. Like a cannibal it feeds on human beings. In my article "A Study of the Mob" I point out that the mob has a self of its own; that the personal self is suppressed, swallowed up by it, so much so that when the latter comes once more to the light of day it is frequently horrified at the work, the crime, the mob self had committed; and that once the mob self is generated, or, truer to say, brought to the surface, it possesses a strong attractive power and a great capacity of assimilation. It attracts fresh individuals, breaks down their personal life, and quickly assimilates them; it effects in them a disaggregation of consciousness and assimilates the

subwaking selves. Out of the subwaking selves the mob-self springs into being. The assimilated individual expresses nothing but the energy [of the] suggestion, the will of the entranced crowd; he enters fully into the spirit of the mob. (p. 304)

How did people come to be this way? Sidis says that when animals begin to move about in large groups that they must become more suggestible; they must become more receptive to the emotions of their comrades and be able to imitate them and respond appropriately when their survival depends on it. When danger is drawing near, it is adaptive for the other members of a herd to respond with fear to the expression of fear in a single member of the herd; the most suggestible run away with the first fearful individual and survive, while those who are less suggestible and remain behind are killed. Over many generations, the less suggestible are culled and the suggestible have the most offspring, and so the species becomes, as a rule, highly suggestible. Suggestibility is the only means of rapid communication that brutes possess, and social life would be impossible without it:

> WHEN animals, on account of the great dangers that threaten them, begin to rove about in groups, in companies, in herds, and thus become social, such animals, on pain of extinction, must vary in the direction of suggestibility; they must become more and more susceptible to the emotional expression of their comrades, and reproduce it instantaneously at the first impression. When danger is drawing near, and one of the herd detects it and gives vent to his muscular expression of fear, attempting to escape, those of his comrades who are most susceptible reproduce the movements, experience the same emotions that agitate their companion, and are thus alone able to survive in the struggle for existence. A delicate susceptibility to the movements of his fellows is a question of life and death to the individual in the herd. Suggestibility is of vital importance to the group, to society, for it is the only way of rapid communication social brutes can possibly possess.

Natural selection seizes on this variation and develops it to its highest degree. Individuals having a more delicate susceptibility to suggestions survive, and leave a greater progeny which more or less inherit the characteristics of their parents. In the new generation, again, natural selection resumes its merciless work, making the useful trait of suggestibility still more prominent, and the sifting process goes on thus for generations, endlessly. A highly developed suggestibility, an extreme, keen susceptibility to the sensori-motor suggestions, coming from its companions, and immediately realizing those suggestions by passing through the motor processes it witnesses, is the only way by which the social brute can become conscious of the emotions that agitate its fellows. The sentinel posted by the wasps becomes agitated at the sight of danger, flies into the interior of the nest buzzing violently, the whole nestful of wasps raises a buzzing, and is thus put into the same state of emotion which the sentinel experiences.

Suggestibility is the cement of the herd, the very soul of the primitive social group. A herd of sheep stands packed close together, looking abstractedly, stupidly, into vacant space. Frighten one of them; if the animal begins to run, frantic with terror, a stampede ensues. Each sheep passes through the movements of its neighbour. The herd acts like one body animated by one soul. Social life presupposes suggestion. No society without suggestibility. Man is a social animal, no doubt; but he is social because he is suggestible. Suggestibility, however, requires disaggregation of consciousness; hence, society presupposes a cleavage of the mind, it presupposes a plane of cleavage between the differentiated individuality and the undifferentiated reflex consciousness, the indifferent sub waking self. Society and mental epidemics are intimately related; for the social gregarious self is the suggestible subconscious self. (p. 308-310)

The rules, customs, and laws of a society must be absolutely obeyed by the individuals who compose it, on pain of death. Blind obedience is a social virtue, but it is also the essence of suggestibility, and so we must all exist, in part, as our disaggregated subwaking selves. Sidis believes that society is prone to all sorts of mobs, manias, and crazes as a result of this fact. I would imagine that certain economic phenomena, like bank runs and economic bubbles, are also included in this category:

> The very organization of society keeps up the disaggregation of consciousness. The rules, the customs, the laws of society are categorical, imperative, absolute. One must obey them on pain of death. Blind obedience is a social virtue. But blind obedience is the very essence of suggestibility, the constitution of the disaggregated subwaking self. Society by its nature, by its organization, tends to run riot in mobs, manias, crazes, and all kinds of mental epidemics. (p. 310-311)

As a society develops and its institutions become more and more differentiated, its rules become more and more numerous and detailed, and they constrain the individual more and more in his voluntary movements, and contract his field of consciousness and inhibit all extraneous ideas. These are the conditions which create the disaggregation of consciousness, and which make suggestion effective. When something striking like a brilliant campaign or a glittering holy image fixes the attention of the public, the subwaking social self can be aroused into mob behavior:

> With the development of society the economical, political, and religious institutions become more and more differentiated; their rules, laws, by-laws, and regulations become more and more detailed, and tend to crimp the individual, to limit, to constrain his voluntary movements, to contract his field of consciousness, to inhibit all extraneous ideas—in short, to create conditions requisite for a disaggregation of consciousness. If, now, something striking fixes the attention of the public—a brilliant campaign, a

glittering holy image, or a bright "silver dollar"—the subwaking social self, the demon of the demos, emerges, and society is agitated with crazes, manias, panics, and mental plagues of all sorts. (p. 311)

Not only that, but individuality is crushed under the force of convention. It is the suggestions of the herd that decide what we will wear, how we will speak, what we will think, and so on. A socialized individual is one made into an automaton by the demands of social organization:

With the growth and civilization of society, institutions become more stable, laws more rigid, individuality is more and more crushed out, and the poor, barren subwaking self is exposed in all its nakedness to the vicissitudes of the external world. In civilized society laws and regulations press on the individual from all sides. Whenever one attempts to rise above the dead level of commonplace life, instantly the social screw begins to work, and down is brought upon him the tremendous weight of the socio-static press, and it squeezes him back into the mire of mediocrity, frequently crushing him to death for his bold attempt. Man's relations in life are determined and fixed for him; he is told how he must put on his tie, and the way he must wear his coat; such should be the fashion of his dress on this particular occasion, and such should be the form of his hat; here must he nod his head, put on a solemn air; and there take off his hat, make a profound bow, and display a smile full of delight. Personality is suppressed by the rigidity of social organization; the cultivated, civilized individual is an automaton, a mere puppet.

Under the enormous weight of the socio-static process, under the crushing pressure of economical, political, and religious regulations there is no possibility for the individual to determine his own relations in life; there is no possibility for him to move, live, and think freely; the personal self sinks, the suggestible, subconscious, social, impersonal self rises to the surface, gets trained and cultivated, and becomes the hysterical actor in all the tragedies of historical life. (p. 311-312)

Laws and mobs are derived from the same cause, according to Sidis. Under normal conditions, social activity works wonders, but when the social mind becomes disaggregated by suppressing the individual personality too much in favor of the unwaking social self, a society can exhibit the worst of mob behaviors. I suspect that this is what happened with the fascist regimes that were created between the World Wars:

> Laws and mobs, society and epidemics—are they not antagonistic? In point of fact they are intimately, vitally interrelated, they are two sides of the same shield.

> Under normal conditions social activity no doubt works wonders; it elaborates such marvellous products as language, folklore, mythology, tribal organization, etc.—products that can only be studied and admired by the intellect of the scientist. When, however, the social conditions are of such a nature as to charge society with strong emotional excitement, or when the institutions dwarf individuality, when they arrest personal growth, when they hinder the free development and exercise of the personal controlling consciousness, then society falls into a hypnoid condition, the social mind gets disaggregated. The gregarious self begins to move within the bosom of the crowd and becomes active; the demon of the demos emerges to the surface of social life and throws the body politic into convulsions of demoniac fury. (p. 312-313)

Sidis goes on to talk about religious revivals, crusades, witch hunts, economic bubbles, and other examples of mob behavior.

Sidis says that the Middle Ages were a time of extreme suggestibility, although people don't behave fundamentally differently today. He talks about how the mania for retaking the holy lands and holy relics became universal in Christendom. The Pope was a ringleader, but so were Peter the Hermit and Walter the Penniless. A single animal in a social species can stir up an entire herd, he says. Horses behave just like humans do. A "horse hero" can set off a stampede.

The Imitation of Invention

There is another author whose work I think is important for understanding the mechanisms of the crowd mind—the late nineteenth century French sociologist Gabriel Tarde. Tarde (1890/1903) says in his book, *the Laws of Imitation*, that social behavior in animals, including humans, can be explained by just two factors: invention and imitation. He says that social behaviors begin as the inventions of a single animal, and these spread to the other animals by imitation. Tarde was influenced by an old book on animal behavior, *Societes animales* by Alfred Espinas, which argued that imitation of invention accounts for social behavior in ants. Espinas thought very highly of the inventiveness of individual ants, apparently; I don't know if he's right, but it's an interesting thesis. Tarde thinks the imitation of invention is the cause of social behavior in people and I think he is right in our case at the very least. What is interesting about the following passage is that Tarde anticipates the modern synthesis in evolutionary theory by making an analogy of the principle of the imitation of invention, while in our day meme theorists (who agree with Tarde on many points) are trying to explain social behavior in terms of the modern synthesis:

> If we consider the science of society from this point of view, we shall at once see that human sociology is related to animal sociologies, as a species to its genus, so to speak. That it is an extraordinary and infinitely superior species, I admit, but it is allied to the others, nevertheless. M. Espinas expressly states in his admirable work on *Societes animales*, a work which was written long before the first edition of this book, that the

labours of ants may be very well explained on the principle "of individual initiative followed by imitation." This initiative is always an innovation or invention that is equal to one of our own in boldness of spirit. To conceive the idea of constructing an arch, or a tunnel, at an appropriate point, an ant must be endowed with an innovating instinct equal to, or surpassing, that of our canal-digging or mountain-tunnelling engineers. Parenthetically it follows that imitation by masses of ants of such novel initiatives strikingly belies the spirit of mutual hatred which is alleged to exist among animals. M. Espinas is very frequently impressed in his observation of the societies of our lower brethren by the important role which is played in them by individual initiatives. Every herd of wild cattle has its leaders, its influential heads. Developments in the instincts of birds are explained by the same author as "individual inventions which are afterwards transmitted from generation to generation through direct instruction." In view of the fact that modification of instinct is probably related to the same principle as the genesis and modification of species, we may be tempted to enquire whether the principle of the imitation of invention, or of something physiologically analogous, would not be the clearest possible explanation of the ever-open problem of the origin of species. (p. 3-4)

He says further:

Among the higher species of ants, according to M. Espinas, "the individual develops an astonishing initiative" [*Des Societes animates*, p. 223; Alfred Espinas, Paris, 1877. The italics are M. Tarde's. Tr.]. How do the labours and migrations of ant-swarms begin? Is it through a common, instinctive, and spontaneous impulse which starts from all the associates at the same time and under the pressure of outward circumstances which are experienced simultaneously by all? On the contrary, a single ant begins by leaving the others and undertaking the work; then it strikes its neighbours with its antennae to summon their aid, and the contagion of imitation does the rest. (p. 4)

[...]

And now my readers will realise, perhaps, that the social being, in the degree that he is social, is essentially imitative, and that imitation plays a role in societies analogous to that of heredity in organic life or to that of vibration among inorganic bodies. If this is so, it ought to be admitted, in consequence, that a human invention, by which a new kind of imitation is started or a new series opened, the invention of gunpowder, for example, or windmills, or the Morse telegraph, stands in the same relation to social science as the birth of a new vegetal or mineral species (or, on the hypothesis of a gradual evolution, of each of the slow modifications to which the new species is due), to biology, or as the appearance of a new mode of motion comparable with light or electricity, or the formation of a new substance, to physics or chemistry. (p. 11-12)

[...]

All resemblances of social origin in society are the direct or indirect fruit of the various forms of imitation, custom-imitation or fashion-imitation, sympathy-imitation or obedience-imitation, precept imitation or education-imitation; naïve imitation, deliberate imitation, etc. In this lies the excellence of the contemporaneous method of explaining doctrines and institutions through their history. It is a method that is certain to come into more general use. It is said that great geniuses, great inventors, are apt to cross each other's paths. But, in the first place, such coincidences are very rare, and when they do occur, they are always due to the fact that both authors of the same invention have drawn independently from some common fund of instruction. This fund consists of a mass of ancient traditions and of experiences that are unorganised or that have been more or less organised and imitatively transmitted through language, the great vehicle of all imitations.

In this connection we may observe that modern philologists have relied so implicitly upon the foregoing proposition, that they have concluded, through analogy, that Sanskrit, Latin, Greek, German, Russian, and other kindred tongues, belong in reality to one family, and that it had a common progenitor in a language which was transmitted, with the exception of certain modifications, through tradition. Each modification was, in truth, an anonymous linguistic invention which was, in turn, perpetuated by imitation. In the next chapter I will return to the development and re-statement of our third proposition. (p. 14-15)

Tarde says that people do not just imitate each other consciously; they imitate each other unconsciously. They also counter-imitate, or do the opposite of what they see others doing. They may also invent new ideas or behaviors, and these spread to other people. He says that counter-imitation is sometimes mistaken for invention but it is not the same thing. There is also non-imitation; in this, people neither imitate what they see around them nor counter-imitate it; they carry on as if the people they are not imitating are not there. This is an anti-social response. Non-imitation is often a response to foreign influences which are considered undesirable. And when a new generation is trying to shake off the habits of its forefathers it simply stops imitating them.

Tarde says that ideas spread as if by contagion. So technologies spread in this way, and so do language dialects and fashions:

The well-known laws of Malthus and Darwin on the tendency of the individuals of a species to increase in geometrical progression, are true laws of human radiation through reproduction. In the same way, a local dialect that is spoken only by certain families, gradually becomes, through imitation, a national idiom. In the beginning of societies, the art of chipping flint, of domesticating dogs, of making bows, and, later, of leavening bread, of working bronze, served both as model and copy. Nowadays the diffusion of all kinds of useful processes is brought about in the same way, except that our increasing density of population and our advance in civilisation prodigiously accelerate their diffusion, just as velocity of sound is proportionate to density of medium. Every social thing, that is to say, every invention or discovery, tends to expand in its social environment, an environment which itself, I might add, tends to self-expansion, since it is essentially composed of like things, all of which have infinite ambitions. (p. 17)

The reason why ideas do not just keep spreading forever is that they meet resistance from competing ideas.

Tarde says that ideas may support each other. These fortuitous combinations he calls discoveries. His discussion sounds to me like associationist psychology, as I noted in the introduction. He says that there may be a propitious interference of two beliefs, of two desires, or of a belief and a desire. With regard to the "propitious interference of two beliefs," he says that:

If a conjecture which I have considered fairly probable comes into my mind while I am reading or remembering a fact which I think is almost certain, and if I suddenly perceive that the fact confirms the conjecture of which it is a consequence (i.e., the particular proposition which expresses the fact is included in the general proposition which expresses the conjecture), the conjecture immediately becomes much more probable in my eyes, and, at the same time, the fact appears to me to be an absolute certainty. So that there is a gain in belief all along the line. And the perception of this logical inclusion is a discovery. Newton discovered nothing more than this when, having brought his conjectured law of gravitation face to face with the calculation of the distance from the moon to the earth, he perceived that this fact confirmed his hypothesis. (p. 26)

So what he is saying is that new beliefs can strengthen one's conviction in old beliefs, if the new ones appear to confirm the old ones.

With regard to a propitious interference of two desires, he gives the example of a hypothetical medieval merchant who was both vain and avaricious but who was unwilling to give up either commercial wealth or social position, and who found a way to obtain both: he used his wealth to buy a title of nobility for himself and his family. This is an example of a discovery, and it was imitated by countless other people. Tarde says that after this unhoped-for prospect, it was probable that both of the merchant's desires redoubled in strength. Gold increased in value in his eyes, as he found out that it could buy titles, as did his vanity, since his wish for a title had been fulfilled. Tarde gives other examples. He says that he might be in love and have both a passion for rhyming; so he might combine the two of these, and both his love and his rhyming mania would be intensified. Tarde offers more examples in addition to this. He thinks commerce, industry, law, and the arts all began as a result of this process.

Tarde thinks that the propitious interference of desire and belief has been of the most importance historically. He says that a belief, given to someone by a friend that he has a gift for oratory, might combine with existing ambition; the two will strengthen each other so that his belief in his oratorical skills increases his ambition; his ambition itself contributed to his conviction. Tarde says that it is this sort of combination which is to be counted among the chief forces which rule the world. The patriotism of the Greeks and Romans was, he says, nothing but a passion nourished by an illusion and *vice versa*. The Christians and Arabs and Jacobins and modern revolutionaries were also motivated by illusion-fed passions and passion-fed illusions. These things always arise in just one person and then spread by contagion to a large number of other people. In this way a whole people may be converted to a religious or political doctrine.

Tarde's work suggests to me that even if his associationist psychology is not exactly right (though it seems perfectly plausible to me), some more exact and elaborate psychology might be able to take its place in his system. So ideas are combined in the mind somehow, and however that happens, once new combinations are formed they can spread to countless other people by imitation. Crowd psychology almost certainly plays a role in determining how ideas are spread, and how people who invent new ideas and attempt to spread them are treated.

Tarde thinks that ideas spread in a wave motion, like the waves in physics—light and sound for example. What that suggests to me is that if it is really true that the spreading of ideas happens in a wave motion then whatever mathematical models exist to describe waves might also apply in this instance. Perhaps the models that describe the contagion of disease might apply as well. I have not investigated the matter, so it's only conjecture for now.

Tarde says that "[t]he indefinite and inexhaustible continuation of these intricate and richly intersecting radiations constitutes memory and habit. When the multiplying repetition in question is confined to the nervous system, we have memory; when it spreads out into the muscular system, we have habit. Memory, so to speak, is a purely nervous habit; habit is both a nervous and a muscular memory" (p. 74). He says that "if the remembered idea or image was originally lodged in the mind through conversation or reading, if the habitual act originated in the view or knowledge of a similar act on the part of others, then these acts of memory and habit are social as well as psychological facts, and they show us the kind of imitation of which I have already spoken at length" (p. 75). So memories and habits can belong to the collective as well as to the individual. Individual memories and habits become group memories and habits by imitation.

Tarde talks about how people imitate each other through the medium of subconscious suggestion; back then they called it animal magnetism or somnambulism. So Tarde's theory is in agreement with Sidis's theory on the subject of the subconscious, and although they don't talk about exactly the same things they do not appear to contradict each other. Tarde says that certain individuals command greater influence than others; they are said to have greater prestige. Prestige does not correspond exactly to power relationships, since invading barbarians are often dazzled by the civilizations they conquer, and end up adopting their ways of doing things. Tarde believes that in the big city, with its large population and with all its sights and sounds and general busyness, many more impressions are made upon the mind than in the country, and ideas and behaviors are communicated to large numbers with great rapidity. People sometimes think that they have escaped suggestive influence by moving away from one social group, like the family, but they become beholden to some other suggestive influence, like those of a school teacher or a popular fellow student. The somnambulism of young children is apparent to many people, but it is only an illusion that we awake from it in adulthood; that we imitate more numerous and more complex ideas and habits does not mean that we are no longer somnambulists.

Tarde says that the people who are completely comfortable with their environments tend to be those who are the most suggestible. They abandon themselves completely to the ideas and gestures of those around them. Timidity is a conscious and therefore incomplete magnetization. Those who strongly rebel against assimilation and who are really unsociable remain timid their whole lives. People who never experience any real timidity upon entering a new situation are sociable to the highest degree; that is, they are excellent copyists, devoid of any particular avocation or any controlling ideas; they speedily adapt themselves to their environments.

Tarde says that inventions and discoveries are never undertaken as a result of persuasive suggestion. The credulity and docility of the highly suggestible renders them uninventive; whatever they think and do is copied from those to whom they defer. To innovate, a person must awake for an instant from his dream of home and country; the individual must escape from his social surroundings. This unusual audacity makes a man super-social rather than social.

Tarde says that inventions do not arise in response to needs, or at least not the specific need for the inventions. He asks the reasonable question of how a person could want something which does not yet exist. So modesty developed after clothing was invented; clothing was not invented because of modesty. A person with no conception of clothing could not possibly desire it. My suspicion is that inventions are responses to *general* needs, but never to specific ones. So clothing was invented in order to keep warm, probably, and later people developed the specific desire for clothing. So the specific desire for sodas did not exist before sodas were invented, but the desire to quench one's thirst and the desire for sweet things did exist, and soda was almost certainly invented to satisfy those desires.

Tarde says that inspirations are due to a very small number of innate but vital wants, but also to the mere pleasure of discovery. Many inventions were the result, probably, of nothing more than the play of naturally creative imaginations.

He also says that new inventors are always influenced by older inventors, who were in turn influenced by still older inventors, and that this process goes back to the simplest inventions, meant to satisfy the most basic needs.

Tarde says that every civilization, even the ones that appear to be the most original, is a combination of the imitations of other peoples. Carroll Quigley made a similar argument in his *Evolution of Civilizations*. Anyway, Tarde says that Arabian art, in spite of its distinctive features, is merely the fusion of Persian and Greek art. Greek art borrowed certain processes from Egyptian and perhaps from other sources. Egyptian art was formed from or amplified by many successive Asiatic and even African contributions.

Tarde says that lack of communication hinders imitation. He talks about how modern technologies like the telephone improve communications between places far distant in space; this speeds up the spread of new ideas.

Tarde suggests that perhaps the disinterested pursuit of truth which was allowed to develop into modern science over the last three centuries (from his day) will not survive in the twentieth century, but will be sacrificed to some state-imposed consoling and comforting illusion. This actually happened in many countries, most notably Russia and Germany.

Tarde considers obedience to be a kind of imitation. He says that the energetic and authoritative man wields an irresistible power over feebler natures; he gives them the direction which they lack. Obedience, to them, is not a duty but a need. "Obedience, in short," he says, "is the sister of faith. People obey for the same reason that they believe; and just as their faith is the radiation of that of some apostle, so their activity is merely the outgoing of some master will. Whatever the master wills or has willed, they will; whatever the apostle believes or has believed, they believe. And it is because of this that whatever the master or apostle subsequently does or says, they, in turn, do or say or are inclined to do or say" (p. 198). It follows that those persons and classes whom one is most inclined to imitate one is also most docile in obeying. So the common people tend to imitate the kings and upper classes. Tarde argues that commands begin as examples; originally the led simply copied their leaders, but in time the leaders were able to get the led to execute their commands by some sign or signal without having to perform the action themselves.

Tarde says that as social inequalities become more superficial, superiors cease to be able to keep their inferiors in awe, and they lose their social function. After they have been softened down to a certain point they cease to produce either admiration or credulity or obedience, all of which make for social strength. At this point the awe of the inferiors becomes envy. This envy helps make the superiors disappear. The led continually raise up idols only to bring them down later. Tarde says that it is not primarily fear that keeps people in subjection but admiration. The positive regard that one party feels for another is not necessarily reciprocated. But it doesn't have to be.

Tarde says that envy effects the assimilation of inferiors to the ideas and habits of superiors. But once the process is completed, envy disappears; everyone is equal. He says that the need for individual divergence, or dissimilation, or "liberty" (as people are in the habit of calling it), is born from the equality born of resemblance. He thinks that mankind would return to savagery if new sources of inequality did not arise, but they always do.

Tarde says that people who live in close contact with each other find it difficult to avoid imitating each other. Superiors sometimes do imitate their inferiors in certain particulars when they live together, as in the case of a master and his household servants. However, the imitation tends to work primarily in one direction.

Tarde says that one of the great advantages of aristocracy is its ability to adopt superior customs from foreign countries and have them be adopted by the mass by imitation. The aristocracies of all times and places have been more receptive to new ideas than the mass. When an aristocracy has become unwilling to accept new ideas, entrenching itself in tradition, its decline has set in.

Tarde says that if the distance between two people or classes is great that imitation is discouraged. A period is called democratic as soon as the distance between all classes has lessened enough to allow of the external imitation of the highest by the lowest.

Tarde says that the people of the cities tend to dominate those of the provinces. Being a Frenchman, this idea must have come naturally to him, as Paris has dominated the rest of France for centuries. Anyway, he says that the cities attract the most capable and energetic people. The aristocracy of the cities holds the mass in contempt just as much as the old aristocracy ever did; it's as selfish as they were, too, and subject to many of its vices; it must be constantly replenished from new elements rising from below in order to keep from succumbing to its vices.

Tarde says that in a democratic age—one in which no one is very much dissimilar from anyone else—it becomes the majority that enjoys the prestige, just as in previous ages a monarch or a nobility enjoyed prestige, and therefore it is the majority that people emulate and submit to. "In times of equality," he quotes Tocqueville as saying, "men have no faith in one another because of their mutual likeness; but this very resemblance inspires them with an almost unlimited confidence in the judgment of the public; for it seems improbable to them that when all have the same amount of light, the truth should not be found on the side of the greatest number" (p. 230). Tarde says that in fact, though, nearly all of the votes in a democracy are mere echoes of the judgments of the people's leaders.

The social superiority of a man is determined by the traits which his society values most highly. So in the past physical strength or agility or skill at handling weapons gave one an advantage over one's fellows. But in our day, Tarde says, "it is useless for a man to be muscular and well-proportioned; unless he also possesses that cerebral hypertrophy which was once abnormal and disastrous, but which is now normally exacted by the exigencies of modern civilization, he is condemned to defeat" (p. 238). He says that "[b]etween these two extremes there is, perhaps, no peculiarity of race or temperament, no morbid or monstrous trait which has not had its day of glory and expansion" (p. 238). He says that many of our instinctive criminals and madmen might have been heroes had they been born in another age. So it seems to me that it's not entirely true, as some people say, that it is entirely up to us whether or not we are successful in life. I don't doubt that that is a useful belief to have if you really do have what it takes to succeed, because it can bolster your resolve; however, if you were born into a civilization which only rewards cleverness and you are not very clever, nor ever will be, then you might be condemned to failure unless there are alternative pathways to success. So in our day a strong or fast but unintelligent person might still become successful if he becomes good at some sport. But it is doubtful even then that he will reach the highest ranks of society.

Tarde says that from the point of view of temporary, if not lasting, social peace, it is much more important that beliefs should be held in common than that they should be true. This is the cause of the supreme importance of religions, he says. This appears to me to explain, also, why organization men are as hostile to geniuses as they are. And that suggests another problem. Almost certainly, the great majority of people can't follow the most sophisticated arguments. The great majority will never understand what Plato and Einstein were saying. Does that mean, then, that everyone should be compelled to think, or at least speak, only those thoughts which the dullest person in his group can grasp? That is what must happen if everyone's beliefs are to remain uniform. This problem of not everyone being able to keep up with the best is one reason why aristocracies are good to have. It is possible to allow freedom of thought and speech for a minority, and to allow them to develop themselves to the fullest. But they must remain distinctly separate from the mass. They must have rights and privileges which the great majority do not have. In this way, the mass can remain uniform without degrading or destroying the very best people. Those born to the mass should have some means of escaping it, but the best among them have always found ways to force themselves into aristocracies.

Tarde says that a period in time can be enamored either of novelty or custom. In times of fashion, what is novel has prestige; in times of custom, what is customary has prestige, and those things are what people defer to, respectively. Independently of any contact with other civilizations, a given people must, he says, inevitably grow in numbers, and they must inevitably as a consequence become more urbanized. This progress causes the nervous excitability which develops aptitude for imitation. In primitive rural communities people can only imitate their fathers and so they acquire the habit of turning toward the past for instruction; the only period in their lives when they are susceptible to the impressions of a model is childhood, when they are under paternal guidance. Tarde says that the nervous plasticity and openness to impressions of adults in cities is sufficient to allow them to model themselves upon new types brought in from the outside. He says that civilizations pass through periods of innovation only to return to periods of custom, where the ideas and habits accumulated during the period of freedom are fixed and consolidated. After periods of urbanization rural life is allowed to grow again at the expense of the cities. He thinks that Europe is going to become more rural again in the future, as unlikely as it sounds. So far this has not come to pass, and he was writing more than a century ago. But that doesn't mean it won't happen. It does seem to have become less innovative than it was in the nineteenth century, though. There are still major breakthroughs like the personal computer and the expansion of the Internet, but nothing on the scale of the changes that the nineteenth century saw.

Tarde says that there are in every community two parties—the party of conservatism and the party of innovation, or to put it another way the party of custom and the party of fashion. These two groups differ in their receptivity to new ideas. The party of conservatism prefers the old ideas; the party of innovation prefers new ones. If the new ideas triumph the party of conservatism, in time, adopts them as its own.

So in summary, we can safely assume that novel ideas and behaviors originate in individuals in a social species and spread through the medium of the subconscious according to certain rules. Social superiors are much more likely to be imitated than social inferiors. Whenever a new idea or behavior enters circulation in a group some support it and others oppose it, and there is always conflict between these two parties; sometimes one party has the upper hand, and at other times the other party does. People gathered together in crowds are more likely to be influenced by a crowd leader and by each other than are people who gather in small groups. The conscious mind is what prevents people from imitating every idea and behavior that they meet with, though it can be disaggregated from the subconscious mind under the right conditions. Crowds tend to consume isolated individuals, and their suggestive power grows with their size. I'll assume all of these things in the following pages.

Chapter 2: Crowd Characteristics

I mentioned many of the characteristics of crowds in the last chapter; in this chapter I'll talk about some more of them and explain them in greater detail.

The Crowd

Gustave Le Bon (1895/1896) gave perhaps the most famous description of crowds in his book *the Crowd*. Most of his major ideas were adopted by the other crowd psychologists.

Le Bon opens the book by talking about how so many of the old ideas had been discredited in the popular mind, and about how so many of the old sources of authority had been destroyed. The only source of authority left standing was the crowd, and it was threatening to absorb all others. We were entering an era of crowds. I'm fairly certain that we still live in that era.

Le Bon says that the crowd was intentionally destroying what was left of our worn-out civilization in order to free itself from its last remaining constraints. He says that when the moral forces on which a civilization has rested have lost their strength that its final dissolution is brought about by brutal crowds known as barbarians. He argues that crowds can only destroy; they can never create. Only a small intellectual aristocracy can support civilization.

He says that even men of distinction make stupid decisions when they form into crowds. Crowds just do not have the ability to do complex reasoning, or to think dispassionately. He says that it is not all the world that has more wit than Voltaire but Voltaire who has more wit than all the world, if by "all the world" crowds are meant.

Le Bon says that an individual may accept contradiction and discussion but a crowd will never do so. If you contradict a crowd, and persist in this after you have aroused its fury, only armed authorities can save you from getting trampled.

Le Bon then talks about how crowds understand and respect authoritativeness and intolerance, but are unimpressed by kindness, which seems to them to be a form of weakness. Their sympathies have never been bestowed on on easy-going masters, but on tyrants who have vigorously oppressed them. The crowd has spasms of rebellion but it is not fundamentally rebellious. After a period of revolt it turns instinctively to servitude.

Le Bon talks about how the French schools did a poor job preparing Frenchmen for life after school. It made them unable to act on their own initiative, so they had come to depend on the state. Most wished to become state functionaries, but not all were accepted; those who were not able to obtain jobs in this way became enemies of the state. Le Bon thinks that a sure way to make someone an enemy of the state is to fill his mind with knowledge which he is unable to make use of. People in this state of mind are ready for any kind of social disturbance to improve their lots.

One thing Le Bon talks quite a bit about is how he thinks different crowds have different natures. So he thinks Latin crowds are more excitable than Anglo-Saxon crowds. This seems to me to be consistent with experience. For whatever reason, the English-speaking countries are just not as prone to tumult as France, Italy, Spain, and the other Latin countries. I don't think this is necessarily due to heredity, though some of it might be. Such factors as culture, climate, geography, and historical experience probably play the largest part in determining the particular behaviors of national crowds. It seems to me that crowds are motivated by the same basic mechanisms but differ in their specific beliefs and behaviors and in how suggestible they are.

Le Bon says that philosophy has not yet produced an ideal which can charm the masses. And their illusions they must have at all costs. They turn to the rhetoricians who will give them their illusions. The masses have never thirsted after truth.

Le Bon says that reason has no effect on crowds; only appeals to their sentiments work. He notes that the great events of history were not very reasonable at all. Reason does little to move men.

Le Bon talks about crowd leaders. He says that crowds always organize themselves under a chief; they are servile flocks who are incapable of doing without a master. The leader often starts off as one of the led. He is himself thoroughly possessed by the idea. These are men of action, not thinkers. They are excitable, nervous, and half-deranged. No matter how absurd their goal may be, they remain undeterred in pursuit of it; reason has no effect on them. Contempt and persecution don't deter them. They sacrifice everything for the cause. These men are strong-willed, and the crowd submits to the strong-willed man, as they become will-less as individuals when they are in a crowd. Le Bon doesn't deny that conscious deceivers can have a great influence on the masses, but it is fleeting; he thinks the self-deceived have a much more enduring influence over the course of events.

Le Bon says that great historical events are caused by obscure persons of great faith, and rarely ever by philosophers or skeptics:

> The arousing of faith—whether religious, political, or social, whether faith in a work, in a person, or an idea--has always been the function of the great leaders of crowds, and it is on this account that their influence is always very great. Of all the forces at the disposal of humanity, faith has always been one of the most tremendous, and the gospel rightly attributes to it the power of moving mountains. To endow a man with faith is to multiply his strength tenfold. The great events of history have been brought about by obscure believers, who have had little beyond their faith in their favour. It is not by

the aid of the learned or of philosophers, and still less of sceptics, that have been built up the great religions which have swayed the world, or the vast empires which have spread from one hemisphere to the other (p. 120).

Le Bon says that there are two kinds of crowd leaders. There are men who are energetic and possess much strength of will, but only intermittently; and then there are men who possess enduring strength of will. The leaders of intermittently strong will are capable of leading the masses in daring enterprises on the spur of the moment; however, they don't have as much influence on the course of events as the men of enduring strength of will. The latter sort of men are the founders of religions and great undertakings.

The means of action of the leaders are affirmation, repetition, and contagion. It is important that the crowd has first been prepared by certain circumstances and it is important, above all, that the person attempting to move a crowd possess prestige, which he will talk about later. I will quote Le Bon extensively here because this is an important section and I can't put it better than he can:

> When it is wanted to stir up a crowd for a short space of time, to induce it to commit an act of any nature—to pillage a palace, or to die in defence of a stronghold or a barricade, for instance—the crowd must be acted upon by rapid suggestion, among which example is the most powerful in its effect. To attain this end, however, it is necessary that the crowd should have been previously prepared by certain circumstances, and, above all, that he who wishes to work upon it should possess the quality to be studied farther on, to which I give the name of prestige.
>
> When, however, it is proposed to imbue the mind of a crowd with ideas and beliefs—with modern social theories, for instance—the leaders have recourse to different expedients. The principal of them are three in number and clearly

defined—affirmation, repetition, and contagion. Their action is somewhat slow, but its effects, once produced, are very lasting.

Affirmation pure and simple, kept free of all reasoning and all proof, is one of the surest means of making an idea enter the mind of crowds. The conciser an affirmation is, the more destitute of every appearance of proof and demonstration, the more weight it carries. The religious books and the legal codes of all ages have always resorted to simple affirmation. Statesmen called upon to defend a political cause, and commercial men pushing the sale of their products by means of advertising are acquainted with the value of affirmation.

Affirmation, however, has no real influence unless it be constantly repeated, and so far as possible in the same terms. It was Napoleon, I believe, who said that there is only one figure in rhetoric of serious importance, namely, repetition. The thing affirmed comes by repetition to fix itself in the mind in such a way that it is accepted in the end as a demonstrated truth.

The influence of repetition on crowds is comprehensible when the power is seen which it exercises on the most enlightened minds. This power is due to the fact that the repeated statement is embedded in the long run in those profound regions of our unconscious selves in which the motives of our actions are forged. At the end of a certain time we have forgotten who is the author of the repeated assertion, and we finish by believing it. To this circumstance is due the astonishing power of advertisements. When we have read a hundred, a thousand, times that X's chocolate is the best, we imagine we have heard it said in many quarters, and we end by acquiring the certitude that such is the fact. When we have read a thousand times that Y's flour has cured the most illustrious persons of the most obstinate maladies, we are tempted at last to try it when suffering from an illness of a similar kind. If we always read in the same papers that A is an arrant scamp and B a most honest man we finish by being convinced that this is the truth, unless, indeed, we are given to reading another paper of the contrary opinion, in which the two qualifications are reversed. Affirmation and repetition are alone powerful enough to combat each other.

When an affirmation has been sufficiently repeated and there is unanimity in this repetition—as has occurred in the case of certain famous financial undertakings rich enough to purchase every assistance—what is called a current of opinion is formed and the powerful mechanism of contagion intervenes. Ideas, sentiments, emotions, and beliefs possess in crowds a contagious power as intense as that of microbes. This phenomenon is very natural, since it is observed even in animals when they are together in number. Should a horse in a stable take to biting his manger the other horses in the stable will imitate him. A panic that has seized on a few sheep will soon extend to the whole flock. In the case of men collected in a crowd all emotions are very rapidly contagious, which explains the suddenness of panics. Brain disorders, like madness, are themselves contagious. The frequency of madness among doctors who are specialists for the mad is notorious. Indeed, forms of madness have recently been cited--agoraphobia, for instance—which are communicable from men to animals.

For individuals to succumb to contagion their simultaneous presence on the same spot is not indispensable. The action of contagion may be felt from a distance under the influence of events which give all minds an individual trend and the characteristics peculiar to crowds. This is especially the case when men's minds have been prepared to undergo the influence in question by those remote factors of which I have made a study above. An example in point is the revolutionary movement of 1848, which, after breaking out in Paris, spread rapidly over a great part of Europe and shook a number of thrones.

Imitation, to which so much influence is attributed in social phenomena, is in reality a mere effect of contagion. Having shown its influence elsewhere, I shall confine myself to reproducing what I said on the subject fifteen years ago. My remarks have since been developed by other writers in recent publications.

"Man, like animals, has a natural tendency to imitation. Imitation is a necessity for him, provided always that the imitation is quite easy. It is this necessity that makes the influence of what is called fashion so powerful. Whether in the matter of opinions, ideas, literary manifestations, or merely of dress, how many persons are bold enough to run counter to the fashion? It is by examples not by arguments that crowds are guided. At every period there exists a small number of individualities which react upon the remainder and are imitated by the unconscious mass. It is needful however, that these individualities should not be in too pronounced disagreement with received ideas. Were they so, to imitate them would be too difficult and their influence would be nil. For this very reason men who are too superior to their epoch are generally without influence upon it. The line of separation is too strongly marked. For the same reason too Europeans, in spite of all the advantages of their civilisation, have so insignificant an influence on Eastern people; they differ from them to too great an extent.

"The dual action of the past and of reciprocal imitation renders, in the long run, all the men of the same country and the same period so alike that even in the case of individuals who would seem destined to escape this double influence, such as philosophers, learned men, and men of letters, thought and style have a family air which enables the age to which they belong to be immediately recognised. It is not necessary to talk for long with an individual to attain to a thorough knowledge of what he reads, of his habitual occupations, and of the surroundings amid which he lives."[17]

[17] Gustave le Bon, "L'Homme et les Societes," vol. ii. p. 116.

1881.

Contagion is so powerful that it forces upon individuals not only certain opinions, but certain modes of feeling as well. Contagion is the cause of the contempt in which, at a given period, certain works are held—the example of "Tannhauser" may be cited—which, a few years later, for the same reason are admired by those who were foremost in criticising them.

The opinions and beliefs of crowds are specially propagated by contagion, but never by reasoning. The conceptions at present rife among the working classes have been acquired at the public-house as the result of affirmation, repetition, and contagion, and indeed the mode of creation of the beliefs of crowds of every age has scarcely been different. Renan justly institutes a comparison between the first founders of Christianity and "the socialist working men spreading their ideas from public-house to public-house"; while Voltaire had already observed in connection with the Christian religion that "for more than a hundred years it was only embraced by the vilest riff-raff."

It will be noted that in cases analogous to those I have just cited, contagion, after having been at work among the popular classes, has spread to the higher classes of society. This is what we see happening at the present day with regard to the socialist doctrines which are beginning to be held by those who will yet be their first victims. Contagion is so powerful a force that even the sentiment of personal interest disappears under its action.

This is the explanation of the fact that every opinion adopted by the populace always ends in implanting itself with great vigour in the highest social strata, however obvious be the absurdity of the triumphant opinion. This reaction of the lower upon the higher social classes is the more curious, owing to the circumstance that the beliefs of the crowd always have their origin to a greater or less extent in some higher idea, which has often remained without influence in the sphere in which it was evolved. Leaders and agitators, subjugated by this higher idea, take hold of it, distort it and create a sect which distorts it afresh, and then propagates it amongst the masses, who carry the process of deformation still further. Become a popular truth the idea returns, as it were, to its source and exerts an influence on the upper classes of a nation. In the long run it is intelligence that shapes the destiny of the world, but very indirectly. The philosophers who evolve ideas have long since returned to dust, when, as the result of the process I have just described, the fruit of their reflection ends by triumphing (p. 126-132).

Le Bon talks about prestige next. Great power is given to ideas propagated by affirmation, repetition, and contagion; in time they acquire what Le Bon calls prestige. He says that whatever has been a ruling power in the world has always maintained its authority by prestige. Everyone grasps the meaning of the term immediately, he says, but it's somewhat more difficult to define. Prestige may involve admiration or fear, but it may exist without them. The greatest prestige is possessed by the dead, by people of whom we don't stand in fear, like Alexander, Caesar, Mohammad, and Buddha. But there are also fictive beings who we don't admire, like the monstrous divinities of the subterranean temples of India, but who nevertheless are endowed with great prestige.

Le Bon says that prestige is in reality a sort of domination exercised on the mind by an individual, work or idea. It paralyzes the critical faculty, fills us with astonishment, and commands respect. The sentiment provoked is somewhat inexplicable, but he thinks it's similar to the fascination which a person experiences when he's been hypnotized (or magnetized, as Le Bon puts it). He says that neither gods, kings, nor women have ever reigned without it.

Next Le Bon talks about the two main kinds of prestige: acquired prestige and personal prestige. Acquired prestige results from name, fortune, and reputation, and it may be independent of personal prestige. Personal prestige is peculiar to the individual and may coexist with the elements of acquired prestige, or it may be strengthened by them, but it may also exist without them. Acquired prestige is more common by far. It is obtained by the mere fact that an individual occupies a certain position, possesses a certain fortune, or bears certain titles. One interesting aspect of acquired prestige is how much outward displays are responsible for it. So a soldier would be stripped of much of his authority without his uniform, and a judge would be stripped of much of his authority without his robes.

In addition to the prestige which people possess, opinions, literary and artistic works, and other things may also have prestige. Le Bon thinks this kind of prestige is the result of accumulated repetitions:

> The prestige of which I have just spoken is exercised by persons; side by side with it may be placed that exercised by opinions, literary and artistic works, &c. Prestige of the latter kind is most often merely the result of accumulated repetitions. History, literary and artistic history especially, being nothing more than the repetition of identical judgments, which nobody endeavours to verify, every one ends by repeating what he learnt at school, till there come to be names and things which nobody would venture to meddle with. For a modern reader the perusal of Homer results incontestably in immense boredom; but who would venture to say so? The Parthenon, in its present state, is a wretched ruin, utterly destitute of interest, but it is endowed with such prestige that it does not appear to us as it really is, but with all its accompaniment of historic memories. The special characteristic of prestige is to prevent us seeing things as they are and to entirely paralyse our judgment. Crowds always, and individuals as a rule, stand in need of ready-made opinions on all subjects. The popularity of these opinions is

independent of the measure of truth or error they contain, and is solely regulated by their prestige (p. 135-136).

Personal prestige is independent of all titles and all authority, and is possessed by a small number or people who exercise a magnetic fascination on those around them. This is despite the fact that the fascinator may be the equal of those he dominates, and he may lack all ordinary means of domination. Le Bon says that leaders with this kind of prestige force acceptance of their ideas and sentiments on those around them and "are obeyed as is the tamer of wild beasts by the animal that could easily devour him." Le Bon cites Buddha, Jesus, Mohammad, Joan of Arc, and Napoleon as examples of leaders with personal prestige. They owe their positions to their prestige. Le Bon says that Gods, heroes, and dogmas win their way in the world of their own inward strength and are not to be discussed; they disappear as soon as they are discussed. Le Bon then goes on to talk about how Napoleon was able to fascinate, and thereby dominate, everyone around him even though he rose from obscurity. Napoleon was obeyed and admired even though he treated people badly, massacred them by the millions, and was the cause of invasion upon invasion. Le Bon concludes that all is permitted you if you possess enough prestige and the skill necessary to uphold it.

Le Bon says that not all examples of personal prestige are so unusual; a private individual who tries to dazzle his neighbors by a new coat or decoration is also possessed of some degree of personal prestige.

Le Bon says that prestige constitutes the fundamental element of persuasion. Whatever is prestigious is imitated:

Between the extreme limits of this series would find a place all the forms of prestige resulting from the different elements composing a civilisation--sciences, arts, literature, &c.--and it would be seen that prestige constitutes the fundamental element of persuasion. Consciously or not, the being, the idea, or the thing possessing prestige is immediately imitated in consequence of contagion, and forces an entire generation to adopt certain modes of feeling and of giving expression to its thought. This imitation, moreover, is, as a rule, unconscious, which accounts for the fact that it is perfect. The modern painters who copy the pale colouring and the stiff attitudes of some of the Primitives are scarcely alive to the source of their inspiration. They believe in their own sincerity, whereas, if an eminent master had not revived this form of art, people would have continued blind to all but its naive and inferior sides. Those artists who, after the manner of another illustrious master, inundate their canvasses with violet shades do not see in nature more violet than was detected there fifty years ago; but they are influenced, "suggestioned," by the personal and special impressions of a painter who, in spite of this eccentricity, was successful in acquiring great prestige. Similar examples might be brought forward in connection with all the elements of civilisation (p. 144).

How does a thing become prestigious? Le Bon says that success has always been one of the most important factors. Whatever is successful ceases to be called into question. Prestige is usually lost following failure. Someone who the crowd acclaimed yesterday may be insulted today if he has been overtaken by failure. The crowd views the fallen hero as an equal and takes revenge for having bowed to a superiority which it no longer admits. Prestige can be worn away more slowly by being subjected to discussion, and this method is, he says, exceedingly sure. Gods and men retain their prestige only as long as discussion is not tolerated.

Le Bon then talks about how there are two kinds of beliefs: a relatively fixed kind, which endure for centuries, and which constitute the real framework of civilization, and the changeable opinions of crowds, which are fleeting and mobile and which do not arise from the fixed beliefs.

Le Bon says that the fixed beliefs are doomed as soon as they start being called into question. The reason why is that every general belief is little more than a fiction and can survive only when it is not subjected to examination. Once a fixed belief is doomed, so is everything that rests upon it. When a nation has lost its fixed beliefs it is condemned at the same time to change all of the other elements of its civilization.

Le Bon says that intolerance is indispensable for the defense of fixed beliefs. However, many thinkers and inventors and other innocent people were persecuted or else died in despair as a result. He says that the only real tyranny is the tyranny of fixed beliefs. The tyranny of a Genghis Khan, Tiberius, or Napoleon pales in comparison.

Le Bon says that the philosophic absurdity that often marks general beliefs has never been an obstacle to their triumph. Also, he thinks that socialist beliefs are inferior to traditional religious beliefs because the old beliefs, having posited paradise in the next world, were beyond contest, while the socialist ideals are vulnerable to contradiction as soon as the first efforts towards their realization are made.

Le Bon talks next about the changeable opinions of crowds. Above the substratum of fixed beliefs are a number of ideas which are constantly emerging and dying out. Some of these exist for only a day, while the more important barely outlive a generation. He talks about how, in France between the years 1790 and 1820, a period of just thirty years, the opinions of the crowd had changed dramatically:

> As an example, let us take a very short period of French history, merely that from 1790 to 1820, a period of thirty years' duration, that of a generation. In the course of it we see the crowd at first monarchical become very revolutionary, then very imperialist, and again very monarchical. In the matter of religion it gravitates in the same lapse of time from

Catholicism to atheism, then towards deism, and then returns to the most pronounced forms of Catholicism. These changes take place not only amongst the masses, but also amongst those who direct them. We observe with astonishment the prominent men of the Convention, the sworn enemies of kings, men who would have neither gods nor masters, become the humble servants of Napoleon, and afterwards, under Louis XVIII., piously carry candles in religious processions (p. 156).

But that isn't the only case when beliefs changed dramatically. Le Bon talks about the reversals in opinion from 1820 to 1890 (Le Bon's day):

> Numerous, too, are the changes in the opinions of the crowd in the course of the following seventy years. The "Perfidious Albion" of the opening of the century is the ally of France under Napoleon's heir; Russia, twice invaded by France, which looked on with satisfaction at French reverses, becomes its friend.

> In literature, art, and philosophy the successive evolutions of opinion are more rapid still. Romanticism, naturalism, mysticism, &c., spring up and die out in turn. The artist and the writer applauded yesterday are treated on the morrow with profound contempt (p. 156-157).

Le Bon says that the opinions which are not linked to any general belief or sentiment are open to every change in surrounding circumstances. He thinks that in his day the number of changeable opinions of crowds were greater in number than they ever were, and he gives three different reasons for this opinion. The first was that the old beliefs were losing their hold over the public mind, and so they were ceasing to shape the more ephemeral beliefs. This made it easier for haphazard opinions without a past or future to spring up. The second reason is that the power of crowds was increasing, and it was being less and less counterbalanced by other forces. This meant that the extreme mobility of ideas, which is a peculiarity of crowds, could manifest itself without hinderance. The third reason is the recent development of the newspaper press, which was continually bringing the most contrary opinions to the attention of crowds. The suggestions that might have resulted from each individual opinion were destroyed by contrary suggestions. The consequence of this was that no opinion succeeded in becoming widespread, and none lasted very long.

Le Bon says that it was a phenomenon new in the world's history for governments to be unable to direct public opinion, but it was a thing most characteristic of his age (and our age, too). In the not very distant past from Le Bon's day, the action of governments and the influence of a few writers and a very small number of newspapers constituted the real reflectors of public opinion. In Le Bon's day the writers had lost all influence and the newspapers ceased to be able to direct opinion. The statesmen of the day did not direct opinion either but strived only to follow it. They feared it and responded unstably to it at times. The opinion of crowds was becoming more and more the supreme principle in politics. According to Le Bon, who was close to the French establishment of the day, the Franco-Russian alliance was solely the outcome of a popular movement. Students of history will recognize this as the beginning of what would become the Triple Entente, which included Great Britain as well, and which opposed the Triple Alliance of Germany, Austria-Hungary, and Italy. Italy switched sides after the war started, however; its place as the third major power in the alliance was taken by the Ottoman Empire. These were the two alliances that fought the First World War.

Le Bon finds it fascinating to observe popes, kings and emperors conducting interviews as a means of submitting their views to the judgment of crowds. He says that formerly it was perhaps the case that politics was not a matter of sentiment, but he's not sure the same can be said now. Politics was being guided more and more by the impulses of changeable crowds, who were impervious to reason and could only be guided by sentiment.

Le Bon denies even that the press had much influence over public opinion. It was obliged to pander to the tastes of the public because of the competition for readers. They were compelled to renounce any attempt to enforce an idea or doctrine. No paper was rich enough to allow its contributors to air their personal opinions, and in any event if such views had been expressed they would not have influenced readers very much; readers demanded only to be kept informed or to be amused.

Governments watched the course of public opinion closely, and nothing was more mobile and changeable than the thought of crowds. It was common for them to execrate today what they applauded yesterday. Without guidance, people were becoming either utterly skeptical or else extremely unstable in their opinions. Le Bon says that just a few decades ago people were relatively more stable in their views. You could be pretty sure of what a person believed if you knew what faction he belonged to. If he was a monarchist, it was a sure thing that he rejected the theory of evolution and held the French Revolution in disdain; if he was a republican he accepted the theory of evolution and thought well of the French Revolution. But things had changed a lot since then. Because of discussion and analysis, all opinions were losing their prestige and their distinctive features were being rapidly worn away. Few survived that were capable of arousing enthusiasm. The man of those times was becoming more and more indifferent to everything.

Le Bon says prophetically that although all of this is a sign of decadence, nevertheless, given the present strength of crowds, if a single opinion were to acquire sufficient prestige to enforce its general acceptance, it would have such tyrannical strength that it would bend everything before it, and the era of free discussion would be closed for a long time. That was actually what happened in Germany, Russia, Italy, and a number of smaller countries just a few decades later. The German and Italian regimes were defeated in the Second World War but the Russian regime survived until a couple decades ago. Le Bon says that crowds are occasionally easy-going masters, but they are also violently capricious. Crowd rule is also at the mercy of too many chances to endure for long. He thinks that the extreme instability of opinions might actually be serving to prolong the reign of crowds because of the indifference which it cultivates.

Le Bon says that an orator with good arguments but without prestige will not be taken seriously. However, an orator with feeble arguments but with great prestige will be able to sway large crowds.

Le Bon thinks well of parliamentary assemblies, as he thinks that philosophers, thinkers, writers, artists, and learned men thrive best in parliamentary regimes. But he says that these regimes have two serious problems. He says that financial waste is inevitable in them and that they tend over time to constrain the freedom of the individual with more and more rules and regulations. The reason why parliamentary governments are spendthrifts is because their constituents are shortsighted in their demands, but the representatives can't go very often against the demands even if they know they are extravagant, because they would be risking their positions. Le Bon says that many European countries, like Portugal, Greece, Spain, and Turkey, had become insolvent, while others, like Italy, were on their way to bankruptcy. I should quote this, given how familiar this must sound to people who read the news:

> Many European countries—Portugal, Greece, Spain, Turkey—have reached this stage, and others, such as Italy, will soon be reduced to the same extremity. Still too much alarm need not be felt at this state of things, since the public has successively consented to put up with the reduction of four-fifths in the payment of their coupons by these different countries. Bankruptcy under these ingenious conditions allows the equilibrium of Budgets difficult to balance to be instantly restored. Moreover, wars, socialism, and economic conflicts hold in store for us a profusion of other catastrophes in the period of universal disintegration we are traversing, and

it is necessary to be resigned to living from hand to mouth without too much concern for a future we cannot control (p. 222).

As for the inevitable restrictions on liberty, these are the result of representatives passing innumerable laws which always constrain the freedom of the individual. Parliaments are blind to the long-term consequences of their actions. Also, as taxes increase, people become less and less free to spend their money as they please. Eventually people grow accustomed to accepting burdensome restrictions and they end in desiring servitude. They lose all spontaneous energy. The individual seeks outside of himself the forces he no longer finds in himself and he finds them in the state. The state becomes an all-powerful god. Le Bon says that outward displays of license conceal just how much people are actually constrained.

The Herd Instinct

Wilfred Trotter (1916/1919) wrote after Gustave Le Bon and Boris Sidis did, and he cites their work. He says that the chief quality of herds is homogeneity, and that a member of the herd can only be a leader if he does not diverge so far from its usual behaviors as to mark himself as not belonging to it. Original behaviors are suppressed. Members of a herd are sensitive to their fellow members, so when one gives an alarm to some danger the rest are able to respond quickly, and in this way the herd is more perceptive of dangers than any one individual would be. Also, hunting packs have advantages that individual hunters lack. So there are great advantages to being a gregarious animal. A wolf pack forms an organism more formidable than a solitary organism like a lion or tiger. However, if an individual wolf does not follow the impulses of the herd he will starve. Likewise, the sheep that does not respond to the flock will be eaten. The individual member of the herd will treat the herd as his normal environment and will resist any attempt to separate him from it.

In humans, the herd instinct extends into matters of opinion and conduct, and in dress, religion, politics, and other matters; we feel compelled to seek out others with similar predispositions for the support without which we feel loneliness or terror; this accounts for the tendency of people to segregate into classes. Even the most apparently eccentric person is supported by the agreement of some class, and it is the smallness of the class that accounts for his seeming eccentricity.

Trotter talks about the manifestations of the herd instinct. Simple ones include the desire not to seem conspicuous, such as in shyness and stage fright. But there is another, with important consequences for what was once called "progress": it is man's resistance to the suggestions of sense experience. He notes that the steam engine was resisted by people until it almost invented itself. When man is faced with two suggestions, the one which the greatest bulk of the herd is behind is the one he will tend to accept.

Trotter says that in the early days of man, when the faculty of speech first appeared, the scope and the power of herd suggestion must have increased considerably. There would have been decrees for almost everything owing to man's desire for certitude, and each individual would have known what he could and could not do, and what would happen if he disobeyed. Man had not yet begun to take account of facts, which could have interfered with the suggestions. Upon this primitive, comfortable state of man intruded the alien and hostile power of reason. Sense experience has been resisted everywhere and at all times because it conflicts with instinctive beliefs. This is why new sciences always meet with resistance.

Trotter says the average man has opinions about all sorts of things, even on subjects about which the experts say the questions are not yet settled. The rational response when one has not thoroughly investigated a subject is to suspend judgment, so it follows that the bulk of a man's opinions have a non-rational origin—that is, they have their origins in herd suggestion. He says that people come up with rationalizations for their instinctive beliefs, but the rationalizations are not why people believe what they do. Clever people can come up with ingenious rationalizations for their instinctive beliefs, but their beliefs are no less instinctive on account of that cleverness.

Trotter says that suggestibility is not entirely a bad thing, even if it causes man to sometimes behave irrationally; it is what makes social life possible, and it enables altruistic behavior. So although man's irrationality has given social reformers much grief, it would be unwise to make man rational by breeding suggestibility out of him.

Trotter says that the best plan of making man more rational may be to work with his suggestibility rather than against it. If rationality were to be made respectable, as it is in science, it's possible that people could come to see irrationality in the same light as they do in using the wrong implement at the dinner table.

Trotter talks about what people do when experience conflicts with herd suggestion. The two normal reactions are indifference and rationalization. Skepticism of herd suggestion is another possible reaction, but it is less common. Regular use of the first two methods produces a type of person who is mentally stable relative to skeptics. Such a mindset is common to the bulk of mankind by middle age. The prevalence of such persons within the state gives it considerable stability, but it tends also to result in the prevalence of people at the helm of the state who are relatively insensitive to feeling or suffering, and who are disinclined to accept ideas suggested by sense experience when they conflict with herd tradition. Early in man's history most people would have been of this type because sense experience was still relatively simple, and so its powers of suggestion were relatively weak. Mental conflicts would have been resolved by simple rationalizations, and the average man could have lived a life free of psychological tension. Narrow patriotism would have characterized the average man, and his leaders could have been arrogant, bigoted, bloodthirsty, and reactionary with no apparent consequences as long as no great change in behavior were necessary; in fact, such a group would have dominated, and historically they often did so. This type persisted to Trotter's day among the elites of many leading countries. But the world had become more complex, and so the advantages of belonging to this statistically normal type were no longer so great. An insensitivity to sense experience meant that the views of such persons would always be narrow; they could never possess the full range of intellectual abilities of which man is capable. That is the price of mental comfort.

Trotter says that there is another major psychological type than the "resistive" type whose adherence to herd suggestion cannot be shaken by experience: this is a mentally unstable type, whose ranks were growing in his day. He says that the increase of mental instability is due to the increase of facts which the non-resistive individual is neither able to assimilate nor to dismiss. They remain in the mind as irritants, causing mental conflict. Trotter thinks that some people use alcohol or drugs as a means to deal with mental conflict. He does not blame them.

Trotter makes a sketch of the mentally unstable type. He says that those of this type tend to be skeptical of everything which is a usual target of ambition because of some experience which cannot be disregarded, and so they tend to be weak in energy and lacking in willpower. However, because their skepticism is incomplete, they are easily won to new causes and religions and quacks, which they just as easily abandon. He says that while the mentally unstable type loses in energy and willpower it gains in adaptability relative to the mentally stable type. Each has something the other lacks, so that neither is capable of the full possibilities of the human personality. What has happened historically, he says, is that nations have started out with the mentally stable type being dominant, but the expansion of experience caused them to become less mentally stable, less energetic, and weaker of will; the result is that they were easily conquered by peoples who were dominated by the more stable type.

Trotter says that the kindly condescension of the old towards the young is in fact the concealed jealousy of the old, whose failing powers cannot match the energy and enterprise of the young. Herd instinct always favors the majority and the ruling powers, and hence age, over youthful zeal.

Trotter makes some comments that might be of interest to those following the kin selection versus group selection debate in evolutionary biology. For those new to this, kin selection was the theory originally formulated by the biologist William Hamilton and then refined by his colleagues; it was popularized by Richard Dawkins in his famous book *the Selfish Gene*. At the moment it's the dominant theory in evolutionary biology and the behavioral sciences, and it's had some influence in some of the social sciences as well.

The basic idea of kin selection is that the most important level of natural selection is not the individual nor the group, but the gene. Groupish behaviors like altruism can be explained in terms of selection at the level of the gene. As Dawkins puts it, "[w]e are survival machines—robot vehicles blindly programmed to preserve the selfish molecules known as genes." We behave altruistically toward others not for the good of the group but either because we are related to them and are helping our shared genes to spread, or else because we expect them to do us favors in exchange, if not immediately then sometime in the future. This idea is called reciprocal altruism and it was proposed by another influential evolutionary biologist, Robert Trivers.

Group selection theories posit that natural selection can happen more than a trivial amount of the time at the level of the group, though it also happens at the level of the individual (when individuals compete with other individuals) and at the level of the gene (where genes compete to spread throughout a population).

My understanding is that while the kin selection theorists concede that natural selection could conceivably happen at the level of the group, competition at lower levels—between individuals and between genes—tends to undermine it, and selection at these lower levels is practically always stronger. So it is highly unlikely that any traits will evolve in individuals that increase the group's competitiveness with rival groups at the expense of the individual's competitiveness with others of his group. The individuals without such traits would outcompete them within the group.

Group selection theory has become more popular recently, and E.O. Wilson, one of the most distinguished living biologists, is supporting it. Wilson was perhaps the one most responsible for the widespread adoption of Hamilton's theory many decades ago. However, now he thinks that group selection theory (or as it has been rebranded, multi-level selection theory) is the best theory for explaining how groupish behaviors have evolved. E.O. Wilson frequently teams up with David Sloan Wilson (they're not related), who is one of the most prominent of the new group selection theorists. The Wilsons are particularly interested in explaining how more complex organisms evolve from simpler ones by means of natural selection. It is now commonly accepted that multi-cellular organisms evolved from the joining together of single-celled ones; how did this happen if not by group selection? E.O. Wilson thinks that social organisms, like the ants which are his speciality, form super-organisms which may with reason be considered organisms in their own right. Natural selection acts upon these groups as if they were individuals, just as natural selection began acting upon multi-cellular organisms as if they they were individuals.

Ever since E.O. Wilson publicly announced his support for group selection (it's been several years now) the debate between the the two parties has grown increasingly intense. The chief area of contention is altruism. The kin selection supporters just can't see how selection can act at the level of the group when selection at the level of the individual and the gene seems to undermine it.

The new group selection theorists argue that selfish individuals may win out within groups, but groups of altruists win out in competitions with groups of selfish individuals; therefore, at least when competition between groups is intense, group selection at least some of the time to win out over lower levels of selection.

Wilfred Trotter proposes a theory which sounds a lot like a group selection theory, however, unlike any evolutionary theory now proposed, it doesn't explain social behavior in terms of altruism. The herd instinct takes its place. This may provide a solution to the problems altruism has, while still being able to explain a wide variety of social behaviors and even the evolution of complex lifeforms from aggregates of simpler ones.

One important difference between Trotter and both sides of the modern theorists is that Trotter focuses on conformity versus deviance while modern theorists focus on altruism versus selfishness. Trotter argues that altruism is a byproduct of the herd instinct—if it is the group custom to behave altruistically the members of the group will behave altruistically—but if the altruism assumes novel forms the altruist will be punished just the same as if he were a malcontent. I don't know if any modern theorists talk about this; they seem to all assume that only the selfish get punished. Another significant difference between Trotter and the modern theorists is that Trotter does not believe that deviants (the analogue of selfish "cheaters") prosper in conformist groups (conformism is the closest analogue to altruism). Deviants tend to struggle in groups, although they may have some advantages over conformists. Modern theorists know about social control—punishing cheaters, as they put it—but for some reason they seem not to take it into account when they say that selfish people (deviants) prosper in altruistic (conformist) groups. I'm not saying that deviants can't prosper, but they have to be able to avoid or endure punishment and have some other advantage to compensate for the risk. So a deviant might prosper if he has developed a new idea or behavior which allows him to exploit his environment better than the conformists can.

Trotter says that gregariousness allows an indefinite enlargement of the unit upon which natural selection acts; the individual is shielded from the immediate effects of natural selection and is exposed only to the special selective pressures that exist within the group. As a result, the individuals within a group are allowed to undergo modifications which would have been untenable if they were alone, and so the individuals become differentiated in their functions, much like the cells of a multicellular organism. This sounds very much like what E.O. Wilson and David Sloan Wilson have been saying about the major transitions from simpler organisms to more advanced organisms being due to higher levels of selection (that is, at the level of the group). I'll quote Trotter on this:

> I have pointed out elsewhere that the fundamental biological meaning of gregariousness is that it allows of an indefinite enlargement of the unit upon which the undifferentiated influence of natural selection is allowed to act, so that the individual merged in the larger unit is shielded from the immediate effects of natural selection and is exposed directly only to the special form of selection which obtains within the new unit.

> There seems little doubt that this sheltering of the individual allows him to vary and to undergo modifications with a freedom which would have been dangerous to him as an isolated being, but is safe under the new conditions and valuable to the new unit of which he now is a part.

> In essence the significance of the passage from the solitary to the gregarious seems to be closely similar to that of the passage from the unicellular to the multicellular organism— an enlargement of the unit exposed to natural selection, a shielding of the individual cell from that pressure, an endowment of it with freedom to vary and specialize in safety.

> Nature has thus made two great experiments of the same type,

and if one be reasonably careful to avoid arguing from analogy, it is possible to use one case to illuminate the other by furnishing hints as to what mechanisms may be looked for and in what directions inquiry may profitably be pursued.

The sporadic occurrence of gregariousness at widely separated points of the animal field—in man and sheep, in ant and elephant—inclines one to suppose that multicellularity must have arisen also at multiple points, and that the metazoa did not arise from the protozoa by a single line of descent. It suggests also that there is some inherent property in mobile living organisms that makes combination of individuals into larger units a more or less inevitable course of development under certain circumstances and without any gross variation being necessary to initiate it. The complex evolution which multicellularity made possible, and perhaps enforced, can scarcely fail to make one wonder whether the gregarious animal has not entered upon a path which must of necessity lead to increasing complexity and co-ordination, to a more and more stringent intensity of integration or to extinction. (p. 103-104)

Trotter talks about the varying degrees to which gregariousness has developed in other species. In the bumble bee there are small, weak families; in the wasps, large and strong colonies which are nevertheless unable to survive the winter; and in the honey bee the social instinct has reached perfection. One of the chief advantages of social life, he says, is the specialization of functions in the individual organisms. However, while individuals may gain new functions, they lose old ones, and in the end become unable to live autonomously. Also, a need is created for a system that can coordinate the activities of these specialized individuals; in individual organisms it is the nervous system which coordinates the activities of the specialized parts of the body:

The varying degrees to which the social habit has developed among different animals provide a very interesting branch of study. The class of insects is remarkable in furnishing an almost inexhaustible variety of stages to which the instinct is developed. Of these that reached by the bumble bee, with its small, weak families, is a familiar example of a low grade; that of the wasp, with its colonies large and strong, but unable to survive the winter, is another of more developed type; while that of the honey bee represents a very high grade of development in which the instinct seems to have completed its cycle and yielded to the hive the maximum advantages of which it is capable. In the honey bee, then, the social instinct may be said to be complete.

It is necessary to examine somewhat closely into what is denoted by the completeness or otherwise of the social habit in a given species.

To return for a moment to the case of the change from the unicellular to the multicellular, it is obvious that in the new unit, to get the full advantage of the change there must be specialization involving both loss and gain to the individual cell; one loses power of digestion and gains a special sensitiveness to stimulation, another loses locomotion to gain digestion, and so forth in innumerable series as the new unit becomes more complex. Inherent, however, in the new mechanism is the need for co-ordination if the advantages of specialization are to be obtained. The necessity of a nervous system—if progress is to be maintained—early becomes obvious, and it is equally clear that the primary function of the nervous system is to facilitate co-ordination. Thus it would seem that the individual cell incorporated in a larger unit must possess a capacity for specialization, the ability to originate new methods of activity, and a capacity for response—that is, the ability to limit itself to action co-ordinated suitably to the interests of the new unit rather than to those that would have been its own if it had been a free unit in itself. Specialization and co-ordination will be the two necessary conditions for success of the larger unit, and advance in complexity will be possible as long only as these two are unexhausted. Neither, of course, will be of avail without the other. The richest specialization will be of no good if it cannot be controlled to the uses of the whole organism, and the most perfect control of the individual cells will be incapable of ensuring progress if it has no material of original variation to work on (p. 104-105).

Here is where Trotter says that altruism is a byproduct of the herd instinct, and that altruists are punished when their altruism takes novel forms. The most important thing for the herd is that homogeneity be maintained; disagreement is never tolerated, however benign it may seem:

Again, a fourth corollary of gregariousness in man is the fact expounded many years ago by Pearson that human altruism is a natural instinctive product. The obvious dependence of the evolution of altruism upon increase in knowledge and inter-communication has led to its being regarded as a late and a conscious development—as something in the nature of a judgment by the individual that it pays him to be unselfish. This is an interesting rationalization of the facts because in the sense in which "pay" is meant it is so obviously false. Altruism does not at present, and cannot, pay the individual in anything but feeling, as theory declares it must. It is clear, of course, that as long as altruism is regarded as in the nature of a judgment, the fact is overlooked that necessarily its only reward can be in feeling. Man is altruistic because he must be, not because reason recommends it, for herd suggestion opposes any advance in altruism, and when it can the herd executes the altruist, not of course as such but as an innovator. This is a remarkable instance of the protean character of the gregarious instinct and the complexity it introduces into human affairs, for we see one instinct producing manifestations directly hostile to each other—prompting to ever advancing developments of altruism, while it necessarily leads to any new product of advance being attacked. It shows, moreover, as will be pointed out again later, that a gregarious species rapidly developing a complex society can be saved from inextricable confusion only by the appearance of reason and the application of it to life.

When we remember the fearful repressing force which society has always exercised on new forms of altruism and how constantly the dungeon, the scaffold, and the cross have been the reward of the altruist, we are able to get some conception of the force of the instinctive impulse which has triumphantly defied these terrors, and to appreciate in some slight degree how irresistible an enthusiasm it might become if it were encouraged by the unanimous voice of the herd. (p. 46-47)

Chapter 3: Extraordinary Popular Delusions

The World Outside and the Pictures in our Heads

One of William James's favorite students, Walter Lippmann, became one of the twentieth century's most prominent journalists. He was also close to the circles of power and influence. He advised presidents from Teddy Roosevelt, who called him "the most brilliant young man of his age in all the United States," to Lyndon Johnson, with whom he had a bitter falling out over the Vietnam War. Most of Woodrow Wilson's Fourteen Points were actually written by Lippmann. Lippmann's columns shaped the thinking of countless other important people. He and public relations founder Edward Bernays were key propagandists during the First World War, despite still being in their mid-twenties. Both were experts for the American delegation at the Paris Peace Conference that ended the war. Both had read the works of the crowd psychologists. So Lippmann had a good understanding of what was really going on in the world, and he also had a good understanding of how the public can be misled by appearances, and also by their own shortcomings. Lippmann (1922) wrote an influential book about it called *Public Opinion* in which he talks about just how little understanding the public has of the world beyond their immediate experience. And yet it was this ill-informed public opinion that decided public policy in a democratic state. Lippmann thought that the experts should make the important decisions and the public should be educated to accept those decisions, rather than having decision-makers act according to the whims of the public. This is an idea he develops in his later book, *the Phantom Public*.

Lippmann says that there is a difference between the world as it actually exists and the world as it is represented in our minds. But it is the world inside our heads that we act upon, regardless of whether that world represents the real one accurately. He gives a remarkable example of this from the First World War. There was an island in the ocean whose inhabitants included people from nations that were at war with each other, but they did not get the news until after the war was well under way. In their ignorance, they carried on as if they were still at peace. And they continued fighting each other after the war had ended, although they were actually at peace. Lippmann says that this is nothing new. People have believed in and acted upon false mental pictures of reality throughout history.

Lippmann says that great men, even during their lifetimes, have two different personas—a public one and a private one. Most people believe the public image of the great man; this image exaggerates his virtues and achievements and conceals his flaws. People treat the private man as if he actually were his public persona. Lippmann says that these public personas are often the spontaneous creations of the mind of the crowd; people project upon him their ideas of what they think he should be.

If Lippmann is right, as I think he is, then technological advances in the media would explain why there are few heroes today. It is exceptionally difficult for important people to keep their private and public lives separate. But how can you maintain an idealized public persona if anyone anywhere can, with a cell phone camera, reveal it to be a myth? It seems to me like such myths are, if not indispensable to leadership, then a great boon to it. People will follow a person if they believe him to be the great man of their imaginations; they are less willing to follow him if they perceive him to be just a regular guy like you and me, which of course he is, in the sense that no one can live up to an idealized persona. The alternative to people following idealized personas appears to be for them to be managed by unfeeling, often unthinking, bureaucracies. Bureaucracies don't have heroes. They have routines and people who do them well or poorly. But if this is granted, then perhaps it is not such a bad thing *per se* that public relations people portray people as being better than they really are. But then people are making decisions on public policy based on emotion, and on false information. This wouldn't be so bad if the public were not expected to make decisions about public policy, but in a democracy, however flawed, they do have some say—at least as a crowd. So leadership by myth might work well in a monarchy or aristocracy, but is likely to become demagogy in a democracy; in the former two government types it doesn't matter if the public believes things that aren't true because they aren't the ones making the decisions about what the state should do.

Lippmann says that people have no choice but to reconstruct in their mind's eyes simplified pictures of the outside world. The problem is that the world is just too vast and complex for anyone to get a perfectly accurate representation of it. So it's not just that they may have only second-hand accounts of what is going on somewhere they have never been before; even if they have been there, even if they were able to observe the events taking place there in real-time, the world is still too complex for anything but a simplified mental representation of it. So the generals in the Great War knew better than other people what was happening on the war front, but they were not capable of imagining millions of soldiers; they thought in terms of hundreds of regiments. Lippmann says that a person hearing about the war from his home might imagine two military or political leaders engaging in a sort of duel, perhaps with a bunch of little soldiers in the background; anything else would be too difficult for him to imagine.

Lippmann gives an example of politicians from the two American political parties receiving, and believing, a false report about what was happening with the American troops in Europe. Both sides believed the fiction because some kind of fiction was necessary for understanding what was going on. Anyway, the Republicans, who were against the League of Nations, were angry that American troops were, they believed, being ordered to war by a foreign government (the British or the Supreme Council) without the consent of Congress. The Democrats defended the action by saying that it was necessary and legal because peace had not yet been concluded because the Republicans were delaying it. Each side believed what they believed because of their partisanship.

But as it turned out, the report was false; the American troops had not been ordered to attack Italians by a foreign government but had been requested by the Italian government to protect Italians in the Adriatic. Lippmann points out that these men were trained as lawyers, and the point he means to make is that even people who have been trained to defer judgment until the facts are in find it difficult to do so when their passions incline them toward false beliefs.

Lippmann says that what men do is not based on direct and certain knowledge but on the mental pictures made by or given to them, and so if a man believes the Earth is flat, he will take care not to go too close to its edges, and if he believes that somewhere there exists a fountain of youth, he might go off in pursuit of it. Lippmann says that even if you explain social life as pursuing pleasure and avoiding pain, that still does not explain why a man thinks one course more likely than another to produce pleasure. It does not explain how people conceive of their interest one way rather than another way. In order to do this, the construction of pseudo-environments, mental pictures of the world, is necessary. When men theorize this is what they are doing.

Lippmann talks about how different groups of people conceive of the world in different ways, and this explains in large part why they behave in different ways. He says that propaganda is the attempt to change the mental pictures of a group so that they will behave in some desired way. The creation of class consciousness is a particular case of propagandizing. Lippmann also talks about national consciousness, and about how each side in a war can earnestly believe that they are defending themselves against the aggression of the other side.

Lippmann talks about how public opinion was managed during the war. He talks about a French officer who wrote propaganda according to the preferences of the generals who were fighting it: the news was tilted either to give people hope or to make them despair. Few knew that their mental pictures were being manipulated in this way.

News which would have demoralized people or which would have caused them to lose faith in the competence of their military leadership was censored. So when the casualties were high on both sides, the French government preferred to emphasize the high numbers of German casualties rather than any territorial gains the Germans made, and this distracted people from the territorial losses. Lippmann says that in order for propaganda to work, though, people cannot be allowed to know what actually happened. The propagandists may know the truth, but they have to censor it. With these conditions met, pseudo-environments can be created in the minds of the public which do not correspond to the world that actually exists. Nevertheless, they act upon the mental pictures presented to them by the authorities. One reason why the wars the great powers have waged since World War II have usually turned out badly is because it is very difficult to censor the information that reaches the public now; the television was responsible for that initially, but now the Internet and cell phone cameras make it virtually impossible to censor what is really going on. If the troops commit some atrocity, as sometimes happens in war (and which used to happen all the time), then the public will almost certainly know about it; the government can't censor it. So people can become demoralized easily, and if they lose patience the military will be forced to withdraw regardless of whether they have achieved their strategic objectives. The generals are forced to fight on two fronts—with the enemy before them and public opinion to their rear—and the troops can't just go against what the generals want to do. The generals can't just do what they want because their bosses, the politicians, are accountable to public opinion. Without the ability to censor information about the war front, public opinion cannot be controlled.

But it isn't just public affairs in which people censor information, says Lippmann. People do it in their everyday lives when they insist upon privacy. Some things are considered not to be anyone else's business, and so they are censored. So much of what goes on between a man and his wife is considered private, and is censored, and how much money a man makes is often considered private, and a man's credit rating is usually considered private, and certain information that passes between lawyer and client and doctor and patient is considered private. But people's ideas about what should be public knowledge and what should be private changes over time. A man's theology used to be considered a public, not a private, matter as it often is today. Infectious diseases were once considered to be private matters, although now they are public ones. It seems to me that in all of the cases Lippmann talks about, and in many more ones also, it has become much more difficult to censor information, especially if one is broadly known to the public. I suspect this has not been a desirable change. There were many great people in the past who might not have become great if everything was known about them, because in many respects public opinion is intolerant. Most people like us because they don't know everything about us; privacy may be the thing that makes social life possible.

Next Lippmann talks about the Creel Committee (or Committee on Public Information) that was responsible for building support in the United States for the country's entry into the war. This was a massive effort. Lippmann brings it up to show just how much effort is required to make opinion uniform in a country:

> Mr. Creel had to assemble machinery which included a Division of News that issued, he tells us, more than six thousand releases, had to enlist seventy-five thousand Four Minute Men who delivered at least seven hundred and fifty-five thousand, one hundred and ninety speeches to an aggregate of over three hundred million people. Boy scouts delivered annotated copies of President Wilson's addresses to the householders of America. Fortnightly periodicals were sent to six hundred thousand teachers. Two hundred thousand lantern slides were furnished for illustrated lectures. Fourteen hundred and thirty-eight different designs were turned out for posters, window cards, newspaper advertisements, cartoons, seals and buttons. The chambers of commerce, the churches,

fraternal societies, schools, were used as channels of distribution. Yet Mr. Creel's effort, to which I have not begun to do justice, did not include Mr. McAdoo's stupendous organization for the Liberty Loans, nor Mr. Hoover's far reaching propaganda about food, nor the campaigns of the Red Cross, the Y. M. C. A., Salvation Army, Knights of Columbus, Jewish Welfare Board, not to mention the independent work of patriotic societies, like the League to Enforce Peace, the League of Free Nations Association, the National Security League, nor the activity of the publicity bureaus of the Allies and of the submerged nationalities.

Probably this is the largest and the most intensive effort to carry quickly a fairly uniform set of ideas to all the people of a nation. The older proselyting worked more slowly, perhaps more surely, but never so inclusively. Now if it required such extreme measures to reach everybody in time of crisis, how open are the more normal channels to men's minds? The Administration was trying, and while the war continued it very largely succeeded, I believe, in creating something that might almost be called one public opinion all over America. But think of the dogged work, the complicated ingenuity, the money and the personnel that were required. Nothing like that exists in time of peace, and as a corollary there are whole sections, there are vast groups, ghettoes, enclaves and classes that hear only vaguely about much that is going on (p. 46-48).

Lippmann says that a man's income influences the quantity and quality of the information he receives about the world. With money you can overcome almost every tangible obstacle of communication. This argument doesn't hold quite as well for our own day as it did back then, though. The Internet makes it possible to find out almost anything about almost anything. It's still expensive for the average person to travel a lot, but not as expensive as it once was. There are applications like Google Maps that allow a person to see the world with information obtained from satellites, but this is still not quite as useful as actually being somewhere.

But there are other reasons why people don't have access to all the information they need to form an accurate mental picture of the world. A lot of people, says Lippmann, are just not very curious about what is going on around them and prefer to spend their time and devote their attention to amusements.

Most people's ideas are determined by their social sets. It is their social sets that decide what ideas are to be paid attention to, and which ones are to be accepted and which ones rejected. They decide which sources of information are admissible and which ones are not. Lippmann says that the social set is not so rigidly defined for people living in the big cities who have wide interests and the means of moving about, but even there there are quarters where self-sufficing social sets can be found. In smaller communities there may exist a freer circulation during working hours but few people do not know which set they really belong to, and which ones they do not belong to.

The distinguishing mark of a social set is usually the presumption that the children may intermarry. Marrying outside the set may still be possible, but nevertheless it usually involves at least a moment of hesitation. Lippmann says that there is a hierarchy of social sets. Between social sets of the same level, association is easy and individuals are quickly accepted. However, contact between sets that are "higher" and "lower" always involves some discomfort and consciousness of difference. Lippmann notes that social barriers are not so rigid in a country like the United States where individuals pass relatively freely from one set to another. He says that social class is not determined entirely by income; it has more to do with the nature of a man's work.

Lippmann says that whatever the tests of admission are, the social set behaves like a biological clan. He talks about how social leaders act as custodians and interpreters of the social pattern, and how they decide who is allowed in and who is not. They keep an eye on what other social sets are doing. The leaders bind the hierarchy together and at each level there is a social set of the social leaders. The people who bind these sets of social leaders together vertically are exceptional people who pass in and out of social groups and maintain contact among them all. Tarde's laws of imitation operate through these channels, Lippmann says. But there are large sections of the population that don't maintain such contacts. Often these groups form their own, separate social hierarchies.

Lippmann says that social superiors tend to be obeyed by social inferiors, and the holders of power tend to be imitated by subordinates, and the more successful tend to be imitated by the less successful, and the rich tend to be imitated by the poor, and those from city tend to be imitated by those from the country. He says that the ruling set of the West is an international set centered in many ways (in his time) in London. He says that "[i]t counts among its membership the most influential people in the world, containing as it does the diplomatic set, high finance, the upper circles of the army and the navy, some princes of the church, a few great newspaper proprietors, their wives and mothers and daughters who wield the scepter of invitation." It is a great circle of talk and a real social set. But its importance comes from the fact that the distinction between public and private affairs practically disappears for this group. The private affairs of the set are public matters, and public matters are its private, often even its family affairs. The opinions of the members of this group filter down to people whose social circle may only be that of a small town.

Lippmann says that most people do not spend very much time informing themselves by reading newspapers, and he cites studies which show this to be the case. He says also that thoughts about the world outside our heads are usually conveyed by words, and yet words are an imperfect vehicle for their conveyance; the meanings of words change over time and the same words can mean more than one thing depending on who hears them. He says that there are all sorts of ways in which public opinion is misled:

Thus the environment with which our public opinions deal is refracted in many ways, by censorship and privacy at the source, by physical and social barriers at the other end, by scanty attention, by the poverty of language, by distraction, by unconscious constellations of feeling, by wear and tear, violence, monotony. These limitations upon our access to that environment combine with the obscurity and complexity of the facts themselves to thwart clearness and justice of perception, to substitute misleading fictions for workable ideas, and to deprive us of adequate checks upon those who consciously strive to mislead (p. 76).

Lippmann says that the power to dissociate superficial analogies, attend to differences, and appreciate variety is lucidity of mind. It's a relative faculty, and the differences can be considerable. A newborn infant is almost wholly lacking in it, and a botanist examining a flower possesses it in abundance. People possess lucidity about the things with which they have become familiar, and lack it in areas outside of their personal experience. The ability had been examined in the psychological laboratories of Lippmann's day.

Lippmann says that life in the cities in the industrial age is not conducive to thought. Thought has become a burden:

If the comparatively simple conditions of a laboratory can so readily flatten out discrimination, what must be the effect of city life? In the laboratory the fatigue is slight enough, the distraction rather trivial. Both are balanced in measure by the subject's interest and self-consciousness. Yet if the beat of a metronome will depress intelligence, what do eight or twelve hours of noise, odor, and heat in a factory, or day upon day among chattering typewriters and telephone bells and slamming doors, do to the political judgments formed on the basis of newspapers read in street-cars and subways? Can anything be heard in the hubbub that does not shriek, or be seen in the general glare that does not flash like an electric sign? The life of the city dweller lacks solitude, silence, ease. The nights are noisy and ablaze. The people of a big city are assaulted by incessant sound, now violent and jagged, now falling into unfinished rhythms, but endless and remorseless. Under modern industrialism thought goes on in a bath of noise. If its discriminations are often flat and foolish, here at least is some small part of the reason. The sovereign people determines life and death and happiness under conditions where experience and experiment alike show thought to be most difficult. "The intolerable burden of thought" is a burden when the conditions make it burdensome. It is no burden when the conditions are favorable. It is as exhilarating to think as it is to dance, and just as natural.

Every man whose business it is to think knows that he must for part of the day create about himself a pool of silence. But in that helter-skelter which we flatter by the name of civilization, the citizen performs the perilous business of government under the worst possible conditions. A faint recognition of this truth inspires the movement for a shorter work day, for longer vacations, for light, air, order, sunlight and dignity in factories and offices. But if the intellectual quality of our life is to be improved that is only the merest beginning. So long as so many jobs are an endless and, for the worker, an aimless routine, a kind of automatism using one set of muscles in one monotonous pattern, his whole life will tend towards an automatism in which nothing is particularly to be distinguished from anything else unless it is announced with a thunderclap. So long as he is physically imprisoned in crowds by day and even by night his attention will flicker and relax. It will not hold fast and define clearly where he is the victim of all sorts of pother, in a home which needs to be ventilated of its welter of drudgery, shrieking children, raucous assertions, indigestible food, bad air, and suffocating ornament.

Occasionally perhaps we enter a building which is composed and spacious; we go to a theatre where modern stagecraft has cut away distraction, or go to sea, or into a quiet place, and we remember how cluttered, how capricious, how superfluous and clamorous is the ordinary urban life of our time. We learn to understand why our addled minds seize so little with precision, why they are caught up and tossed about in a kind of tarantella by headlines and catch-words, why so often they cannot tell things apart or discern identity in apparent differences (p. 72-74).

Next Lippmann talks about stereotypes. Not even direct experience is safe to rely on in forming conceptions of the outside world because our minds rarely receive raw sensations. These we get only when a thing is actually an entirely novel experience to us. Most of the time our previously formed mental categories inform our perceptions of things. When we report back to others what we have seen we are also communicating our biases. But it is necessary for us to conceive of the world in terms of these categories because the world is too complex to think about it in any other way. The word "stereotype" has acquired a negative connotation in our day but it's important to emphasize that while stereotypes can be misleading and cause people to behave in irrational or unfair ways, they can also be fairly accurate and useful, and in any event there is, again, no other way to deal with a complex environment other than to make use of them.

Lippmann elaborates on the subject of stereotypes. He talks about how Americanization is really the substituting of American stereotypes for European ones. I would imagine that other cases of assimilation work the same way. He also talks about how we tend to understand the people with whom we are personally acquainted as individuals rather than as instances of stereotypes. But for most other people we think in terms of categories. If we learn that a person graduated from Harvard, or from Yale, or that he is an intellectual, or a plutocrat, or that he's an old army sergeant, or that he's a regular guy, we make certain assumptions about him based on those categories. We can be made aware of our use of stereotypes by education, but we can never entirely abandon them. Some of them are reasonably accurate and the economizing of our attention is inevitable given how limited it is and how much we have to deal with.

Lippmann says that those who wish to censor the arts wish to do so because they vaguely feel that the mental categories acquired through fiction tend to be imposed on reality. The censors don't want anyone discovering anything not sanctioned by them. Lippmann doesn't agree with aggressive censorship but he does agree that fiction influences our mental categories. He thinks that the power of fiction to shape these categories has increased as it has become better able to appeal visually to the imagination.

Lippmann says that there's another reason why we hold to our stereotypes when we could adopt more disinterested views of the world. Our systems of stereotypes might be the core of our personal tradition, the defenses of our position in society. Our stereotypes are an ordered, more or less consistent picture of the world, to which our habits, tastes, capacities, comforts, and hopes have adjusted themselves. This is a world that we understand, have a place in, and feel comfortable with:

> THERE is another reason, besides economy of effort, why we so often hold to our stereotypes when we might pursue a more disinterested vision. The systems of stereotypes may be the core of our personal tradition, the defenses of our position in society.
>
> They are an ordered, more or less consistent picture of the world, to which our habits, our tastes, our capacities, our comforts and our hopes have adjusted themselves. They may not be a complete picture of the world, but they are a picture of a possible world to which we are adapted. In that world people and things have their well-known places, and do certain expected things. We feel at home there. We fit in. We are members. We know the way around. There we find the charm of the familiar, the normal, the dependable; its grooves and shapes are where we are accustomed to find them. And

though we have abandoned much that might have tempted us before we creased ourselves into that mould, once we are firmly in, it fits as snugly as an old shoe (p. 94-95).

Lippmann says that any disturbance of our stereotypes seems to us like an attack upon the foundations of the universe. It is an attack on the foundations of *our* universe. Where important things are at stake, we do not readily admit that there is any distinction between our universe and the real universe. It is intolerable for most of us to be compelled to admit that the people we honor are unworthy, or that the people we despise are noble. There is anarchy if our order of precedence is not the only possible one. It would shake the foundations of our self-confidence if our ways of valuing people and things were totally inverted:

No wonder, then, that any disturbance of the stereotypes seems like an attack upon the foundations of the universe. It is an attack upon the foundations of *our* universe, and, where big things are at stake, we do not readily admit that there is any distinction between our universe and the universe. A world which turns out to be one in which those we honor are unworthy, and those we despise are noble, is nerve-racking. There is anarchy if our order of precedence is not the only possible one. For if the meek should indeed inherit the earth, if the first should be last, if those who are without sin alone may cast a stone, if to Caesar you render only the things that are Caesar's, then the foundations of self-respect would be shaken for those who have arranged their lives as if these maxims were not true. A pattern of stereotypes is not neutral. It is not merely a way of substituting order for the great blooming, buzzing confusion of reality. It is not merely a short cut. It is all these things and something more. It is the guarantee of our self-respect; it is the projection upon the world of our own sense of our own value, our own position and our own rights. The stereotypes are, therefore, highly charged with the feelings that are attached to them. They are the fortress of our tradition, and behind its defenses we can continue to feel ourselves safe in the position we occupy (p.

95-96).

Lippmann then talks about how Aristotle's theory of natural slavery was a classic framing of a stereotype. The idea that some men were naturally suited to command and others to obey helped justify the social order of Aristotle's day.

Lippmann says that stimuli received from the outside world are colored by stereotypes. What we receive is a blending of the two. If what we are looking at corresponds successfully with what we anticipated, then the stereotype is reinforced for the future. So he says that if a man thinks that the Japanese are dishonest and he happens to run across two dishonest Japanese, he will be confirmed in his stereotype. But if experience contradicts the stereotype, one of two things can happen. If the man is set in his ways or if some powerful interest makes it inconvenient for him to rearrange his stereotypes, then he'll reject the experience as an exception which proves the rule. But if he is still curious and open-minded, the new experience will be taken into account in his picture of the world. If the incident is striking enough, he might feel uncomfortable with his entire scheme of things. He might be shaken so much as to distrust all accepted ways of looking at life, and he might come to expect that normally a thing will not be what it is generally supposed to be. If he's a literary man he might develop a passion for inverting the moral canon by making Judas, Benedict Arnold, or Caesar Borgia the hero of his story.

Next Lippmann talks about the American stereotype of "progress" and how it influenced so many aspects of American life. Basically, this was the idea that whatever was bigger, faster, stronger, more numerous, more expansive, more up-to-date, and so on was necessarily better. This led to an obsession with means to the near exclusion of ends, or rather, these things were considered to be ends in themselves. It was easy enough for Americans to figure out how to fight the Great War—just make and send to the front the best and the most stuff they could put out. But when the war was over it wasn't clear to most Americans what should be done with the victory. That would have required thinking in terms of different stereotypes from the ones which they had grown accustomed to. So the United States was not able to fully capitalize on its victory.

Lippmann talks some more about stereotypes. He talks about how the industrialists and their critics had very different stereotypes about business. The industrialists viewed themselves as the agents of progress and the creators of wealth and wished to be left alone to do their important work. The people who lost in the competition with the industrialists saw only the waste and unfairness of the great trusts. Lippmann also talks about how an American editor claimed that there were no classes in America while *the Communist Manifesto* claimed that history was the history of class struggles. Both sides sincerely believed what they said. He says that the inability that most people have to consider that each party in a dispute is equipped with a different version of the facts requires them to question the good faith of their antagonists. To admit that an opponent might have a different version of the facts would imply that one's view of reality is not the whole truth about it. That could threaten a person's system of stereotypes and is therefore avoided as an explanation.

Lippmann talks about how stereotypes mislead people about things like geography and time.

Lippmann talks in one part of the book about the strategic use of ambiguity. If politicians are specific about what they mean then sometimes they will alienate supporters. Sometimes the positions of different factions among their supporters just can't be reconciled. But there are slogans and symbols which nearly every supporter will respond well to, and these can be appealed to to maintain party unity, however tenuously.

Lippmann says that symbols and slogans can be made more and more general until you get something like the Rights of Man or the World Made Safe for Democracy which can mean all things to all people. He says that while you may preserve the emotional connection among people for a time with something like these, you lose the intellectual connection. The agreement which these things seem to generate is only apparent, not real; everyone has his own private understanding of what they mean. So Woodrow Wilson's 14 Points meant something different for each of the European powers. Everybody expected everything and demanded everything. It was difficult for each nation to think beyond the national symbols which they were accustomed to; the symbol of Europe was too general for the statesmen of that day.

Lippmann talks about how, in America before 1789, most people identified with their states, not with the union as a whole. Their states and communities seemed real to them while the union did not. Their experiences and symbols had until then been confined to the states, which they rarely ventured outside. Lippmann argues that their experiences did not match their real environment, though, which was at least as large as the 13 states. The states needed a common defense as well as a financial and economic regime as large as the Confederation. But it was difficult for them to think in terms of the union as long as the pseudo-environment of the state encompassed them and state symbols exhausted their political interest. He talks about how Alexander Hamilton had no state loyalties, but only national loyalties, owing to the fact that he had been born in the West Indies. So Hamilton was able to conceive of a larger union and work to realize it. Lippmann thinks that people like Hamilton are always behind the crystallizing of a common will.

Lippmann says that symbols are made congenial and important because they are introduced to us by congenial and important people. We first learn about the world beyond our immediate experiences through our elders, and though we might learn more about it on our own as we grow up, there are still vast parts of the world that remain unknown to us. We are compelled to relate ourselves to that through authorities. Where all the facts are out of sight a true report and a plausible error will read and sound alike, and except where our own knowledge is great we cannot tell the difference between them. So we have to choose between trustworthy and untrustworthy reporters.

However, even that is difficult. Not even the experts know who is most expert among them. Also, the appropriate expert might be too busy to be consulted or impossible to get at. But there are people who we can identify easily enough because they are at the head of affairs. Parents, teachers, and masterful friends are the first people of this sort we encounter. We trust such people in learning anything that is beyond our immediate experience. Lippmann says that it is sometimes considered undignified or sheep-like to trust authorities like this, but he says that there is no practical way around it. It is impossible for anyone to live completely independently of such influences. Hermits are the closest among us to being completely independent, but even then they have been subject to many of the same influences as everyone else before they become hermits. They have learned from others how to keep warm and how to keep from being hungry, and about what the great questions are.

The utmost independence that we can exercise, says Lippmann, is to multiply the authorities to whom we give a friendly hearing. Our quest for truth requires that we seek out the experts and force them to answer any heresy that has the accent of conviction. However, although we might be able to tell who among the experts has won the dialectical victory, we are virtually defenseless against a false premise which none of the debaters has challenged, or against a neglected aspect that none has brought to the argument. Lippmann says that conventional democratic theory assumes the opposite of what he is assuming here. It assumes for the purposes of government an unlimited supply of self-sufficient individuals.

The people who we depend on to learn about the outside world are also the people who seem to be running it. Lippmann says that the leaders are in direct contact with their environment. They may have a limited notion of what they ought to define as the environment, and they are still prone to stereotyped vision, but they are not dealing wholly with abstractions. They decide, give orders, and bargain, and something definite, perhaps not what they imagined, actually happens.

Lippmann talks about how every organization has an oligarchy (he uses the term machine) based on a system of privileges. There is no avoiding having a system of leaders and led. He says that it's not necessary to invent a collective intelligence in order to explain why the judgments of a group are usually more coherent and often more true to form than the remarks of a man in the street. One mind or a few can pursue a train of thought but a group trying to think in concert can do little more than assent or dissent. The members of a hierarchy have a corporate tradition in which apprentices learn the trade from masters, who in turn learned the trade when they were apprentices. In any enduring society the change of personnel within the governing hierarchies is slow enough to permit the transmission of certain great stereotypes and patterns of behavior. These ways become familiar and are recognized as such by the mass of outsiders.

Lippmann says that all organizations are governed by a small number of people. This is true even when, theoretically, a much larger number of people are supposed to govern. One machine can be replaced by another in an election, and revolutions can abolish particular machines altogether, but machines never disappear entirely. The idyllic theory of democracy is nowhere realized—not even in trade unions, socialist parties, or communist governments. There is always an inner circle surrounded by concentric circles which fade out gradually into the disinterested or uninterested rank and file.

Lippmann says that democrats have never come to terms with this inevitable fact of group life, but regard it as perverse. There are two main theories of democracy. One presupposes the self-sufficient individual, which Lippmann rejects, and the other presupposes an Oversoul regulating everything. Lippmann says that there is nothing that the Oversoul explains that cannot be explained by the actions of actual human beings. I assume he means the oligarchies.

Lippmann says that the most that the masses can do without an organization is say "yes" or "no" to the actions proposed by a hierarchy. In order to act collectively they must place themselves under the leadership of others. He says that initiatives, referendums, and direct primaries cannot replace machines. This is because no amount of balloting can obviate the need of creating an issue, whether it be a measure or a candidate, on which the voters can say either "yes" or "no." There is no such thing a direct legislation. When citizens receive a ballot they vote "yes" or "no" on those amendments that are presented to them and no others. The most brilliant amendment in the world might occur to one of them but nevertheless he votes on what's on the ballot. Lippmann says that you'd have to do violence to the English language to call that legislation. He concludes his discussion by saying that the many can elect after the few have nominated.

Lippmann says that the cultivation of symbols serves the same purpose for the rank and file as privileges do for the hierarchy—that is, it conserves unity. These symbols are things like the totem pole or the national flag; they could be something like a wooden idol or God the Invisible King; they could be some magic word or some diluted version of Adam Smith or Jeremy Bentham. Symbols have long been cherished by leaders, many of whom were themselves unbelievers because they were the focal points where differences merged. Detached observers may scorn such things, but only when symbols have done their work does the leader have a handle by which to move a crowd. In a symbol emotion is discharged at a common target and the differences of real ideas are disregarded. Leaders tend to hate destructive criticism because the symbols and their supporting rituals cannot withstand criticism, and when they go so does the unity of the mass. The people break up into bickering or warring sects. Free spirits think highly of the debunking of what they regard as nonsense, but clear definitions and candid statements are poor tools of leadership.

Lippmann elaborates on the importance of symbols. He says that they enable people to work toward a common end, but they can also be an instrument by which a few can fatten on the many, deflect criticism, and seduce men into facing agony for objects which they do not understand.

Lippmann says that these things are not flattering if we choose to think of ourselves as realistic, self-sufficient, and self-governing personalities. But again, they can't be dispensed with; they might be the only means by which collective action may be efficiently organized. He even says that there are times when one wrong opinion is preferable to two right opinions because the wrong opinion maintains unity while the two right opinions dissolve it. The dissolution of unity can sometimes lead to disaster, as for example in a time of war. There is also a conspiracy of silence among the leaders at such times. Even if they disagree with the actions of their colleagues and superiors they hold their tongues because of the dissolution of unity that would be the result.

Lippmann says that traditional democratic assumptions serve best during times of tranquillity and harmony, and not for emergencies and dangers. Where the masses must cooperate in an uncertain and eruptive environment, it is usually necessary for the leaders to secure unity and flexibility without real consent. The symbol is what does this.

Lippmann talks a bit more about how the leaders deal with the public. He says that democratic politicians pay the most attention to the highly influential, who can usually be won over with favors, and the least influential, because courting them makes the leaders seem magnanimous. The leaders can't act as valets to everybody, though; they don't have enough time or enough favors; the anonymous multitude therefore receive propaganda. Lippmann says that all leaders are necessarily propagandists, since they have access to information which the public does not, and must decide what the public should know and what it shouldn't. For the reasons given previously they can't tell people everything they know.

Lippmann says that the knowledge of how to manufacture the consent of the public had increased dramatically in recent years as the result of psychological research and modern means of communications, and it could be improved still more. He says that a revolution was taking place that was infinitely more significant than any shifting of economic power. Within the life of the generation then in control of the government, mass persuasion had become a self-conscious art and an organ of popular government:

That the manufacture of consent is capable of great refinements no one, I think, denies. The process by which public opinions arise is certainly no less intricate than it has appeared in these pages, and the opportunities for manipulation open to anyone who understands the process are plain enough.

The creation of consent is not a new art. It is a very old one which was supposed to have died out with the appearance of democracy. But it has not died out. It has, in fact, improved enormously in technic, because it is now based on analysis rather than on rule of thumb. And so, as a result of psychological research, coupled with the modern means of communication, the practice of democracy has turned a corner. A revolution is taking place, infinitely more significant than any shifting of economic power.

Within the life of the generation now in control of affairs, persuasion has become a self-conscious art and a regular organ of popular government. None of us begins to understand the consequences, but it is no daring prophecy to say that the knowledge of how to create consent will alter every political calculation and modify every political premise.

Under the impact of propaganda, not necessarily in the sinister meaning of the word alone, the old constants of our thinking have become variables. It is no longer possible, for example, to believe in the original dogma of democracy; that the knowledge needed for the management of human affairs comes up spontaneously from the human heart. Where we act on that theory we expose ourselves to self-deception, and to forms of persuasion that we cannot verify. It has been demonstrated that we cannot rely upon intuition, conscience, or the accidents of casual opinion if we are to deal with the world beyond our reach (p. 248-249).

Lippmann talks about the history of political philosophy next. He talks about the debates between aristocrats and democrats, and their common acceptance of the intellectual framework created by Aristotle. Lippmann says that what hardly any of these thinkers considered was how the ruler, whether he was a king or an aristocrat or a man of the people, was to get his information. Knowledge was necessary for making good decisions, but the political philosophers just took knowledge of the world for granted. Aristotle recognized the importance of citizens having direct knowledge of their environments, however:

In deciding who was most fit to govern, knowledge of the world was taken for granted. The aristocrat believed that those who dealt with large affairs possessed the instinct, the democrats asserted that all men possessed the instinct and could therefore deal with large affairs. It was no part of political science in either case to think out how knowledge of the world could be brought to the ruler. If you were for the people you did not try to work out the question of how to keep the voter informed. By the age of twenty-one he had his political faculties. What counted was a good heart, a reasoning mind, a balanced judgment. These would ripen with age, but it was not necessary to consider how to inform the heart and feed the reason. Men took in their facts as they took in their breath.

[. . .]

But the facts men could come to possess in this effortless way were limited. They could know the customs and more obvious character of the place where they lived and worked. But the outer world they had to conceive, and they did not conceive it instinctively, nor absorb trustworthy knowledge of it just by living. Therefore, the only environment in which spontaneous politics were possible was one confined within the range of the ruler's direct and certain knowledge. There is no escaping this conclusion, wherever you found government on the natural range of men's faculties. "If," as Aristotle said, [Footnote: *Politics*, Bk. VII, Ch. 4.] "the citizens of a state are to judge and distribute offices according to merit, then they must know each other's characters; where they do not possess this knowledge, both the election to offices and the decision of law suits will go wrong" (p. 358-359).

The problem was most difficult for the democrats, and it remains a problem.

Lippmann talks about how in small, self-contained, self-governing communities it is possible for the people to know their environments very well, because the environment doesn't extend very far beyond the small community. Democracy is possible, and it works well. Lippmann says that Jefferson understood intuitively that America had to remain a nation of small farmers if it was to maintain its democratic way of life. Entanglements with the outside world had to be avoided, and that included foreign commerce in addition to foreign alliances. It was better not to have a foreign policy at all if it could be helped. But America did change. It became a great industrial and commercial country. Most of the facts with which the ordinary person had to deal were outside of his reach. So political institutions have had to adapt to this new state of affairs.

Lippmann talks about how the Federalists, like Hamilton and

Washington, had wanted union, not democracy. They wanted to limit the influence of local interests and strengthen the federal government. They didn't want deadlock within the government; they wanted a government that could formulate and execute policy across all of the states. At first the federalists looked to the gentry for support, but the gentry was not strong enough to struggle for the succession. Jefferson came to office in 1800 and established a new tradition of democratic government. He stereotyped the images, ideas, and many of the phrases of democracy. The Constitution came to be regarded as the instrument of democratic government. Lippmann says that the framers of the constitution with all their sagacity had failed to see that a frankly undemocratic constitution would not be tolerated for long.

Andrew Jackson had consolidated and expanded the democratic tradition that Thomas Jefferson had created. He began the practice of turning public office into patronage. The principle of rotation in office with short terms was regarded as a great reform at the time. The system prevented a privileged class from monopolizing government positions and appeared to open careers to talent. It also prevented the establishment of a powerful permanent bureaucracy. This system, called the spoils system, was regarded by most people in Lippmann's day as corrupt. People were given positions because they helped the president get elected, and not for any other reason. Lippmann doesn't think too badly of patronage, though, because, he says, it weakened the local spirit and brought together in some kind of peaceful cooperation the provincial celebrities who, if they had not felt a sense of common interest, would have torn the union apart.

Lippmann talks about guild socialism for a bit. Since it no longer seemed possible in the industrial era to make the small township the basic unit of democracy, some of the thinkers of Lippmann's day thought that the workshop might be able to fulfill the role. Lippmann is skeptical of the idea. He thinks that even if each workshop were really able to make its own decisions that there would be a chaos of bickering workshops. Also, he wondered how the workers of a small workshop would be able to grasp the unseen environment of an entire industry, much less other aggregates and the relations among them.

Lippmann then talks about how the public expects newspapers to deliver the truth about the unseen environment upon which they base their political decisions for next to nothing. That is if the truth is not believed to arise spontaneously from the hearts of the citizens. And he says that students of political science hardly pay attention to how the news is created, despite its overwhelming importance. He talks a bit more about the economics of the news business. The newspapers can't survive without advertising. And although a paper can alienate advertisers and survive, the one group which they cannot alienate is the buying public. These are not the very poor, but those with enough disposable income to buy the things that advertisers want to sell. The surest guarantee of a newspaper's independence is the loyalty of its readers. If a paper's readers will support it no matter what then it will wield a power greater than that which any one advertiser can wield, and it can break up any combination of advertisers. If a newspaper betrays its readers for the sake of an advertiser, then it is probably the case that either the publisher sincerely shares the views of the advertiser or else he thinks, possibly mistakenly, that he cannot count on the support of his readers if he openly resists dictation.

Lippmann talks about how reporting is theoretically the foundation for the whole newspaper business, and yet it is one of the most poorly paid and least regarded of positions. Able men go into it only out of necessity or for experience, and with the intention of being promoted as soon as possible. Another problem is that reporters can't be everywhere at once. They are also not clairvoyant. Yet they must cover a very broad range of subjects. Newspapers don't try to keep an eye on all mankind but have watchers stationed at certain places, like Police Headquarters, the Coroner's Office, the Country Clerk's Office, City Hall, the White House, the Senate, the House of Representatives, and so on. They watch, or rather in the majority of cases they belong to associations which employ men who watch a comparatively small number of places where the life of anyone departs from ordinary paths or when events worth telling about occur.

Lippmann talks about press agents. The enormous discretion as to what facts and what impressions shall be reported was steadily convincing every organized group of people that whether it wanted to secure or avoid publicity, discretion could not be left to reporters. So they were hiring press agents to act as intermediaries between their organizations and the press. He says that the temptation to exploit a press agent's position once they've hired him is great. Lippmann quotes one writer as saying that many direct channels to the news had been closed and the information for the public was first being filtered through publicity agents. The great corporations, banks, railroads, and all organizations of business and social and political activity had them. Even statesmen had them. They were the media through which the news came.

The press agent makes a reporter's job easier than it would otherwise be. However, he is responsible only to his employers and their interests, not to the public and its interests, and he presents accounts of the facts which he would prefer the public to accept, not a dispassionate portrait of reality. The publicity man is a censor and propagandist.

Lippmann says that news and truth should be distinguished. The news is not the truth. The function of the news is to signalize an event, while the function of truth is to bring to light the hidden facts, to set them into relation with each other, and to make a picture of reality on which men can act.

Lippmann says that the best public policy is made when there is a division of labor between the people taking account of the facts and the people acting upon them. It would be best, he says, if the people doing the intelligence work did not have a "policy," but simply presented the facts as they were and left it to others what to do with those facts. He lays out a detailed plan for an intelligence agency modeled after British institutions, which he thought did a good job collecting, analyzing, and acting upon facts about the world.

The Madness of Crowds

Memoirs of Extraordinary Popular Delusions and the Madness of Crowds by Charles Mackay (1841/1852) has long been popular with people interested in crowd behavior, and especially with stock traders and investors. Mackay gives excellent accounts of how economic bubbles form and what happens when they burst, but he also talks about alchemy, the crusades, witch-hunts, prophecies, fortune-telling, animal magnetism, the influence of politics and religion on the way head and facial hair are worn, murder through poisoning, haunted houses, popular follies of great cities, popular admiration of great thieves, duels, and relics. Mackay says at the beginning of the book that men go mad in herds and recover their senses one by one, and it's hard to disagree with him after reviewing his evidence.

Mackay begins the first volume of his book with a discussion of John Law's Mississippi Bubble. Law was a financier and gambler from a Scottish banking family who was forced to escape Britain after he killed a man in a duel. The Duke of Orleans became his patron. The Duke became regent after the death of Louis XIV and could execute the scheme Law had developed; it was for a joint-stock company with a monopoly to exploit the wealth of France's Louisiana territory west of the Mississippi, which was thought to abound in precious metals. The company was to have the exclusive right to farm taxes and coin currency. The stocks were to be backed by paper money, which Law had made more creditable with the public by measures like requiring notes to be payable on sight and at the value at which they were issued, and by requiring death for bankers who issued notes without having sufficient security to answer all demands. Law's paper money became more valuable than metal currency because it was common then for the government to depreciate the value of metal currency.

The paper money experiment was tried with France itself first, and this revived the commerce of the country. Law's paper currency had done so much good for France that any promises of the future that Law gave were readily believed. This is what fueled the frenzy of speculation that became the Mississippi Bubble. But the Regent thought that if paper money could work such miracles, it could do better than complement metallic currency; it could replace it. Mackay says that this was one of the Duke's fundamental errors.

The company was granted greater and greater privileges until it was erected into the Royal Bank of France. But both Law and the Regent forgot Law's principle that a banker who issued paper currency without the funds necessary to provide for them should be put to death. After the company went from being a private institution to being a public one, the Regent printed 1000 million livres of paper money, which was far more paper than they had security for. Mackay blames the Regent rather than Law for what happened; Law had never printed more than 60 million livres of paper when he had control of the company.

The value of the stock had increased owing to the zeal of its purchasers, and the more it increased the more people wanted to buy the stock to improve their fortunes. But this couldn't go on forever and it didn't. The bubble burst and France experienced a terrible economic collapse. Law, who had previously been the country's most popular man, became despised. He fled France, and despite his attempts to repair his fortunes, he died in poverty.

What happened was that the Prince de Conti was upset with Law because Law wouldn't allow him to buy shares of India stock at his own price; in order to get even with Law, the Prince demanded a huge amount of specie all at once from his bank, an example which, if imitated, would threaten the entire scheme. Law complained to the Regent and the Regent forced the Prince to refund two-thirds of the specie which he had withdrawn from the bank. The Prince was an unpopular man and people did not readily follow his example, but felt that Law had been unfairly treated. However, some of the shrewder speculators began withdrawing specie in small amounts over time because they had anticipated that the scheme would not last forever. They transported the specie along with expensive jewelry and other valuables out of the country to England and Holland.

Law's bank had no trouble procuring the necessary specie until this point. But France continued to lose specie to England and Holland, and what little specie was left was carefully hidden away, so that the bank had a difficult time meeting its obligations. Law got laws passed depreciating the value of specie relative to paper money, but this did not restore public confidence in the paper, but had the opposite effect. Law, out of desperation, tried to forbid the use of specie altogether. He made it illegal to own specie in excess of five hundred livres; those who broke the law were subject to a heavy fine and had the excess confiscated by the government. It was forbidden to buy up jewellery, plate, and precious stones, and people were encouraged to inform on those who did it, and were rewarded half of the amount they discovered. This turned servants against masters and turned citizens against neighbors, and in time it became enough for an informer to say that he suspected someone of concealing money in his house for a search warrant to be granted.

Law and the Regent had become extremely unpopular. People lost faith in the value of the paper money and in Law's Mississippi Company. Mackay says that France came close to revolution then. The government made a desperate effort to convince people that the western bank of the Mississippi really did have all the precious metals it was reputed to have, and they sent around six thousand of the poorest dregs in France to work in the imagined mines. Most sold their tools for what they could get and immediately returned to their old way of life. Within three weeks half of them were back in Paris. Many extremely gullible people believed that specie would soon be found again in France, however.

Everything got worse for Law and his system from here. The system fell apart and left countless people in difficult circumstances. Law was not safe to walk the streets without an escort. He did manage to escape France but, despite his efforts, he was unable to repair his fortunes and he died in poverty in Venice.

Mackay also talks about England's South Sea Bubble, which also happened during the early eighteenth century and which was similar to, and was inspired by, France's Mississippi Bubble. The people who engineered it thought that they could make Law's scheme work for England if they were careful. They would expand credit to its most extreme limit without allowing the system to break. There were prominent naysayers but their warnings were disregarded. Pessimism about the venture was unpopular. Almost everyone, it seemed, hoped to get rich quick, and without much thought for the consequences.

Joint-stock companies appeared everywhere and were given the apt name of "bubbles." Some of the companies lasted for only a week, or a fortnight, and were never heard from again, and others didn't survive even that long. The highest of the aristocracy were as eager in these projects as any stock jobber. Many fools were impoverished and many rogues were enriched. Speculators took the first opportunity of a rise to sell out, and the next morning the scheme was at an end. One of the projects which received great encouragement was for a company "to make deal-boards out of saw-dust." Mackay thinks this was meant to be a joke, but dozens of other companies that were hardly more reasonable were bought into by countless dupes who lost a great deal of money as a result. One of the projects was for a wheel for perpetual motion, and the company had a capital of one million pounds; another was "for encouraging the breed of horses in England, and improving of glebe and church lands, and repairing and rebuilding parsonage and vicarage houses." The most absurd scheme was for a "company for carrying on an undertaking of great advantage, but nobody to know what it is." Lots of people bought into this, despite its absurdity, and after they did the guy who started it sold out, left for the continent, and was never heard from again.

Eventually the government decided that the bubbles had gotten out of hand and it put an end to them. The South Sea Company itself took a while longer to burst. The directors made all sorts of efforts to keep up the stock price. However, public confidence could not be maintained forever, and the bubble finally burst, ruining many, though a few did well in the end. The directors had made a last-ditch effort to get the Bank of England to save the company but, although the Bank made an effort, it was not enough. The Bank floated some of the company's bonds in response to overwhelming public demand, but when it became clear that this wasn't helping, and the company was going under, and runs were being made on bankers and goldsmiths all over the country, the Bank distanced itself from the South Sea Company. The Bank of England managed to survive, but all sorts of other damage was done to the country, not least to the character of the people. It all happened within the space of eight months.

The people regarded themselves as the innocent victims of a gang of rogues and demanded harsh punishment for the directors and their accomplices. The directors had most of their property confiscated, but were allowed to keep a portion of it, depending on the merits of each case, so that they could repair their fortunes if they were able to. One of the directors was a Mr. Edward Gibbon, who was the grandfather of the famous historian. The elder Gibbon was able to rebuild his fortune after the South Sea Company had collapsed.

After Mackay talks about the stock bubbles, he talks about the tulip mania in Holland. Tulips were introduced into Western Europe in the middle of the sixteenth century and had grown in prestige until 1637 when the bubble burst. Just before then it was considered disreputable for a Dutchman of means to be without some. Mackay presents a list of the goods exchanged for one *Viceroy* tulip, which cost 2500 florins. The goods included two lasts of wheat (448 florins), four lasts of rye (558 florins), four fat oxen (480 florins), eight fat swine (240 florins), twelve fat sheep (120), two hogsheads of wine (70 florins), four tons of beer (32 florins), two tons of butter (192 florins), one thousands pounds of cheese (120 florins), a complete bed (100 florins), a suit of clothes (80 florins), and a silver drinking cup (60 florins).

Mackay talks a bit about some awkward and unfortunate incidents that resulted from the exorbitant price of tulips. One sailor had eaten a merchant's prized tulip mistakenly thinking that it was an onion, and this sent the Dutch establishment into an uproar and it caused the sailor to be thrown in jail for months on a felony charge. In another case, an English traveller who happened to be an amateur botanist dissected a valuable bulb and made learned notes on it, only to be discovered by its owner. He was led through the streets, followed by a mob, and was presented before a magistrate, who informed him that the bulb was worth four thousand florins, and had him locked in prison until he found securities for the payment of this sum.

But this couldn't last forever. People began buying tulips in order to earn profits by speculation. But then people started thinking that in the end someone was going to be ruined. As this conviction spread, people began selling the bulbs and the price fell dramatically, never to rise again. People had a hard time selling their bulbs at the prices they bought them for, and it soon became difficult to sell them even at a substantial discount. A lot of people were indeed ruined. An atmosphere of mutual suspicion had developed.

Mackay talks next about the love people have for relics—for things bearing some relation to a great or beloved person. So the handkerchief that a king blew his nose in would, in the past, have been highly prized, and so would the toe-nail of an apostle. Centuries ago people were known to buy and sell the supposed tears of Jesus or Mary at exorbitant prices. Mackay says that people have a fondness for the relics of great criminals, too. So the ropes which hung famous criminals were often sold at high prices.

Mackay says that people become more credulous during times of calamity.

He then talks about the fashions of wearing hair, and the sometimes odd reasons for them. So at times it is the fashion for men to have beards, and at other times it's the fashion for them to shave all their facial hair. At one point it was the exclusive right of European kings to wear long hair, but this was in time imitated by others, and then the kings started wearing their hair short. The cavaliers and roundheads of the English civil war knew each other by the way they wore their hair: the cavaliers wore it long and the roundheads wore it short.

The next thing Mackay talks about is duels.

Mackay has a chapter titled "the Love of the Marvellous and the Disbelief of the True." Mackay thinks that the reason why people prefer to believe extravagant falsehoods over truth is because the falsehoods have long been believed; newly discovered truths are regarded as intruders and are treated as such. Mackay makes the interesting observation that Kepler could gain neither bread nor credence when he told people that the Earth revolved around the Sun, but when he pretended to tell fortunes and cast nativities everyone flocked to him and paid enormous fees for his services.

Mackay talks about how the great scientists and inventors of the past were originally disbelieved, and were often thought to be mad or guided by the devil. When Roger Bacon invented the telescope and the magic lantern, nobody believed that unaided human ingenuity was responsible for it; on the other hand, no one cast doubt on the accusation that Bacon was given his knowledge by the devil. No one believed Bacon when he suggested that saltpeter, sulphur, and charcoal, when mixed together in certain proportions, would produce effects similar to thunder and lightning; oracles, on the other hand, were believed for ages. In the days of Cardinal Richelieu, Solomon de Cans conceived of the idea of a steam engine and was locked away in the Bastille because he was thought to be a madman. When Harvey proved the circulation of the blood, he was widely despised. People believed it to be a wicked attempt to undermine the belief that the king's touch had the power to cure disease. As Mackay says, "[t]hat a dead criminal's hand, rubbed against a wen, would cure it, was reasonable enough; but that the blood flowed through the veins was beyond all probability." That vaccination could inoculate people against disease was widely disbelieved in Mackay's day, but it was readily believed that vaccination could give a person the qualities of a cow.

Mackay gives another example of the ready disbelief of the true and the ready belief in the fantastic. One Jesuit attempted to explain to the natives of Peru how a powerful lens of his worked. He used it to magnify the sun's rays and burn a man's arm, but his explanation of how it was done was not believed. The natives attempted to seize and destroy the lens because they thought that the Jesuit was in league with infernal gods to draw down the fire of Heaven upon them.

Mackay gives another example similar to this one. He talks about a Brahmin in India who possessed a love of learning, and was initially happy to learn new things from Westerners. However, when he was shown a microscope and had it explained to him how it worked, he became morose. He insisted that the Englishman who showed it to him let him have it, and at last the Englishman gave in. Then the Brahmin destroyed it. He said that the device unsettled his beliefs and he didn't want it to unsettle the beliefs of the others in his country. He was now forever perplexed, a solitary individual among fifty million people who were all educated in the same beliefs that he was and happy in their ignorance. With the microscope destroyed, their minds would remain undisturbed. Mackay says that many learned men will smile at the ignorance of the Peruvian and the Hindoo, but those men may also be ignorant and prejudiced. Mackay talks about how, in his own country, the science of geology was regarded as trying to "hurl the Creator from his throne" and justify atheism.

Mackay concludes the chapter reiterating what he said before, that people are readily deceived when established beliefs are appealed to, but will not believe a truth when it is new.

The next thing Mackay talks about is the fad phrases that the people of the great cities use. These rise to popularity for a time, when they are almost universally heard, but then they fall out of use and are replaced by some other phrase which has its day and is also forgotten. I don't think things have changed very much since Mackay's day. Phrases like "groovy," "far-out," and "rad" were popular decades ago—in the United States at least. I don't hear "cool" very often anymore but I remember that it was popular when I was growing up. "Bad" was also popular when I was a kid, as was "tight"; I haven't heard either in a long time. In London many years before Mackay's day the fad word was Quoz, which was supplanted by "What a shocking bad hat!" Quoz appears to have been a term of reproach, but beyond that it had no fixed meaning.

After "What a shocking bad hat!" it was "Walker!," which lasted only two or three months. Then it was "there he goes with his eye out," and "there she goes with her eye out." But people grew tired of these just like they grew tired of the other phrases. For a brief time "Has your mother sold her mangle?" was popular, but its progress was impeded by the fact that it couldn't be applied well to the older members of society. Its successor, "Flare up!," which emerged at the time of the Reform riots, was far more popular and had a much longer career. In fact, it drove all other slang out of the field. Merely saying it made the humblest Englishman feel like he still had some self-respect.

But "Flare up!," too, became passe. The next fad phrase was "Does your mother know you're out?," which was addressed to young men with more than reasonable swagger. But this greatly offended young men who were approaching but had not quite reached adulthood. In any event, this phrase also fell out of use. The next phrase was "Who are you?" It was uttered quickly, and if a person looked puzzled or responded slowly it was thought to be very amusing. A number of phrases were inspired by popular culture, and they overlapped each other to some extent. So one fad was "Cherry ripe! Cherry ripe!" Another was "Tom and Jerry." Another was "The Sea!, the Sea!" "All Round my Hat" and "Jim Crow" were also popular; street minstrels blackened their faces in order to give proper effect to the latter song.

Mackay mentions in the next chapter that showing anger with a crowd only makes things worse for an individual who does it. It's taken to be a sign of weakness.

He talks in the chapter after that about a group of hereditary murderers in India called the Thugs. Their job was to murder travelers and take their belongings. They sincerely believed their calling to be sanctioned by religion, and they brought up their children to behave as they and their parents and grandparents did. Mackay says that the fact that they believed this made them more dangerous than people who kill for the sake of greed, since a greedy killer might tire of his work after he became rich. The Thugs believed that killing was their noblest duty; they could never stop. There was also a sect that kidnapped children and sold them into slavery.

The next chapter is about the Crusades, and he talks about these in detail. People all over Christendom had been overcome by the desire to take back the holy lands and the sacred relics that were supposedly kept there. They sold their property at low prices and left, almost wholly unprepared, for their destination. That was how it was at first, anyway. The original group was just a mob. However, the crusaders became better organized as they fought with the Muslims for control over Palestine. The crusades were authorized by the popes, and nobles and even kings led them. But strange characters like Peter the Hermit were also ringleaders. The Jews were massacred during the crusades and even Constantinople was sacked, on account of the lingering mistrust between Western and Eastern Christendom. The Byzantines thought of the Westerners as little better than barbarians, while the Westerners thought of the Byzantines as insincere in their faith and basically untrustworthy. Mackay says that Western Christendom became more sophisticated as a result of the crusaders' contact with people more sophisticated than themselves. In the end the crusaders were driven out of Palestine by the Khwarezmians, who had been pushed out of Persia, which they formerly ruled, by the Mongol hordes. The Khwarezmians lost control of the Holy Lands to their Muslim rivals. In any event event that was the end of the crusaders' presence in the holy lands. The ardor of the people had cooled substantially and they could not be persuaded to exert themselves in retaking the lost territories.

In the next chapter Mackay talks about witch hunts. During the middle ages people were incredibly superstitious. No one believed himself to be secure from the machinations of the devil and his agents. Whenever someone was a victim of some calamity he blamed it on a witch. People were quick to accuse others of witchcraft, and thousands and thousands became victims of the delusion. Although it appears that most of the charges were made in all sincerity, Mackay says the powerful used the accusation of witchcraft to ruin the weak when no other pretext could be found for it.

In 1488 Pope Innocent VIII, who was sincerely alarmed by all the reports of witchcraft, delivered a bull calling upon the nations of Europe to rescue the church of Christ upon earth. He appointed inquisitors in every country and granted them the apostolic power to convict and punish. This is when the witch mania began in earnest. Mackay talks a lot more about the history of witch hunts, and he says that belief in witchcraft ended around the middle of the eighteenth century, except among the most vulgar.

In the next chapter Mackay talks about how poisoning people became more common in the early sixteenth century and spread uncontrollably in the seventeenth century. Poison was commonly used by women in order to get rid of their husbands.

Poisoning was most prevalent in Italy, where it was looked upon as a perfectly justifiable means of getting rid of an enemy. Mackay says that the Italians of the sixteenth and seventeenth centuries poisoned their opponents with as little compunction as an Englishman of his day brought an action at law against someone who had done him injury. He says that ladies put poison bottles on their dressing-tables as openly and used them with as little scruple upon others as the dames of his day used perfume or lavender-water on themselves. He comments that the influence of fashion is so powerful that it can even cause murder to be regarded as a venial peccadillo.

The poison mania had become particularly virulent in France. It was encouraged among the people by some well-publicized accounts of the nobility using it.

After this chapter Mackay talks about haunted houses.

The next chapter is about alchemy. Many of the alchemists were charlatans who told people that they had the ability to turn base metals into gold, or else they would soon know how to do it. Even princes were deceived by them. The charlatans used their claims to live off of the credulity of others. There were some alchemists who were entirely sincere, though, and who worked tirelessly and risked their own fortunes on what was, in the end, a fruitless enterprise. Mackay says that nevertheless, some important discoveries in chemistry were made as byproducts of these pursuits, and a lot was learned about what didn't work, so he doesn't think it was a complete waste.

The next chapter is about the many kinds of fortune-telling. As I noted before, Kepler earned his living with astrology, though he would have preferred to devote himself entirely to astronomy. Mackay quotes Kepler's defense of his actions:

> The best excuse ever made for astrology was that offered by the great astronomer, Keppler, himself an unwilling practiser of the art. He had many applications from his friends to cast nativities for them, and generally gave a positive refusal to such as he was not afraid of offending by his frankness. In other cases he accommodated himself to the prevailing delusion. In sending a copy of his "Ephemerides" to Professor Gerlach, he wrote that they were nothing but worthless conjectures; but he was obliged to devote himself to them, or he would have starved. "Ye overwise philosophers," he exclaimed, in his "Tertius Interveniens;" "ye censure this daughter of astronomy beyond her deserts! Know ye not that she must support her mother by her charms? The scanty reward of an astronomer would not provide him with bread, if men did not entertain hopes of reading the future in the heavens" (p. 261).

Mackay's last chapter is about magnetizers. Animal magnetism was a popular strand of the fad, and it was the ancestor of modern hypnotism. Mackay concedes that hypnotism is possible, but he denies that it happens for the strange reasons that the magnetizers gave, or that people had supernatural powers while magnetized. But the claims were broadly believed during the eighteenth century.

Chapter 4: Manipulating the Masses for Power and Profit

The Origins of Mass Persuasion

Edward Bernays, a nephew of Sigmund Freud, wrote two remarkable books about mass psychology and its applications, *Crystallizing Public Opinion* and *Propaganda.*

Bernays (1923) talks about the history of mass persuasion in *Crystallizing Public Opinion.* The oratorical tradition of classical civilization flourished before the fall of Rome, after which mass persuasion, like many other things, became difficult or impossible. Bernays says that the widespread illiteracy and the destruction of the money economy and the breakup of society into countless self-sufficient, small-scale agricultural groups meant that the prerequisites for mass persuasion did not exist. The forces of custom therefore played a larger role in determining public opinion. The era of mass persuasion began in the closing centuries of the medieval period as the result of two factors: the rapid rise of cities and the invention of printing. These enabled a vigorous exchange of religious pamphlets, sermons, satires, and letters. Propaganda played a decisive role in the Reformation and the Counter-Reformation. The first newspapers were printed in the seventeenth century in England and France. While the battle for public opinion was originally fought along religious lines, politics became an increasingly important subject, and this was especially the case during and after the French Revolution. Bernays talks about how the subject of mass psychology was not seriously studied until the late nineteenth century, when crowd psychologists like Le Bon and Tarde wrote their influential books. This seems to me to have been the case with an important exception—Charles Mackay's 1841 book *Memoirs of Extraordinary Popular Delusions and the Madness of Crowds.*

Anyway, Bernays goes on to talk about the history of press agentry, the ancestor of his profession of public relations. Bernays denies that public relations counsel (what he calls himself) is a euphemism for press agent. Press agents had a bad reputation at the beginning of the twentieth century. They were regarded as people who whitewashed the misdeeds of the powerful by getting favorable pieces in the newspapers for their clients. Bernays says that in the preceding decades the great industrialists didn't care about public opinion; "the public be damned" summarized their attitudes. But as the result of the attacks of the muckraking journalists, which aroused the public against them and hampered their work, they learned the importance of guiding public opinion.

Another thing that Bernays rejects is the idea that public relations is just a euphemism for propaganda. Actually, I don't see how public relations counsel and public relations are not euphemisms for propagandist and propaganda, respectively. And in fact, Bernays is more forward about what he does in his other major book, *Propaganda*. That isn't to say that people like Bernays never do good work, but he is probably trying to improve the image of his profession by denying that a change in terms was meant to mislead people. It probably was, though. Or as we put it today, it was meant to put a positive spin on it.

Bernays says that his field expanded rapidly after World War I after people discovered just how effectively public opinion could be manipulated. He says that he was a member of the Committee on Public Information that was responsible for the propaganda effort for the United States during that war, and he was also a member of the staff at the Paris Peace Conference. So he witnessed these things firsthand. As late as 1928, he says, the only two public relations firms in New York which were widely known were his and Ivy Lee's. Corporations were catching on to the idea of public relations, but it took time for them to accept it fully.

Bernays says that public relations came of age during the Great

Depression. Business had gotten a bad reputation; meanwhile, the New Deal government was emphasizing its role as defender of the common man. Business had a public relations problem, and so it sought out experts to repair its image. It was vigorous in promoting its causes to the public in a way that it never had been before. So by 1940 businessmen ceased to think of their affairs as being private, owing to the necessity of conveying to the public that the interests of business were aligned with the interests of the public.

Bernays cites the definition of public relations as it was given in the *Dictionary of Sociology*; it was based on Bernays's definition:

> "the body of theory and technique utilized in adjusting the relationships of a subject with its publics. These theories and techniques represent applications of sociology, social psychology, economics and political science as well as of the special skills of journalists, artists, organizational experts, advertising men, etc. to the specific problems involved in this field of activity." (p. xlix)

The second meaning was:

> "the relations of an individual, association, government or corporation with the publics which it must take into consideration in carrying on its social functions. These publics can include voters, customers, employees, potential employees, past employees, stockholders, members of antagonistic pressure groups, neighbors, etc." (p. xlix-l)

Public relations counsel was defined as expert in

> "analyzing public relations maladjustments; locating probable causes of such maladjustments in the social behavior of the client, and in the sentiments and opinions of publics; and advising the client on suitable social theories and tested

techniques in solving many of the problems of society." (p. l)

Bernays quotes the crowd psychologists as saying that people don't usually arrive at their opinions on the basis of individual reasoning; rather, they conform to the opinions of their leaders or of the surrounding community, which usually amount to the same thing. He says that men of limited understanding tend to be hostile to opinions with which they disagree. So new opinions are generally met with hostility. There is nothing new in what Bernays says about crowd psychology for people who have read the original works, but it's worth pointing out that he assumes the truth of these works in manipulating public opinion, and he was one of the best people in the world at doing that.

Edward Bernays doesn't think that the public always behaves as the media directs them to behave. He notes how sometimes all of the major newspapers in an area can be against a candidate for office and yet the candidate might still win; and they might all be for a candidate, and yet he might still lose. So Bernays seems to have a more qualified view than some of how effectively public opinion can be manipulated by experts. Media professionals are also, partly, just following the crowd. They produce things that are likely to be received favorably by the crowd, and therefore bought. So they have the profit motive to consider. So, says Bernays, the leaders influence the public and the public influences the leaders.

Bernays quotes Everett Dean Martin's *the Behavior of Crowds* a little bit after his discussion about this. Martin says that people sacrifice their independence in order to remain members of a group. So each group has certain beliefs and a certain code of conduct which it will not allow any of its members to change, because if they were changed the group would be dissolved. It is for this reason that the group does not encourage the critical faculty. Other groups are not permitted to be presented in a fair light among a group's members because to do so could threaten the beliefs of the group. And again, if that happened the group might be dissolved. Groups also portray themselves to members and to outsiders as being just a wonderful group of people. The group alone is "the people" and is superior to all others. They seek to become dominant and lord it over everybody else. Groups are quick to compete with other groups so that they might secure a victory which would enhance their self-importance. Whenever the leaders are attempting to secure recruits for a movement or point-of-view they assume the inevitability of their ultimate victory, and for the reasons just given.

Bernays then talks a bit about Wilfred Trotter's *Instincts of the Herd in Peace and War*. The individual tends to conform to what his group believes because isolation is terrifying for gregarious animals. Also, herds tend toward homogeneity. The group compels conformity. It is a worthwhile tradeoff for individuals to sacrifice themselves to group conformity because a group of gregarious animals is many times stronger than the combined strength of their individual members.

Before Bernays's discussions of Martin and Trotter he talks about Walter Lippmann's *Public Opinion*, and the idea of the stereotype. Bernays accepts Lippmann's view that people don't see things as they really are but according to stereotypes. Stereotypes are broad generalizations about individuals or groups of people, and these can be misleading in particular cases. Each group has its own stereotypes about the outside world.

Anyway, Bernays continues his discussion about Trotter's ideas. According to Trotter, it is this impulsion to conform to group standards that causes people to form classes, which are herds within a herd. Ideas are accepted only if they come from within the herd; outside views are ignored or rejected. It is for this reason that people tend to be insensitive to experience. Each advance in science or engineering ("progress" as it was called back then) seems obvious in hindsight, but each advance was nevertheless resisted until, as Trotter puts it, "the machine almost invented itself." Ideas believed because of the herd instinct tend to be rationalized, but that doesn't change the fact of their origins.

Bernays doesn't rely just on crowd psychology in his public relations work; he says it is also important to appeal to certain basic instincts. In his chapter on techniques and methods Bernays says that there are a limited number of human instincts but they can be manipulated by skillful handling in an infinite number of ways. He talks about how advertisers take into account human needs in selling their products. They appeal to the desire for shelter, the desire for sex, and the desire for food for example. The job of the public relations counsel is to discover in his client's causes ideas which will appeal to the fundamental instincts in man. Bernays gets his basic instincts from the early twentieth century psychologist William McDougall, and among these, in addition to the instincts just mentioned, were flight-fear, repulsion-disgust, curiosity-wonder, pugnacity-anger, self-display-elation, self-abasement-subjection, and parental-love-tenderness. One example that Bernays gives of how to manipulate basic instincts for profit is an advertisement for radiators, which took advantage of the instinctive desire for shelter. The advertisement has a family gathered around a radiator while a storm is raging outside. Another example is that it is effective for public health officials to stress the possibility of a plague or epidemic because it appeals to the emotion of fear and presents the possibility of preventing the spread of the epidemic or plague. Bernays gives more examples besides these, but I won't list them all here.

Bernays says that in order to be effective, a public relations counsel must be able to imagine himself as a member of each of the publics with which he deals. Then he must figure out how to appeal to the largest number of these. He also says that a public relations counsel must make news for his clients in order for his ideas to travel.

The Invisible Government and its Subjects

In his second major book, *Propaganda*, Bernays (1928) says that "[t]he conscious and intelligent manipulation of the organized habits and opinions of the masses is an important element in democratic society" and those who are able to do it constitute an invisible government which, he says, "is the true ruling power of our country." Bernays views opinion leaders as being, apparently, all-powerful. He says that "[w]e are governed, our minds molded, our tastes formed, our ideas suggested, largely by men we have never heard of"; and this is the way things must be if vast numbers of people are to cooperate so as to live together as a smoothly functioning society.

Bernays says that the invisible governors are, in many cases, unaware of the identity of their fellow members in the inner cabinet of opinion-makers. The governors govern by their qualities of natural leadership, by their ability to supply needed ideas, and by their key positions in the social structure. A vanishingly small number of people control what everybody else believes and how they act, and this is the case in politics, in business, and in our social conduct and ethical thinking. This minority who understand the mental processes and social patterns of the masses "pull the wires which control the public mind" and "harness old social forces and contrive new ways to bind and guide the world."

Bernays says that if everyone were to vote for their desired candidates without the aid of the invisible governors that they might vote for dozens or hundreds of candidates and produce nothing but confusion. A party machine is necessary to reduce the number of candidates to two or three from whom the public may choose. Likewise, we would not be able to function as a society if each individual had to study for himself all the abstruse economic, political, and ethical data involved in every question. For this reason people defer to opinion leaders and to the media through which they communicate. So we may get our views from some ethical teacher like a minister, or from a favorite essayist, or merely from prevailing opinion, and most of the time we conform to the standardized code of social conduct which these sources have provided us with. The same argument holds true in the marketplace as well. In theory everybody buys the best and cheapest commodities offered to him on the market, but in practice this is impossible. If everyone went around pricing and chemically testing before purchasing the dozens of soaps or fabrics or brands of bread which are for sale, he says, economic life would come to a standstill. To avoid such confusion, society consents to have its choices narrowed by propaganda. The same thing is happening at any given moment with regard to policies, commodities, and ideas.

Bernays says that we could have a committee of wise men make choices for us instead, but we have chosen the method of open competition. Sometimes propaganda is misused, as with manipulation of the news, inflation of personality, and the general ballyhoo by which politicians, commercial products, and social ideas are brought to the consciousness of the masses, but this is the price we pay for our system.

Bernays talks about how modern technologies of communication and transportation have made it so that ideas can be spread rapidly or even instantaneously over the whole of America. This has made it so that people can be associated and regimented for common action even though they might live thousands of miles apart. When the country was founded, the basic unit of organization was the largely self-sufficient village community. Each one had its own public opinion, generated by direct discussion by the group. So the country has changed dramatically.

Bernays talks about the heterogeneity of the country in his day (the same holds for our own day—in fact, it has become still more heterogenous). There were private associations for practically every kind of interest, and there were publications that influenced the opinions of each one of these groups. There was some overlap in membership, but the impression Bernays conveys is one of great diversity of opinion.

Bernays talks about how the experience of World War I caused intelligent people to wonder about the new possibilities of regimenting the public mind. He says that the leaders of the propaganda effort were able to get the key men in every group to support the war effort, and this had a profound effect because their word carried authority with hundreds or thousands or hundreds of thousands of followers. The propagandists needed only to use the right mental cliches and emotional habits in order to get the public to react in the desired ways.

Bernays gives a remarkable example of how the struggling velvet industry deliberately manufactured a demand for its goods. They had their agents go to the appropriate opinion leaders and convince them to wear velvet. So an intelligent Parisian encouraged distinguished countesses and duchesses to wear velvet, and this influenced the opinion of French clothing designers and manufacturers. As for the presentation to the public, "the American buyer or the American woman of fashion was simply shown the velvet creations in the atelier of the dressmaker or the milliner. She bought the velvet because she liked it and because it was in fashion." Editors of American magazines and fashion reporters of American newspapers were subjected to the actual, though created, circumstance and subjected consumers to the same influences. Big department stores in America, aiming to be style leaders, advertised velvet gowns on the authority of French couturiers. Hundreds of other department stores wanted to be style leaders too. And the idea continued to spread along these lines, so that the demand for velvet exploded. In other words, the demand for a good was completely manufactured by propaganda. How? The propagandists went to the appropriate opinion leaders and influenced them, and everyone beholden to them followed along; the second tier of the opinion hierarchy followed the first tier; the third tier followed the second tier; the fourth tier followed the third tier; and so on, all the way down to the average American consumer—I assume some housewife who wanted to be fashionable.

Bernays makes another interesting comment in *Propaganda*. He asserts that the real reason why people buy one thing rather than another is not because the advertiser claims that it is cheap and of excellent quality, but because it is the group custom to buy some one thing over other things. Bernays says that the real reason why a purchaser is planning to spend his money on a new car instead of on a new piano is because it is, at the moment, the group custom to buy cars rather than pianos.

Bernays talks about how a propagandist would manipulate people into buying pianos. The thing to do is to appeal to some basic sentiment like the home instinct, and then to convince the appropriate opinion leaders, like well known decorators, that pianos are good things to have in homes. So this would get the idea circulating in the producers that pianos should be placed in homes. The propagandist is to convince the public that pianos are desirable to have in homes by staging an event or ceremony. To this ceremony, key people, people known to influence the buying habits of the public, are to be invited. So a famous violinist, a popular audience, and a society leader would be invited. This would give the idea of piano rooms a place in the public consciousness that it did not have before. Influential architects would be persuaded to put a special place in their houses for pianos, and the less influential architects would obey the more influential ones.

As a result of the propagandist's machinations, the music room will be accepted; it will be made "the thing." The man or woman who has a music room or has arranged a corner of the parlor as a musical corner will naturally think of buying a piano, and it will come to him as if it were his own idea. Bernays says that in the past, manufacturers said to prospective buyers, "Please buy a piano," whereas now the process is reversed and the buyer now asks the manufacturer to sell him a piano.

My impression is that mainstream economists don't have the slightest clue about this sort of thing. They're still under the impression that people buy things because they've considered their preferences, weighed the alternatives in a dispassionate way, and chosen the product that maximizes something called "utility" at the lowest possible price. Should we believe Bernays over the average economist? There are reasons for being skeptical about Bernays. Bernays is also selling a product—public relations. If manufacturers read his book they would probably say, "we need to do our own propaganda; let's hire this guy Bernays." So there is a possibility that Bernays exaggerates the power of propaganda. But he draws from examples of where propaganda really worked. And there is no doubt that it was responsible for getting the United States into World War I, and that Bernays's techniques were created or refined in that war. So I believe Bernays is giving a realistic account of what propaganda can do. The works of the crowd psychologists who Bernays has also read suggest that he has an accurate conception about human nature.

Bernays talks more about how the group formation of modern society can be manipulated in order to spread ideas. He gives the example of the nationwide competitions for sculpture in Ivory soap, which were open to school children in certain age groups as well as to professional sculptors. A sculptor of national reputation found Ivory soap to be an excellent medium for sculpture. Procter and Gamble offered prizes for the best sculpture in white soap, and the contest was held under the auspices of the Art Center in New York City, an organization which had a high standing in the art world. School superintendents and teachers throughout the country were glad to encourage the movement as an educational aide for schools. Practice among school children as part of their art courses was stimulated. Bernays says that the campaign was effective because it appealed to a number of basic human instincts. It appealed to the aesthetic, competitive, gregarious, snobbish, exhibitionist, and maternal instincts. Housewives were pleased with it because their children were learning the habits of cleanliness. Artists and educators were pleased with it because aesthetic appreciation was being cultivated in young people. And of course the soap manufacturers were pleased with it because it stimulated demand for their soap. Bernays says that a propagandist should be able to identify the interests of the various groups with which he must deal, and in organizing a campaign he should discover as many overlapping interests as possible and use them to the best possible advantage.

Bernays makes another unorthodox assertion about economics. He says that in the days of handicrafts demand created its own supply; however, in the era of mass production, it is necessary that suppliers create their own demand. A huge manufacturing concern, capable of supplying the demand for an entire continent, can't stand idly by and wait for buyers to demand goods. They must be proactive; they must create their own demand with propaganda.

Bernays does say a little later that public opinion can't be molded arbitrarily. And yet business must take account of it. He says that when business acted as if its activities were of no concern to the public the muckraking press was born and the public turned against it and had laws passed which constrained it. Ever since then business has become more and more dependent on public opinion. It depends on the public in its role as buyers, but it also depends on the public now as holders of stocks and bonds. The great diffusion of wealth is what made it possible for a much broader class of people to own such things. Their feelings and views can't be violated with impunity. Anyway, although public opinion can't be molded at will, it can be influenced. Bernays says that you cannot persuade a whole generation of women to wear long skirts, but you may, by working through leaders of fashion, persuade them to wear evening dresses which are long in the back.

Bernays talks about how a false rumor caused a company's stock to decline significantly. But damage of this sort can be contained by a prudent public relations strategy. What I think is interesting is what this discussion suggests about why stocks are worth what they are worth. What people think determines what a stock is worth, and not people as individuals but as groups. And people can be swayed by false as well as by true information. And yet, I think, based on what I've read, that if a company is really a good company that its stock price will eventually rebound from false rumors. If it is well-led and has a good strategy and the assets it needs to do its best work then it ought to continue to perform well, and this will generate news that will sway public opinion to reevaluate what it thinks the company is worth. Likewise, a company probably could not maintain a high stock price based on good press alone. Sooner or later, as in the case of Enron, the truth comes out and the stock price collapses. But in the short run the public can be swayed by falsehoods. I think people bought the idea of the Iraq War for similar reasons, but it's not so easy to repair the long-term damage caused by a short-term misunderstanding like that. Also, I think that delusions can last for a considerably longer time than a few months or years if they accord with a large number of basic instincts and are instilled early enough in life, and if they are enforced by the authorities, and if people are continually indoctrinated by regular mass gatherings, as in the case of religions. There is no way that all of the great religions are true on all points because they contradict each other on some of their core tenets. And yet each is believed by tens or hundreds of millions or even billions of people. And they have been believed in some cases for thousands of years. So I don't think it is inevitable that people will realize that the information they base their decisions on is false, or that they will act accordingly if they do realize it.

Bernays talks about how propaganda is used in politics. He says that the great political problem in modern democracies is how to induce leaders to lead. If public opinion determines how the government is to act then it seems as if political leaders are forced to be will-less servants of their constituents. Bernays says that no serious sociologist believes that the voice of the people expresses any divine or specially wise and lofty idea. Rather, the mind of the people is made up for it by the group leaders in whom it believes and by people who understand how to manipulate public opinion. Public opinion is made up of inherited prejudices and symbols and cliches and verbal formulas supplied to them by the leaders. Bernays says that fortunately propaganda can be used by political leaders to sway the masses to their point-of-view. And he thinks that indeed they must if they are to lead successfully.

Bernays talks a bit more about the possibilities and limitations of propaganda. He doubts that the public will become impervious to propaganda upon learning its methods. He also doubts that a press agent can make a nobody into a great man by puffery. In order for a person to become a great man in the eyes of the public he has to have something about him that appeals to the public, and if he doesn't appeal to them he is ignored.

Bernays makes an interesting proposal. He thinks that the government should have a Secretary of Public Relations in order to interpret and guide public opinion for the President. A cabinet position was never created, but the White House Press Secretary somewhat resembles what Bernays was arguing for. I think Bernays wanted something like the Committee on Public Information to become a permanent organ of the government. Nazi Germany created the Ministry of Public Enlightenment and Propaganda for Joseph Goebbels, which was kind of like that; however, I don't think Bernays anticipated what such an apparatus could do.

Chapter 5: The Crowd Versus the Individual

These days we hear no end of talk about how great "innovation" is. Even "disruption" is becoming popular. We have been led to believe that social networking on the Internet has something to do with the dawning of a new "creative economy." All sorts of people are selling books and giving talks about how to be more innovative. Government officials tell us that we need to invest in innovation. Schooling (learning by drill, learning by rote, "teaching to the test") has something to do with this, apparently, as does giving a lot of money to academic researchers who obtained their positions for their proven lack of ability to innovate or disrupt. The more money you spend the more innovation you are supposed to get.

All of that is nonsense. Nearly all of the crowd psychologists describe groups as fundamentally intolerant; Tarde appears to be the only dissenter, but that disagreement may only be apparent. Recall that Tarde thought that some groups were amenable to fashion while others resisted it. However, I would imagine that among the fashionable crowds you would get yourself into trouble if you didn't follow whatever happened to be fashionable at the moment. What is fashionable today might be unfashionable a decade from now and you have to keep current or risk derision or exclusion from the group.

One thing is clear, though: new ideas never, ever emerge from groups, as opposed to individuals—never from any governmental or corporate or academic or any other kind of bureaucracy. They don't even emerge from social networks, though a social network might organize around an innovative individual. Notice how on sites like Kickstarter it is individuals who come up with ideas or initiate projects and then the crowd merely follows along, or declines to follow along; it says "yes" or "no" as Lippmann would put it; the groups do not spontaneously organize or initiate projects, but only appear to do so.

Groups tend, by their very nature, to be intolerant of new ideas. They tend to dislike the sort of people who do come up with new ideas, and when groups are unrestrained, they ostracize or destroy innovators. Anyone with the slightest acquaintance with the history of ideas will know that this has always been the case: Socrates and Galileo weren't the only ones who met with group intolerance. Notwithstanding the changed rhetoric of our our day, people behave in fundamentally the same ways. And although it is true that new groups always form around innovators, the groups become intolerant just as soon as they form. So the Christians began as a deviant sect organized around an innovative leader and soon after began excluding those who did not conform to their doctrines. When they obtained power they used it to persecute heretics and rival sects and render opinion uniform.

So new ideas come from individuals—and not just any individuals, but deviant ones. From people who are not members in good standing of some crowd. Almost certainly, new ideas are formed in the minds of individuals by the psychological laws of association. The ideas associated are taken from other people and from the individual's own experiences. So it is true that creative people learn from others, and in that sense and in that sense only is innovation ever a team effort. The only way for any group to be creative is for it to have people in charge who will protect deviant individuals from the rest of the group. Left to fend for themselves, innovators are usually done for. Unfortunately, innovators are often difficult to get along with. William Shockley, co-inventor of the transistor while he was at Bell Labs, as well as one of the founders of Silicon Valley (Palo Alto was his hometown), was regarded by his colleagues as a jerk. His team of researchers (the "Traitorous Eight") abandoned him and started the first wave of Silicon Valley startups. William H. Whyte wrote back in the 1950's that most corporations did not have great researchers because they insisted on micromanaging them and were unwilling to tolerate their personality quirks; Bell Labs was different, though; it allowed scientists a considerable amount of freedom to follow their curiosity.

Social networks don't make intolerant people tolerant. We've been seeing proof of this since the 2011 revolts in the Arab countries against their authoritarian regimes. The religious minorities in those countries now fear for their security. In a pure democracy, one in which there are no constitutional protections for minorities, the majority is free to have its way with everyone else. Given the fundamental intolerance of groups, the current situation could easily have been predicted in advance. The fallen Arab dictators have turned out to be, intentionally or not, champions of religious liberty.

One of the best books about the hostility of crowds towards individuals is Sir Martin Conway's (1915) *the Crowd in Peace and War*. Everett Dean Martin's (1920) *the Behavior of Crowds* is also good. And although William H. White (1957) was not writing in the same tradition as these other writers, his book *the Organization Man* contains a good description of the attitudes of crowd men towards deviant individuals, so I will be talking about that book as well.

Kingdom versus Crowddom

Conway says that party organizers like good party men and them only. If individuals were left to their own devices they would develop their own political opinions and no two people would have exactly the same views. That, for a crowd, is to be avoided at all costs. Crowds swallow people up, says Conway, and then they digest them; the digestion is done by indoctrination. People are expected to believe and behave as the others of the group behave, which is as the party leader directs them to believe and behave. Conway notes that a person cannot retain the same views throughout his life and expect to be regarded as a member in good standing of the group. This is because the views of the group may change. He says that in Great Britain the liberals changed their views after the socialists took over, so that anyone who held the views taught to them by Mill and other classical liberals was ostracized from the group.

Conway says that crowds are not inclined to view the individual as having any great amount of importance. What is important for the crowd is the perpetuation of the group. Individuals die all the time and are replaced by new members. Individuals join the group and they leave the group. But the crowd lives on.

Conway says that conventional people distrust the unconventional man and look upon him with suspicion. This is because a person who violates minor conventions seems likely to violate the more important ones upon which the existence of the crowd depends. The unconventional man is outside of and perhaps opposed to the organized crowd and may become the center of a new and hostile crowd which could threaten the existence of the old crowd. Conway says that crowds form originally around some freely thinking individual and they fear and hate anyone who differs from them. Bees behave the same way. They not only kill stranger bees but bees that have been absent from the hive for a few days. The tribes of the Amazon behave the same way. They kill every Indian who comes their way, and if one of their number is absent for six months or more they kill him too. Rubber agents were aware of this fact and used it to their advantage; if they had one of the Indians for six months or more he was theirs for life.

Conway talks about how religions are manifestations of crowd psychology. Religions are organized around emotions. However, emotions are unstable things. A new emotion may be given expression by a new sect which could grow quickly and overwhelm its parent religion. A single orator is all it takes. For this reason religions have to be intolerant.

Conway says that crowds hate freedom of speech. The crowd does not fear its own conversion, but fears that some orator might use his freedom to create a crowd similar to but inimical to itself. Free individuals—individuals not belonging to a crowd—delight in freedom of speech and the variety of views which it permits. But a crowd can never permit it.

Conway says that the loss of a member to another crowd is worse than having a member die. This is because a conversion is not merely a loss of one member but a gain of one member to a rival crowd. A death might not even be a loss if the member has sacrificed himself for the cause, as this is good for morale.

What I am thinking about is how, as late as the early twentieth century, some people still retained the freedom of thought to comment upon and even denounce the conquest of society by crowds. Few are in a position to do it today, because almost every single person is beholden to some crowd. People who denounce "groupthink" almost always mean someone else's groupthink. Free individuals almost don't exist.

Conway says that people who live in towns become merged into the crowd more readily than people who live in the country. He thinks this is because people live nearer to one another in the towns, whereas in the country people live at some distance from each other. So crowd feeling grows with the density of the population. Conway says that it was in the ancient city-states that crowd-dominion first openly and plainly took shape. The individual wise or strong ruler was tabooed and was forced from lordship to service.

When the public rules, the individual is inclined to be more or less of one mind with it. The public behaves as a crowd, with all the qualities Conway has been describing. One problem with this is that an individual strong and independent enough to form his own opinions for himself will probably be out of harmony with public opinion all or most of the time. For him and others like him, who, says Conway, are the best class of people anywhere, the dominance of the crowd will be not less but much more objectionable than the dominance of a king. A crowd may be as despotic as a king, and even more despotic than that.

Conway talks about how there have only been two forms of government in the history of the world: the kingdom and the crowddom. A kingdom is the rule of one person over the rest, while a crowddom is the rule of the crowd over every individual within a state.

Conway elaborates on the difference between kingdoms and crowddoms. Regal despots, especially the wisest and ablest, are usually out of sympathy with the aspirations of the crowd. They are skeptical about the value and efficiency of crowd-government. Conway then talks about the Treaty of Verona which, he says, "authoritatively set forth the essential points of difference between individual and crowd rule." The treaty condemns representative government and acknowledges that a free press is indispensable to the partisans of it.

Conway says that it's strange that the document does not mention the danger to kingdoms of the right to public meetings. This is just as indispensable to crowd government as a free press. It is by these two means that crowds are initiated and built up. Where the two are prohibited it is extremely difficult to build great national crowds or parties. So public meetings and the popular press are the two chief sources of crowd power and the two chief enemies of individual rule.

Conway says that the members of the executive and legislative bodies of a representative government are not merely elected by, but are amenable and responsible to, public opinion. This means that the leaders of the government must all be crowd-exponents or crowd-representatives. When crowd-compellers are chosen to lead, the people are subordinate to the will of the leader and not the other way around for as long as the leader remains in control of the government. Conway quotes and concurs with another writer who says that there can be no experts in a really representative government, not even experts in government. So there is no place for expertise or science or reason in a really representative government.

Conway cites Byzantium as a case of kingship going wrong, but his criticism seems superficial and half-hearted. He claims that the best form of government is a limited kingdom or a limited crowddom, because they accommodate man's dual nature—individual man and crowd man—best. But I think his sympathies are with kingship.

Conway talks about how the crowd by its very nature tends to diminish the freedom of its members, and not just in one or two aspects but in every aspect. The crowd tends to reduce every individual under its sway to the same uniform pattern. He talks about how, in order to prevent some people from ruining themselves by drink, even those who drink moderately are compelled not to drink. So limitations that would be advantageous for people of low character are not necessarily advantageous for those of high character, and may do positive harm to the latter.

Conway talks about how, if crowd-dominion continued to advance at the current pace, individual freedom would be dangerously threatened. It hardly seems fair to Conway that a man should go abroad to earn enough to live on for the rest of his days only to return and have the government take from him as much of his money as it pleases in order to spend it on things which he may disapprove of. He asks that if he can't drink in London lest a Glasgow engineer should get drunk, then why shouldn't his eating choices be limited as well? And why not the style and cut of his clothes and the size and character of his house, and the way his children are to be taught, and the quality of treatment he is to receive from physicians, and the drugs he is to permitted to take, and the way he is to raise his children? Conway thinks that total crowd-dominion would amount to absolute tyranny over the individual in every sphere of life. And it could not be expected to make these decisions wisely because the crowd lacks the individual's brains. So crowd tyranny is not only all-embracing but dimwitted as well. In the end, all are reduced to service to the collective.

Conway says that individual freedom and the crowd are "normally, necessarily, and for ever hostile to one another," and he maintains that "no true freedom is possible for the individual unless he can be protected against crowd-dominance." He says that the crowd can't be expected to protect the individual from itself, so a country's constitution has to protect him, and this is best done when the crowd's right of free organization is limited. Conway says that the United States is in fact a limited crowddom because the U.S. Constitution safeguards individual rights and a powerful Supreme Court interprets it. But Great Britain has no such protections. He says that the House of Lords could act as a check on the public will but its powers have been curbed dramatically. It no longer has the power of veto. Conway is deeply wary of Winston Churchill, who said that when individual and public interests conflict, individual rights must give way. Conway says that if he is the owner of a rare picture and the crowd wants to see it, he still nevertheless ought to have the right to say "no" to them; individuals ought to retain the exclusive right to some things even if the crowd doesn't like it.

Conway says that when the crowd demands "liberty" what it really means is the liberty of the crowd, not the freedom of the individual. Crowd liberty is the liberty to organize, to make its members into good crowd men, and to expand its influence as far as it possibly can.

Conway says that the crowd always sacrifices the exceptional individuals to the lowest common denominator. Even though the most inept students profit the least by preferential treatment, and the best students would profit the most by it, the crowd nevertheless favors the most inept. This allows them to indulge their sentimentality while stifling the exceptional individuals who they fear to be restive crowd units.

I'm pretty sure Conway is right here. If he is, then how is an exceptional individual to regard the crowd? Unless he has lived an unusually sheltered life, he must know how the crowd regards him. They don't want to cultivate his abilities so that he may more effectively advance the common good. Rather, they want to handicap him. They're like the Emperor Commodus in the *Gladiator* film, who gives a deadly wound to the hero before the big fight. This being so, why should he have any affection for the crowd? It may serve his purposes to flatter them, seeing as they are so strong. But when it is within his power, why should he not exploit them? It would only be returning the favor. That may have been the thinking of some of history's great but treacherous men, like Alcibiades and, I'm fairly certain, Napoleon.

Conway says that conscience is the voice of the multitude. It is the internalized norms of the community in which one lives. Some of these norms may seem completely arbitrary to outsiders. For example, one lady he talks about thought it wicked to play cards, and so she didn't do it, but she felt okay playing with cardboard pieces numbered 1 to 13. When we violate the norms of the community, we feel shame or guilt. It takes someone very strong in his individuality to openly say something unpatriotic or unorthodox. Conway quotes someone as saying that conscience makes people cowards, and this appears to be the case. My suspicion is that if you forced people to choose between dying and being ostracized from their friends and family and community forever, a lot of them would choose death. Conway doesn't condemn conscience, but he says that it can be used to impose absurd restrictions upon the freedom of individuals. Some restrictions are perfectly innocent but are believed by the crowd to be injurious to its interests. Conway says that individuals who conform to the consciences imposed upon them by their communities, whether their communities be on the up-grade or on the down-grade, tend to live comfortable lives. People who stand outside the crowd, whether they be great seers or great criminals, lead harder lives.

Conway says that the Treaty of Verona which articulated the point of view of the old regime was written only about a century ago (from his day), and yet it seems totally antiquated. I was thinking about how a century or so separates us from Conway and yet things have not changed fundamentally since then, except that the power of crowds has increased still more against individuals.

Conway says that the purpose of battles in war is to turn the enemy from an organized group into a mob. An organized group can impose its will on numbers much larger than its own, while mobs yield readily to organized force.

The Crowd as a Creature of Hate

I talked a little bit about Everett Dean Martin when I discussed Bernays's work. Martin shared Conway's loathing of crowds and crowd life. He says in his book *the Behavior of Crowds* that in our age, everyone feels pressured to belong to a crowd in order to have influence, and they sacrifice their principles to the single-minded aim of getting as many people behind them as possible.

Martin alludes to an observation made by William James that people will believe anything as long as it isn't contradicted by something else we've experienced. That doesn't bode well if you consider its implications. The reason why dictators censor the ability of people to express themselves is almost certainly so that no counter-suggestions can emerge that would cause people to doubt what the dictator has told them. If only the dictator's views are allowed to be heard, then that is what all but an exceptional minority will believe. And this is perhaps another reason why the dialectical method is helpful in improving our understandings; it forces us, whenever we learn about a new subject, to expose ourselves to counter-suggestions. If you only teach one side of an issue then you are teaching people to be dogmatic; they are not being taught how to think for themselves. And that is probably the way all but an exceptional minority would have it. If you give people the ability to think for themselves they might think otherwise than you would have them think.

Martin cites Nietzsche as saying that the crowd is an instrument of revenge, a way for the many weak to pass judgment on the few great because they feel emboldened by their numbers. Martin says that crowds are by nature creatures of hate, and always have some object for their hate. So in the Great War Americans hated the Kaiser, although the Kaiser was little more than a symbol. Americans hated King George III during the war for independence, too, although George III was also only a symbol. The objects of hate aren't responsible all by themselves for whatever it is the crowd doesn't like, but they symbolize the things that are responsible. And the crowd is capable of using the psychological mechanism of displacement if it is robbed of the original object of its hate; so if mob in the street is driven back from the object of its attack it will loot another store or two before it disperses.

What the crowd hates more than its opponents is heretics or schismatics. It can tolerate people who fail to live up to their convictions as long as their convictions are the same as those of the crowd; however, to have once accepted the crowd's beliefs and then rejected them is unforgivable. The heretic's name arouses the crowd's fury. Martin explains this as the crowd's self-defense; the nonconformist weakens the hold of the crowd's beliefs on the rest of the group to the extent that they must be taken into account.

Martin says that the crowd-man can save the crowd from being dissolved by a heretic by discrediting the heretic's views—and the heretic himself—in the eyes of the crowd. It is best if he is not even permitted to speak.

Here is a good question, one I've often pondered but which I don't yet have a good answer to: given that this is how people behave in crowds, and we live in an age where one must usually be part of some crowd to wield influence, and, in most cases, even to hold a job, or to run a business if one has one, how can an individual who wishes to free himself from crowd prejudices do so without jeopardizing his well-being? In the past the answer might have been to seek the patronage of an elite which was liberally educated and so was relatively free from crowd psychology; that meant becoming a tutor for one of them, or selling books to them, or taking a position in a university or church controlled by them. Or you could have been a part of the elite itself. But the elites are no longer liberally educated. They themselves are the slaves of crowds. If you want to earn a living as a writer, you have to write for a mass audience, for a crowd. University faculty are no longer liberally educated but are mostly the slaves of crowds. Politicians are beholden to crowds of constituents. The major media outlets ridicule or censure people who deviate from the "mainstream"— that is, from the conventions, however fleeting, of the crowd. It really is as Le Bon and Martin say, that we live in an era dominated by crowds. But it is worse now than it was back then. It seems to me that the freely-thinking individual is now being driven to the margins of society, whereas a century ago he might have been welcomed into high society, as Lippmann was. H.L. Mencken was able to earn a living and even become famous mocking the crowd; today, people guard their speech even when joking; most people are employed at organizations which will abandon them at the first sign of a crowd's displeasure, and in the Internet era it is harder than ever to conceal things from the judgment of crowds.

Martin says that it is not the abuse of power by a ruling crowd that causes it to fall to a revolutionary crowd; if that were the case, he says, then there would be revolutions all the time, since all ruling crowds abuse their power; rather, revolutions have tended to happen after the ruling crowds have made efforts at reform; the masses have endured mistreatment for centuries under their ruling classes without doing anything about it.

Martin says that fads are a manifestation of crowd psychology; to be old-fashioned is, in the mind of the crowd-man, as non-conformist as being a freak or an originator.

Martin doesn't think that democracy necessarily means crowd

rule; he thinks that the conservative writers who say this may be resentful that their own crowd is in danger of being supplanted by a new crowd. But nevertheless, he says that, given the intolerance of crowds, the individual's freedom depends on the number of things which the ruling crowd considers to be its business. This is because the freely acting individual, by not conforming to the crowd, weakens the faith of the rest of the crowd in its beliefs. If it considers few things to be its business, then the individual is relatively free; if it considers everything to be its business, then the individual has little hope of exercising his freedoms. The problem with democracy, as Martin sees it, is that potentially everything is the business of the crowd. In an absolute monarchy, the sovereign can't attend to everything and doesn't want to, and so people are free in the areas he doesn't care to regulate.

Martin says that constitutions are valuable in that they limit the number of things which are the business of the crowd. But when the majority finds that it is no longer limited by constitutional protections of individual liberties, there is no limit to how much it will meddle in everyone's lives. It's worse than autocracy, since in an autocracy there is only one tyrant, while in a tyranny of the majority, there may be 100 million tyrants.

Martin quotes Tocqueville on his reservations about American democracy. Tocqueville was concerned more about the lack of protections for the individual against the tyranny of the majority than about any imagined excess of freedom. Tocqueville says in his book that the majority in the United States has more power than any absolute monarch in Europe, and it is unclear to whom one may go to seek redress if one has grievances. Tocqueville says that he has seen no country in which freedom of opinion is so limited as it is in the United States, and he thinks this is why the country lacks literary genius; I'll quote him here:

> In my opinion the main evil of the present democratic institutions of the United States does not arise, as is so often asserted in Europe, from their weakness, but from their

irresistible strength. . . . I am not so much alarmed by the excessive liberty which reigns in that country, as by the inadequate securities which one finds against tyranny. When an individual or party is wronged in the United States, to whom can he apply for redress?

It is in the examination of the exercise of thought in the United States that we clearly perceive how far the power of the majority surpasses all the powers with which we are acquainted in Europe. At the present time the most absolute monarchs in Europe cannot prevent certain opinions hostile to their authority from circulating in secret through their dominions and even in their courts.

It is not so in America. So long as the majority is undecided, discussion is carried on, but as soon as its decision is announced everyone is silent. . . .

I know of no country in which there is so little independence of mind and real freedom of discussion as in America. In America the majority raises formidable barriers around the liberty of opinion. Within these barriers an author may write what he pleases, but woe to him if he goes beyond them. Not that he is in danger of an *auto-da-fe*, but he is exposed to continued obloquy and persecution. His political career is closed for ever. Every sort of compensation, even that of celebrity, is refused him. Those who think like him have not the courage to speak out, and abandon him to silence. He yields at length, overcome by the daily effort which he has to make, and subsides into silence as if he felt remorse for having spoken the truth.

Fetters and headsmen were coarse instruments . . . but civilization has perfected despotism itself. Under absolute despotism of one man, the body was attacked to subdue the soul, but the soul escaped the blows and rose superior. Such is not the course adopted in democratic republics; there the body is left free, but the soul is enslaved. . . .

The ruling power in the United States is not to be made game of. The smallest reproach irritates its sensibilities. The slightest joke which has any foundation in truth renders it indignant. Everything must be the subject of encomium. No writer, whatever his eminence, can escape paying his tribute of adoration of his fellow citizens.

The majority lives in the perpetual utterance of self-applause, and there are certain truths which Americans can only learn from strangers, or from experience. If America has not yet had any great writers, the reason is given in these facts—there can be no literary genius without freedom of opinion, and freedom of opinion does not exist in America (p. 254-256).

Martin says that even minorities behave tyrannically, because they are too impatient to wait before they become a majority.

Martin says that American democracy permits some freedoms, but these come down to the freedom to vote, the freedom to make money, the freedom to spread propaganda, and the freedom from intellectual and moral responsibility. The freedom to vote is a sham because individuals are herded into crowds by professional peddlers of political influence and they are made to vote as blocs; the crowds are formed by vulgar, insincere, and partisan political propaganda. The individual, as an individual, has little choice in who he votes for. Martin grants that the freedom to make money is a real freedom, but this freedom is accompanied by the freedom from responsibility to other people who are harmed in the making of it. The right to freedom of speech is a sham just like the freedom to vote, however; each crowd demands the freedom to spread its own propaganda while denying other crowds the right to spread theirs. All join together to condemn the non-crowd-man. By freedom from intellectual and moral responsibility Martin means that crowds substitute bureaucratic meddlesomeness for conscience and crowd-tyranny for personal decency.

Martin then argues that the original aim of democracy was to allow more individual freedom but he says that it has been hijacked by rival crowds trying to lord it over everybody else, and who think goodness consists in making everyone the same. The problem with Martin's position is that a lot of the problems that now exist in democratic governments also existed in the ancient democracies; also, it is strange for democracy to go astray not just in the United States but in, apparently, all other Western democracies as well. Except maybe Switzerland; but each canton is a small democracy by itself, and the federal government is weak. Maybe Iceland's democracy functions well but I don't know enough about it to say; it's a small community of people, however. Anyway, if American democracy were a perversion rather than the norm, then we wouldn't see other democracies suffering from the same problems. But I don't think Martin wants to take up the arguments in favor of aristocracy; he says that aristocrats have argued against democracy on the grounds that it is by nature mob rule. Aristocracy is a hard sell in America.

Martin has more to say about why crowd-democracy makes people irresponsible—why, in fact, it demands that people be irresponsible. What he means by this is that the crowd substitutes taboos for individual judgment, and anything that gets past the public censors is deemed permissible. The taboos suit the least disciplined of the community—people who can't be exposed to the slightest temptation without succumbing to it. The more capable minority is burdened by the restrictions because they are more capable of self-discipline when allowed freedom, and freedom is required for them to achieve their full potential.

Martin talks about how so many of the great men since the beginning of the nineteenth century have been treated badly by the crowd. In this, he unwittingly echoes what Sir Robert Filmer, stalwart defender of absolute monarchy, said about democracy long before it became popular. If a man of genius wishes to become popular, says Martin, he has to prostitute his talents to a vulgar majority. I'll quote Martin here:

From the beginning of the nineteenth century until now it has been chiefly the business man, the political charlatan, the organizer of crowds, the rediscoverer of popular prejudices who have been preferred in our free modern societies. Keats died of a broken heart; Shelley and Wagner were exiled; Beethoven and Schubert were left to starve; Darwin was condemned to hell fire; Huxley was denied his professorship; Schopenhauer was ostracized by the elite; Nietzsche ate his heart out in solitude; Walt Whitman had to be fed by a few English admirers, while his poems were prohibited as obscene in free America; Emerson was for the greater part of his life persona non grata at his own college; Ingersoll was denied the political career which his genius merited; Poe lived and died in poverty; Theodore Parker was consigned to perdition; Percival Lowell and Simon Newcomb lived and died almost unrecognized by the American public.

Nearly every artist and writer and public teacher is made to understand from the beginning that he will be popular in just the degree that he strangles his genius and becomes a vulgar, commonplace, insincere clown.

On the other hand steel manufacturers and railroad kings, whose business record will often scarcely stand the light, are rewarded with fabulous millions and everyone grovels before them. When one turns from the "commercialism" which everywhere seems to be the dominant and most sincere interest in democratic society, when one seeks for spiritual values to counterbalance this weight of materialism, one finds in the prevailing spirit little more than a cult of naïve sentimentality.

It can hardly be denied that if Shakespeare, Boccaccio, Rabelais, Montaigne, Cassanova, Goethe, Dostoievsky, Ibsen, Tolstoi, Rousseau, St. Augustine, Milton, Nietzsche, Swinburne, Rosetti, or even Flaubert, were alive and writing his masterpiece in America today, he would be instantly silenced by some sort of society for the prevention of vice, and held up to public scorn and ridicule as a destroyer of our innocence and a corrupter of public morals. The guardians of our characters are ceaselessly expurgating the classics lest we come to harm reading them. I often think that the only reason why the Bible is permitted to pass through our mails is because hardly anyone ever reads it.

It is this same habit of crowd-thinking which accounts to a great extent for the dearth of intellectual curiosity in this country. From what we have seen to be the nature of the crowd-mind, it is to be expected that in a democracy in which crowds play an important part the condition described by de Tocqueville will generally prevail. There is much truth in his statement that it seems at first as if the minds of all Americans "were formed upon the same model." Spiritual variation will be encouraged only in respect to matters in which one crowd differs from another. The conformist spirit will prevail in all. Intellectual leadership will inevitably pass to the "tight-minded." There will be violent conflicts of ideas, but they will be crowd ideas. (p. 268-270)

Martin says that the scholars of the Renaissance revolted against the crowd-mindedness of their age with the aid of the Greek and Roman classical works. A knowledge of the classics enables a person to become a judge of values, and to develop his own likes and dislikes; he is able to become an independent thinker. This makes him an enemy of crowds. Martin says the reason for this is that a student of the classics becomes acquainted with ideas and ways of living which frankly challenge his own; his thoughts tend to travel in what the crowd regards as forbidden paths. But he says that pedagogues have made the learning of the classics so unpleasant that many students never develop the interest to learn what is so great about them.

The Organization Man and the War on Genius

In *the Organization Man*, William H. Whyte describes American society as it had taken shape by the 1950's. The old values of individual freedom and initiative, hard work, thrift, and ingenuity were losing their hold on people in deed if not in word. There were people still affirming the old faith, but the world around them had already been dramatically changed. Now, people increasingly identified with large organizations which provided them with security and a high standard of living in exchange for loyalty. People sought employment and advancement with big business, governmental organizations, universities, non-profits, and other large organizations. New values were needed to thrive in this milieu, and a new kind of person embodied those values: the organization man. The organization man prizes the group over the individual, and is above all a conformist. Whyte argues that organization men were becoming the dominant class in America.

When I was reading the book, I recall thinking that these people sounded exactly like good crowd men. The best explanation I've thought of for the change from the old individualistic values to the new group values in the United States is that during the Gilded Age, a handful of powerful industrial and financial magnates controlled the economic life of the United States, and they acquired and ruled their empires as individuals. Ideologies exist largely to justify power, so individualistic ideologies dominated at the time. But after the captains of industry had passed away, their companies were left in the hands of people who had risen from the ranks and had not created the companies themselves, and had not been formed by the same experiences, and whose interest was primarily in their salaries and not in stock which they owned in their companies. Technical and managerial skills had become relatively more important factors of production than capital or labor, and so power shifted into the hands of the people who had those skills. So I accept, with James Burnham and some other writers of the time, the idea that there was a quiet managerial revolution, and a new class which was not capitalist in a traditional sense had come to power. Whyte doesn't identify his organization men with Burnham's managers, but I think they are talking about the same thing.

As Martin and Tocqueville point out, America has always had a tendency toward crowd-mindedness. I think the difference between the Gilded Age and the 1950's is that in the Gilded Age powerful individuals existed who could act as a counterweight to the crowd, while in the 1950's there really wasn't anyone who could resist it.

Whyte says that organization men do not like those among them with opinions of their own. It is easier for the group to cooperate if everyone conforms to commonly held beliefs. The important thing is to create a consensus, not to develop new ideas. Organization men have argued that new ideas can be devised in groups, but Whyte doubts it; ideas are always developed by individuals and spread to the group. But allowing every individual to develop his ideas and speak more or less freely disrupts the consensus of the group, and there must be a consensus at least on the important things in order for the group to coordinate its actions. So the administrator and the creative genius are natural antagonists. Whyte says that administrators are naturally uncomfortable when asked who came up with what idea, since they would have to point out that an individual came up with them, and they would prefer that everything be viewed as a team effort. According to Whyte, organization men view opinionated people as being authoritarian or aggressive. The top boss is not an organization man; in fact, organization men perceive the top boss to be an authoritarian; they are the managers and technicians below him.

Whyte talks about how organization men blackball geniuses who try to get jobs at big organizations. The organization men believe that geniuses are anti-social; the brilliant man is inclined to disrupt the harmony of the group by clinging to his own ideas when the group disagrees with him; and besides, most of the important ideas have already been thought out, they say; therefore it is best to sacrifice genius to maintain the harmony of the group. Organization men much prefer applied research to basic research. They much prefer incremental improvements to existing paradigms over ground-breaking ideas. Very few scientists under their sway have the opportunity to work independently and on the problems they choose. Peter Thiel has argued that so much of the innovation being done today has been incremental improvements; perhaps crowd psychology explains why. If you think about who came up with the great ideas of the nineteenth century, who came up with the great inventions, who implemented them on a vast scale, it was always exceptionally talented and passionate individuals, and not groups of well-rounded team players.

Whyte says that executives are more suspicious of the organization than the organization men below them are. The top boss does not like being constrained in any way; he wants to dominate and not be dominated; he does not want to have to "play nice" with people. He's typically a hard worker who cares about results. But the people rising through the ranks to executive positions in his day (and almost certainly still in our day) had to be able to go along to get along until they got to the top and could finally do what they wanted to do. One executive Whyte talks about says that the ideal is to be a conformist on the outside and an individualist on the inside. The impression I got is that if executives could have things just as they wanted them to be that they would be complete autocrats; they would have total freedom of action and the people below them would have hardly any freedom of action, because they would be compelled to act according to the boss's dictates. A lot of people think of Steve Jobs as a creative, freedom-loving guy. And he was. But he was also a dictator. And he was no worse an executive for that; he was one of the best in fact. But he did not rise up through the ranks. I don't think he could have; he just was not the type to go along to get along.

Whyte says that the organizations had prospective and current employees take psychological tests in order to make sure that their personnel and particularly their leadership had the qualities that they were looking for. In effect, the organizations used them to weed out nonconformists. Such things as preferring reading to bowling with a group, along with frequent daydreaming, marrying a woman two years older than you, not having children after 17 years of marriage, and valuing aesthetics could all arouse suspicion. Those were actual examples from the book. If you answered "wrongly" on the tests it really would have jeopardized your ability to get a job or get promoted. Whyte advises people to lie on the tests. He says that people tend not to be honest about themselves, and if you were entirely honest you could be jeopardizing your own prospects. Whyte says that it may well be true that all this pruning and selecting helps a company adapt to its existing environment, but what if the company has to take a dramatically different course in order to compete, or just to survive? He says that the dinosaurs were formidable creatures. Whyte says, also, that the profiles tend to be self-confirming. If only a certain type of person is allowed to become an executive, then only people of that type will become executives. If certain types of people are not even permitted to join the organization then those types will not ever become executives.

Whyte says that industry, with few exceptions, has done a terrible job of recruiting and keeping and not stifling the best scientists. That is the case even though, in the past, great scientists have invented products that made their companies huge amounts of money. The trouble is that organization men just cannot understand the conditions under which scientists do their best work. They always insist that the scientists be team players and that they love the company, but the best scientists are fiercely independent; they resist any attempt to give them direction; they may not love the company. They prefer to indulge their curiosity, working on what they want to work on the way they want to work on it. Most of the time organization men just do not hire the most brilliant scientists. And the best scientists in Whyte's day did not want to work for industry (they still don't, with the exception of technology companies like Google). Good scientists are frustrated by management and either they openly balk and get fired or else they just quit. Whyte mentions General Electric and Bell Labs as important exceptions. These companies allowed scientists to work on pretty much what they wanted to work on, and when they discovered something that would be of use to the company they told management about it and it made money for the company. Whyte says that scientists do not have to be paid a lot of money but they do want their freedom.

Whyte says that it's not true that you need a huge amount of money to do great science, except in certain fields. Most great advances were the work of a single individual with perhaps no more than a pencil and some paper, or some other inexpensive items. Great advances tend to come from outsiders who approached an old problem from a new direction. These people paid no heed to the consensuses of the big organizations.

The impression I got from Whyte's chapter on science in industry is that there is almost no chance that any great scientist could thrive there. Even though it would make a company a lot of money to just let a great scientist do whatever he wanted to do on the company's dime, the management would almost always be against it. But I did think of a way that a large company could pull it off. The great scientists would have to be directly accountable to the board of directors. In other words, they would not be subject to management at all. Not even to the CEO. There should not be a parallel hierarchy of scientists. It would be tempting to create something like that, but the trouble is that the scientists in management would almost always be the mediocrities; great scientists always prefer to do science rather than management. The mediocrities would be telling the great scientists what to do, and they would almost certainly ruin everything. The great scientists would either rebel and get fired or else they would quit. So there should be no organization at all; just individual scientists doing whatever they wanted to do. The management would not like this at all, at least at first, and perhaps they never would like it. They would try to get control of it but they should be denied the ability to do this. The shareholders would get their payoff when the company's profits and stock price increased as a result of the work the scientists would do. This is not really such a radical proposal when you consider that letting scientists do what they want *has* worked. Again, it worked for GE and Bell Labs. But my proposal would remove great scientists completely from the control of organization men. The board of directors would see no reason to thwart the scientists because the board represents the interests of the shareholders. Management's material interests are tied to their salaries, which are not affected much regardless of whether they thwart genius. Shareholders suffer if the company thwarts genius.

Another reason I think this is a good idea is that there is not much risk involved. Again, scientists do not need to be paid very much. Even the greatest scientists would be satisfied with average middle class salaries (and possibly less) as long as they could do what they wanted to do. And regardless of what they might say, as Whyte says, the best discoveries are made using very little capital in most cases. Even if they were not given any research funds at all, great scientists can still do amazing things with the money in their pockets and a quick trip to Walmart. Really. You should read Samuel Smiles's *Self-Help* to see what a resourceful scientist can accomplish. The greats of the nineteenth century and earlier had the bare minimum of resources—things like pots, pans, watch-glasses, apothecaries' phials, and pigs' bladders. Many scientists would not believe themselves what they could do with the crudest of instruments. Anyway, the group should not grow so large as to require management. I don't know exactly how large the group should be. It should probably not exceed Dunbar's number, or about 150 people. Dunbar's number is the cognitive limit to the number of people with whom one can maintain stable social relationships. Groups larger than this probably require more restrictive rules, laws, and enforced norms to hold together. But in my opinion, even 150 people is probably too much. In the realm of ideas it is far better to have a few geniuses than to have an army of mediocrities.

I think a great scientist would accept a salary of $50,000 a year if he could do whatever he wanted to do. That's actually a pay raise for non-tenured scientists. If a company hired 150 good scientists that would cost it $7.5 million a year. That's practically nothing for a large company. That's actually, as I understand it, a little bit low for the pay of a CEO. The trouble is that there are probably not 150 *great* scientists in existence, though there may be 150 *good* ones. There might not be a single great scientist in existence if you are talking about scientists of the caliber of Newton or Einstein. How are you supposed to obtain a commodity when it doesn't exist? No price is high enough to buy it. The trouble is that all of the organizations we have to deal with all our lives tend to crush the curiosity and independence necessary to do great science. The universities are no exception. A company following my plan might be better served by having gifted young people trained by older scientists with reputations for excellence rather than sending them to college. So they would be apprentices instead of being trained on an academic assembly line and matriculated to a stifling bureaucracy.

Again, I think that a smaller group could still be very productive, and perhaps more productive than a larger group. Five great scientists could outperform 150 good ones—even if they were only paid $50,000 a year. That works out to a $250,000 per year investment, which is almost nothing for a large company. And the payoff would almost certainly be much larger than that. A $250,000 per year investment in great scientists could produce billions of dollars in future revenues. Even if it didn't, again, $250,000 is practically nothing for a large company. So there is almost no risk for a potentially enormous reward. Why hasn't anybody done it yet? Because everyone thinks that science can be safely entrusted to management and management almost always bungles the job. In my plan, management would not be able to bungle the job. I suppose the board of directors would have to be enlightened, understanding, and patient in order for it to work, though. Some of these people would be difficult to get along with. And management might still find ways to sabotage everything. Perhaps management would not be able to retaliate if the activities of the scientists were kept secret from them. Management would find out about the science on a "need to know" basis.

Perhaps this is a little whimsical, but I think there is a chance of it working, and it shows how an understanding of crowd psychology can be applied to practical problems. The most important point I'm making here, and I'm absolutely convinced of its truth, is that money and organization are not the limiting factors in the development of new ideas; the limiting factor is individual freedom, and this is incredibly scarce. You can develop great ideas alone and with little money as long as you have individual freedom. Without individual freedom, though, it doesn't matter how much money you have or how sophisticated an organization you have; you will not produce new ideas.

Society's Need to Restrain the Individual

The sociologist Edward Ross (1901) takes a more sympathetic view toward groupishness in his book *Social Control*. He makes it clear at the beginning of the book that there is a constant tension between the desires of the individual and the need for social stability. A gain for one is not infrequently a loss for the other. Ross seems to have no problem with people believing falsehoods as long as it makes them more sociable.

Ross talks about how different things like sympathy, praise and blame, beliefs, and laws influence social conduct. He talks about how religion can be used as a form of social control. Heaven and Hell can be used as inexpensive rewards and punishments to supplement the law and public opinion in bringing recalcitrant individuals around to the interests of the whole society. But it is clear to me that if religion is used, it can only work if inculcated while people's capacity for independent judgment is still unformed, and the belief in wild, unproven, and probably false propositions must be punitively enforced if religion is to work at all. But this is likely to earn religion the enmity of some of the most intelligent, best-educated, and most thoroughly honest members of the community, who can't accept the use of falsehoods even if it's for the public good.

Freedom-loving individuals might not like it, but social control is necessary for people to live in harmony with one another and cooperate for mutual advantage. In one passage Ross is critical of radical individualists like Flaubert, Carlyle, Renan, Ibsen, and Nietzsche. Flaubert thought that the people were an immoral beast, and were fundamentally hateful and idiotic and immature, and always at the bottom of the hierarchy of social elements. Ross deems these sentiments "the cult of the ego" and regards its adherents as brilliant megalomaniacs. He thinks their arguments are both untrue and inexpedient. It's a poor substitute, he says, for the approval of one's neighbors. It is fine to combat folly, but he sees no sense in encouraging egotism.

Public opinion was gaining greater strength as a means of social control and it was the means best suited for modern life. Only the criminal and the moral hero don't care what other people think about them. In Ross's day, and also in our own day, most people crave publicity and notoriety. Most of us respond warmly to praise and wilt under general disapproval. There was another trend at work in Ross's day, which has continued into our own day, of increasing economic interdependence. This gives the community hostages for the individual's good behavior. If the individual arouses resentment in his neighbors they can blight his prosperity and alter the whole course of his life. Ross says that "[t]he day of the sturdy backwoodsman, settler, flat-boatman, or prospector, defiant not alone of law but of public opinion as well, is gone never to return." People had become so used to obeying public opinion that they did not notice that they were following it, and did not think to question it. Ross adds:

> They cannot dream of aught but acquiescence in an unmistakable edict of the mass. It is not so much the dread of what an angry public may do that disarms the modern American, as it is sheer inability to stand unmoved in the rush of totally hostile comment, to endure a life perpetually at variance with the conscience and feeling of those about him. (p. 104)

There is something in public opinion that is neither praise nor blame, says Ross, and this is mass suggestion. Our foods and drinks, our dress and furniture, our amusements, our religious emotions, our investments, and even our matrimonial choices are influenced by it. Everything we do is influenced by it, and a great mass of people can be rendered uniform as a result of it, just "as a steam roller reduces bits of stone to smooth macadam":

> Everything we do reveals the pull on conduct exerted by social suggestion. Our foods and drinks, our dress and furniture, our amusements, our religious emotions, our investments, and even our matrimonial choices confess the sway of fashion and vogue. Whatever is common reaches us by way of example or advice or intimidation from a hundred directions. In our most private choices we are swerved from our orbit by the solar attraction—or repulsion—of the conventional. In public opinion there is something which is not praise or blame, and this residuum is mass suggestion. From this comes its power to reduce men to uniformity as a steam roller reduces bits of stone to smooth macadam. Mr. Bryce has termed it "the fatalism of the multitude," and shown that it its something entirely different from the tyranny of the majority. (p. 147-148)

One's social environment determines the extent to which suggestion holds sway over one's opinions. Some people are slaves of it, while those exposed to other environments are relatively more free from it. The writer he cites below is Boris Sidis:

People of narrow orbit—children, farmers' wives, spinsters, peasants, fishermen, humble village folk, often soldiers and sailors—are slaves to an imposed sense of obligation. Prolonged exposure to a circle or group that speaks always with the same decision the same commands, benumbs the will over whole areas of choice. On the other hand, whatever breaks the clench of the environment or invigorates the will,—liberal education, discussion, travel, varied experience, contact with new types of men, leadership, new ideas and wants, changes in general opinion or intellectual progress,—undermines the tyranny of group suggestions. But most people live their lives in a cove; only the few ever reach blue water. In the wilderness, on the border, in the country neighborhood, the individual counts for much. Likewise in a large city with many types of belief and sentiment. But in a military academy, a garrison, a colony, a religious community, a country village, or a provincial town, the many get the upper hand of the one. And when it is not Mrs. Grundy that coerces, it is tradition. Old colleges, universities, monasteries, senates, academies, administrative departments, army and navy, ancient families and quiet neighborhoods become the haunt of traditions that cast a spell over those who come within their reach. So around rank, station, caste, and office cluster powerful precedents and traditions which quietly overpower and regulate the newly initiated.

"In civilized society," says a writer, "laws and regulations press on the individual from all sides. Whenever one attempts to rise above the dead level of commonplace life, instantly the social screw begins to work, and down is brought upon him the tremendous weight of the socio-static press . . . under the crushing pressure of economical, political, and religious regulations, there is no possibility for the individual to determine his own relations in life; there is no possibility for him to move, live, and think freely; the personal self sinks, the suggestible, subconscious, social, impersonal self rises to the surface, gets trained and cultivated, and becomes the hysterical actor in all the tragedies of historical life." (p. 148-150)

Ross says that suggestion works best when one suggestion is not contradicted by other ones. There are other conditions in which suggestion takes hold more firmly, such as when a person is young, or fatigued, or diseased, or nervous. Also, repetition and the authority of the speaker increase the likelihood that suggestion will take hold. Being caught up in the enthusiasm of a mob also increases the power of suggestion:

The force of suggestion depends somewhat on *bodily* and *mental condition*. Fatigue, disease, and "nerves" lessen the power of inhibition, while mobmadness leads men captive to the impressions of the moment. The *source* of suggestion is a vital matter. The strange power of the individual authority or prestige to impose his will on others is well known. The services of this power on behalf of social control will be examined in the chapter on "Personality." *Volume* or *mass* is, of course, to be considered in measuring the importance of suggestion. The orator presses his point by reiteration. The advertiser wants the name of his soap or baking powder to catch the eye at every turn. The politician knows that if much mud be thrown some of it will stick. The ascendency of the mob over a over a newcomer varies directly with its size. The educator estimates his power to influence a child by the number of years allowed him. The officer demands time to train the recruit into a soldier. The missionary finds it is the first batch of converts that costs. It is its cumulative aspect that makes *social suggestion* emanating from the community at large the chief kind to be considered in connection with the conduct of adults. Finally, there is the *purity* of suggestion. The force of a suggestion is vastly lessened if it meets counter-suggestions that inhibit and block it off. It is therefore *social suggestion protected from contradiction* that can best bend down the individual will. (p. 146-147)

Ross says that despite our inherited theories of the "free moral agent" it's easiest just to follow the conventions of those around us, whether they be good or bad. So praise or blame for our actions is due for the most part to the community in which we live. We admire goodness only when it is difficult, since it is so easy to do what is expected of us. Ross cites as evidence of this the fact that many well-behaved people, when removed from the usual social pressures, behave badly. This is what frequently happens when people move to frontier societies:

Despite our inherited theories of the "free moral agent" we all know the ease of drifting, oars in lap, with the current. We admire goodness only when it is difficult; and outside of obituaries we never give any one credit for practising the common virtues. If it is the rose-strewn path that tempts, then respectability constitutes in old and staid communities the greatest of temptations. Merit in fact begins only when we surpass the ordinary practice. Not to lie to the assessor is one thing; to show him overlooked property is another. They are the same in principle, but the latter means more, because it transcends the ordinary practice. We see far greater merit in a lawyer who will not deceive the jury than in one who will not deceive his client. Yet the difference is simply that the one gravitates to the example of his profession, while the other rises sheer above it.

"Nowadays," said Sighele, "the difficulty is not in finding collective crimes, but rather in finding crimes that are not collective." But if there is much badness, there is likewise much goodness, that betrays the complicity of one's surroundings. There is collective righteousness as well as collective crime, and in a just apportionment of responsibility Jones deserves scarcely more credit for his conventional virtues of decency, monogamy, and tolerance than he does for his conventional accomplishments of reading and writing. Between a man and his associates there comes to be a silent, subtle moral osmosis which we are just beginning to perceive; and until we have comprehended this we shall never quite account for good behavior.

The early history of frontier places like Ballarat or Dutch Flat or Skagway shows that many well-behaved persons, when lifted out of the social pressure, become in respect to character as seriously deranged as those deep-sea fishes that are brought to the surface with the air bladder protruding from the mouth. (p. 151-152)

Ross thinks that it's a good thing for people to pretend that human nature is more benign than it really is because the effects of suggestion can help make it so. He says it's a good idea to give others a reputation to live up to; people respond to the expectations of them. So he says that Admiral Horatio Nelson's famous signal, "England expects that every man will do his duty," was more effective than offering material rewards because of its power of suggestion. Ross says that the Anglo-American fiction of his time was no worse than French fiction, despite the protestations of French writers, for glossing over people's moral failings, and making out to be gentlemen and heroes people whose real life counterparts would not be, and this is because, again, it sets high expectations for people to live up to. Ross speaks also about the positive effect of an educator's expectations of students on their conduct. He also talks about how suggestion can have a negative impact upon people, and he talks about how people tried to conceal the darker parts of human nature so that they would not influence people's behavior. It seems to me that if you wanted to influence people's behaviors in the best possible way, the authorities would have to censor what people could be exposed to, or else people would have to censor themselves.

From here, Ross talks more about the power of social expectations, and about how, in his day, it seemed like all of the media in the United States had been censored by public opinion so that no one might be influenced in a bad way.

Ross also talks about education as a means of social control. In traditional societies the young were raised so that they would not, because they could not, question the great religious and ethical teachings of the past. No counter-suggestions were ever permitted to be presented to them, so they assumed that the ancient ways were as natural and inevitable as anything else in their environments.

Ross talks quite a bit about artists, who he says are often inclined to be anti-social. The best artists in his opinion portray people as better than they are in order to create high expectations in others. They provide people with models of conduct which, if acted upon, would be beneficial to the social order. Ross disagrees with the idea that artists should do nothing else but express themselves, something which he regards as narcissistic.

Ross says that artists tend to resent any kind of restraint and incite others to rebel against restraints. He thinks artists invented the idea of "art for art's sake" because they despise having moral obligations thrust upon them.

Another method of social control is the domination of one class over others. Ross talks about the methods that parasitic classes use to maintain their positions:

> The means whereby the minority can physically overpower the majority are many and well understood. They arm, train, and organize themselves as did the Spartans. Like the Normans, they build themselves strongholds and castles. They girdle themselves with mercenaries as the princes of the old regime surrounded themselves with Swiss. They sow the seeds of enmity among their victims after the manner of the Hapsburgs in dealing with their subject peoples. They deprive them of weapons as the Spartans did the Helots. Like the West India planters, they prevent them from meeting, seeing, or communicating with one another. They keep them ignorant, following the policy of the Southern slave owners. They cut off their natural leaders as did the Roman masters. They break their spirit with overwork. They terrorize them with cruelties. They keep them under constant surveillance, as in classic times the slaves on Sicilian estates were chained by day and penned underground by night. By such policies it has been found practicable for a parasitic band to hold down many times their number. (p. 385-386)

Chapter 6: The Kinds of Crowds

Cajolers, Special Pleaders, and Mascots

In his book *the Crowd in Peace and War* Sir Martin Conway (1915) also talks about the different kinds of crowd leaders. There are three: the crowd-compeller, the crowd-exponent, and the crowd-representative. The first type he discusses is the crowd-compeller. These are dominant personalities who come up with fantastic ideas which they force upon everyone else.

One quality that a crowd-compeller needs is foresight. He needs to be able to foresee difficulties and be able to provide against them. The type of foresight which he needs is not the foresight as to what might happen but the foresight as to what he can cause to happen with the human organism under his control.

Conway says that orators commonly belong to the crowd-exponent class, although a crowd-compeller can be a great orator. A crowd-exponent believes what he tries to get the crowd to believe, and feels as the crowd feels; he is carried away by them. The crowd-compeller moves others but is himself unmoved. Conway says that the greatest crowd-compellers are often not orators.

Conway talks more about how crowd-compellers impose their views upon the masses. Then he says that public opinion is created by a succession of crowd-compellers. He says that it is not the public that should be indicted for the actions of a nation but its crowd-compellers. He says that "[a]ll nations are natural born fools."

Conway says that great crowd-compellers are rare in politics. It takes more than capacity for such a man to appear; he must also have the opportunity. If there had been no French Revolution Napoleon would never have become a great crowd-compeller. Conway thinks that Cecil Rhodes did not achieve his full potential. He thinks that Lord Kitchener might have great crowd-compelling abilities but that can only be revealed in the process of time. We know of course that Lord Kitchener never quite became a figure of the stature of Napoleon or Caesar. Winston Churchill appears to have been able to do it, but Conway, who was familiar with his early career, regards him as a crowd-exponent, not a crowd-compeller.

Conway doesn't doubt that crowd-compellers thrived in England on a smaller scale, though. He thinks that England has more men possessed of the power to lead men than perhaps any other country. He thinks the quality is hereditary, though it may be cultivated by education. He also thinks that "certain classes" possess more of it than others do. He says, naughtily by our standards, that the British subaltern "leads the Indian soldier as a sheep-dog controls a flock."

I think that when the British empire still existed, there was a great demand for people with crowd-compelling leadership skills. There were all sorts of subjects all over the world who needed governing. I think the British declined in the number of their capable leaders after the empire was lost for the same reason. There just isn't a big demand for excellent leaders anymore. Or at any rate no big demand for crowd-compellers. It's hard for a person in charge of a democratic government or even a publicly-traded company to be a crowd-compeller. A democratic leader is severely constrained by public opinion; he can't depart from it very much, at least in public. A leader of a publicly-traded company is accountable to his shareholders and to his customers, and also to public opinion. Steve Jobs was a remarkable exception. He didn't accept the conventional wisdom that the CEO's job was to give the customer what he wanted. Jobs thought that people could be made to want the things he thought were great. And they could be. They were. But practically everybody else just gives the customer what he says he wants.

Conway recounts an instance when he observed a British officer's power of command. The officer was able to compel a disorderly group of passengers to become orderly; he just gave brief and clear orders and they stopped doing what they were doing.

The next kind of leader is the crowd-exponent. The crowd-exponent has not created any crowd of his own, but is formed by an existing crowd. He discerns what the crowd believes and then conveys it back to them in pleasing terms. Crowd exponents come to power when a movement is already strong and tending towards the attainment of its object. The originator has usually already died, but sometimes he is still alive. Conway says that this type of person would horrify the crowd-compellers who they owe their existence to.

The voice of the people is the voice of God in the mind of the crowd-exponent. These leaders don't arrive at their opinions by doing laborious research on what a people thinks and then consciously adopting it and voicing it; they are creatures of public opinion and they understand it instinctively. They are carried away by public opinion of their own free will as a rule, but even if they oppose it on some point upon reflection they still have to go along with it.

Conway says that Disraeli was a crowd-compeller and that Gladstone was mainly a crowd-exponent, and he thinks that their two different leadership types explain largely why they did not get along.

Conway says that there is a very mean type of crowd-exponent who is a conscious hypocrite; he follows, and knowingly follows, the crowd he pretends to guide. He anticipates the direction he thinks the crowd will go in and he gets there ahead of them. These people remind me a lot of the people of our day who want to be "on the right side of history." Anyway, Conway says that "the unguided crowd is always a fool, and the man that follows in front of it instead of guiding it must therefore often look like a fool also."

Conway thinks Lloyd George was an excellent example of a crowd-exponent. He was fundamentally without opinions or prejudices of his own; he adopted the views of the crowds with which he had to deal, and he expressed them very well.

Conway says that the third kind of crowd leader is the crowd-representative. A crowd-representative is a picturesque figurehead rather than an individual force. Constitutional monarchs are a good example of this kind of leader. Conway says that a crowd-representative can be one of the preceding two types as well though. So the King of the Belgians was an effective crowd-compeller, but he was an exception. A constitutional king is supposed to be the personification of his people. He speaks with their voice, acts for them, stands for them in the sight of the world. In private he may be whatever he pleases, but in public he has to play his proper role. Conway notes that monarchs tend not to take public notice of events regarding individuals, like the publication of Darwin's *Origin of Species* or Milton's *Paradise Lost*, despite the fact that these events may be of world-historical importance. They will, however, take notice of events that affect the crowd as a crowd. So they will acknowledge when a large number of people die at sea, or in a mining accident.

Conway says that a crowd-representative can do no wrong in the eyes of the crowd. This is because he represents the crowd, and cannot act otherwise than in conformity with it. Conway says that the murder of a king is a more heinous offense than the murder of other individuals because the murder inflicts a more serious wound upon the crowd the king represents.

Paranoiacs and Madmen as Favorite Leaders

The psychoanalytic theorist Wilfred Bion wrote about half a century later than the original crowd psychologists, though he was influenced by that group. In his book *Experiences in Groups*, Bion (1961) discusses the work of Gustave Le Bon, Sigmund Freud, Wilfred Trotter, and William McDougall. So it appears that the serious writers on group behavior all come from the same tradition more or less.

Bion's theory is highly original. Some of the things he says are surprising, such as his contention that group leaders are often chosen because they are paranoid or mad. Anyway, his theory of the types of crowd leaders is different from Conway's, though I don't think it necessarily contradicts it. Bion thinks there are distinct types of groups and that different kinds of leaders are preferable for each group. Conway and the other crowd psychologists seem to assume that there is just one basic kind of crowd and all crowds share the same properties. So Bion's great contribution appears to be the idea that different groups form for different reasons and that this results in the creation of different kinds of groups, each of which has distinct properties.

Bion says that one reason individuals form groups is because they are either fighting something or running away from something. In this type of group, only these two functions, along with the reproductive function, which is tolerated, are considered to be legitimate in group life. That is because all three of these functions ensure the perpetuation of the group. So when someone put in charge of a group organized to fight or flee does not want to fight or flee, the group does not take kindly to him. They think he is not doing a good job as leader. Bion says that in a group he led for the purpose of giving treatment, the group did not trust him and tried to get rid of him and replace him with another leader. They discarded the new leader also and let Bion lead again, but there were members who were trying to sabotage the group.

One thing I was thinking about when I read this was North Korea. An educated person, free to a significant degree from the rude passions of the mob, has a hard time understanding why North

Korea's people could support its leadership given that, apparently, it is the leadership's fault that the country is diplomatically and economically isolated, and therefore squalid. But the worship of the Dear Leader does appear to be sincere and spontaneous. And I think this is because the Dear Leader is their war leader. He is there to face down enemy groups and deliver his people from the vaguely understood terrors coming from abroad. So a good Dear Leader is a Dear Leader who fights or helps the group flee. Some other activity, like increasing international trade or controlling the proliferation of nuclear weapons, is not readily understood. A leader who concerns himself with these things without explaining himself in terms of fight or flight is not understood and is thought to be a bad leader. The group might try to get a new Dear Leader if he persists. Then they can carry on being truculent.

What if North Korea ceased to be in a state of perpetual conflict with its neighbors and with the United States? If Bion is right, many groups are formed with the purpose to either fight or flee something; North Korea appears to be one of those groups. If North Korea made peace with everyone, then for what purpose would the group—North Korea itself—exist? The group—that is, the country—might dissolve. The group would return to being a heterogenous jumble of isolated individuals. As Trotter said, isolation is terrifying, and gregarious animals do whatever they can to avoid it. So from the point-of-view of preserving the group, neither the North Korean leadership nor the North Korean people are being irrational—that is, knowingly using the wrong means to their preferred ends. The end of a group is to preserve the group. It may well be that the individuals within a group will become more prosperous after being absorbed into another group, but gregarious animals do not normally think in such terms. So the people of North Korea would be better off if they joined the South Korean group, but the North Korean group would cease to exist. That would be a terrifying leap for them.

Another thing I just thought about is the conflicts in the Middle East among all the nationalities and tribes and sects. Maybe these groups don't *want* to make peace with each other. If they made peace, they might dissolve into a mass of isolated individuals. That is not to say that these groups can't make peace. They might make peace if they felt that it was necessary to join forces to match some stronger group opposed to some combination of them. This might be how larger aggregates form. If you think about the history of nations, they were born from conflicts—from wars and revolutions. The United States was formed from a loose alliance of colonies against Great Britain. Italy was formed by war and revolution. Germany was formed from an alliance of German states against France, which was perceived to be an aggressor. The NATO alliance was formed in opposition to the Communist bloc. I suppose the last group is not a true nation, but the principle is the same. Such an alliance would have seemed bizarre without the Cold War.

Bion's explanation also provides us with a reason why organizations which were created to serve some purpose become self-serving institutions. The historian Carroll Quigley thought that this process was the chief reason for the decline and fall of civilizations. Originally, a group might be formed for a purpose, but in time it becomes self-serving. From the point-of-view of the group members, this might not seem to be a bad thing, because in the view of groups, the group exists for its own sake. For the individual, the alternative to belonging to the group, however useless it might become to outsiders, is to become isolated. And again, for a gregarious animal that is terrifying. If a department in an organization resists being disbanded, it probably resists for the same reason that organizations and nations do. If you explained to the people in a department that their work was no longer necessary for the organization, they would not understand. The department exists for its own sake. It is evil to disband the department. So Bion's insight about group behavior explains vested interests of all kinds well.

Bion says that the mistake he made when he was warned about sabotage was not exploiting it as an enemy to be resisted. Then he would have been acting as a proper leader, as the group understood leadership. If you can only fight or run away, says

Bion, then you must find something to fight or run away from.

Bion says that it was unusual that his group did not find a substitute leader who satisfied them. Most groups do. Usually it is a man or woman who is strongly paranoid. If the presence of an enemy is not immediately obvious to the group, he says, the next best thing is for the group to choose a leader to whom it is.

Bion makes an interesting observation. He says that individuals in a group are quite capable of doing work, but they are also quite opposed to the idea that they have met for the purpose of doing work; they feel like some important principle has been infringed if asked to work.

Bion says that the three basic assumptions of group life correspond to three distinct kinds of groups. The three basic assumptions are fight-or-flight, which I have been discussing, along with pairing and dependence. The pairing groups are about mating. Dependence groups coalesce around some individual upon whom all are dependent. The individuals in a dependence group view the leader as having magical powers, or something like them. Bion seems to view religions as dependence groups.

Bion says that there are actually two groups within every group. The first group is the basic assumptions group. This is the group that concerns itself with the perpetuation of the group based on fight-or-flight, pairing, or dependence. The second group is concerned with the task which the group is charged with performing. The two groups and their goals sometimes conflict. Again, this idea reminds me a lot of Quigley's analysis of instruments versus institutions. Perhaps instruments are organizations in which the work group is predominant while institutions are organizations in which the basic assumptions group is predominant.

In his section on dependence groups Bion says that when groups are left to spontaneous behavior they often choose as their leader their most ill member—someone thought to be mad or possessed by a devil. And if they don't have such a person they think they should have one. So if I am understanding Bion correctly groups formed based on dependence prefer to depend on madmen. Bion says that the more practical members of this sort of group try, if they can, to make the leader a god instead of a person, so that the leader is not actually a madman.

Bion talks some more about how the dependence group chooses its leaders. They prefer paranoid schizophrenics or malignant hysterics if they can find them, but if they can't find one a psychopathic personality with delinquent trends will do, and if one of those can't be found either, it will pick on a verbally facile high-grade defective. Bion says that he has never experienced a group of more than five people that could not find one of these types to appoint as leader.

Bion says that the work group or "sophisticated group" that tries to ensure that the group behaves rationally and according to its objectives is always a small group. It usually finds itself in conflict with the much larger assumptions group. The work group believes that improvement is possible and desirable; the assumptions group prefers to keep things as they are. So Bion's work and assumptions groups appear to correspond to the innovators (rationalists) and conservatives that appear in the works of Pareto, Tarde, Trotter, and others.

Bion says that in the dependent group, "bibles" are resorted to when the individual who has been made leader of the group proves to be refractory material. The group resorts to bible-making when threatened with an idea the acceptance of which would entail development on the part of the individuals comprising the group. When a dependent or fight-flight group is active, the group struggles to suppress new ideas because it is felt that they threaten the *status quo*. With regard to the fight-flight groups, new ideas, whether they be tanks or a new method for selecting officers, are rejected because they are opposed to the military bible. In a dependent group new ideas threaten the leader on whom all are dependent, whether that leader be a "bible" or person. With regard to the pairing-group, the new idea or person, being equated with the unborn genius or Messiah, must remain unborn if it or he is to fulfill the pairing-group function. People outside of the couple or genius or Messiah must not advocate new ideas as this would be usurping the function of the leader.

Bion says that the pairing group consists of a couple of the opposite sex as well as a surrounding group characterized by hopeful expectation. So this sort of group is animated by different emotions from the fight-flight and dependence groups.

What Bion is saying suggests that all of the messiah myths are pairing-groups. My understanding is that it is not just childbirth but the birth of ideas or the coming of a long-awaited person that people organize around. So the Jewish and Christian and Islamic messiahs seem to be ideas that form pairing-groups. And if the messiah ever did come, then, if I'm understanding Bion correctly, the group would dissolve (or I suppose it could evolve into another kind of group, if that is possible; could it become a dependence group?). The Marxist idea of the inevitable establishment of a communist utopia at the end of history seems to be another pairing-group belief. Nazi Germany's 1000 Year Reich seems to be another belief of this sort. Bion says that aristocracies are also pairing-groups.

One thing I'm wondering about is why the three different assumptions should always form three distinct groups. Could you not have a group that combines two of these or all three of them? Nazi Germany appears to have used all three. So if the 1000 Year Reich was the pairing-group assumption, the persecution of Jews and socialists and attacks on foreign countries was the fight-flight group assumption, and cult of the Führer was the dependence group assumption.

Bion says that it is important that the ideas of the basic

assumption groups never be carried out in practice. They become dangerous to the degree to which they are. All groups must act, hence they must take account of reality; this is why the work group, and science however crude, are indispensable to the success of the group. The work group does not act on the basis of assumption group beliefs. If they can, though, they try to make their realistic understandings of the world into assumption group beliefs.

Bion says that the reason why there are so few people in the sophisticated group is because the majority reject the pains of development. The majority of people are comfortable with platitudes and dogmas and that is the level at which thought becomes stabilized. Bion is reminded of the fear some express that the least cultured members of a society tend to have the most children while the "best" people remain sterile.

What I'm thinking about is how this bodes for democratic government. If people become scarcer with intellectual sophistication, then in a pure democracy the wisest people will never have their views triumph over those of the majority. But in an aristocracy or monarchy they have a fair chance of doing that.

An important point that Bion makes is that a group leader will not be obeyed if he strays from the role assigned to him by the group. His particular role is determined by the type of group he belongs to. What is expected of him will be different depending on whether he is the leader of a fight-flight group, or a dependence group, or a pairing group. Bion says that the leader must share the group's beliefs in order to awaken the group's faith.

Bion rejects the idea that the leader must have a strong and imposing will; rather, Bion thinks that the leader must sacrifice his individual inclinations in order to fulfill a role determined in advance by the group to which he belongs. A person becomes the leader because his inclinations match the group's criteria for leadership. Bion notes that in this he is opposed to the views of

Le Bon and Freud. Who is right? Well, let's consider the case of Napoleon Bonaparte. It is undeniable that he had a unique personality and a strong will. But—he adapted himself to his circumstances as well. His outward behavior was calculated to influence whatever audience he was entertaining at the time. I'm fairly certain that if Napoleon had acted however he felt like he could not have led so many men. So Napoleon was under compulsion. Or perhaps it is closer to the truth to say that Napoleon understood the constraints of social relationships, accepted them, and willingly worked within them. So it is possible for a person with a strong will to become a leader of a group, but he has to have the prudence to adapt his outward behavior to the expectations of others.

Bion doesn't rule out the possibility that the assumption group leader can be the same person as the work group leader, but he doesn't think this is very common. The individual personalities of assumption group leaders tend to be obliterated to make them more acceptable to their followers, while the predispositions of the work group leaders make them unacceptable to the assumption group. Bion notes that the disasters into which assumption group leaders often lead people are readily explainable within this framework.

This discussion brings to mind all the disasters that the Bush administration was responsible for—and the fact that Bush was elected twice. Intellectual observers of George W. Bush have often commented on his lack of curiosity and his imperviousness to the facts, and have condemned him on these grounds. And yet it was these very qualities, almost certainly, that got him elected. There are many people who could have done a better job of managing the state, and yet they were not elected. Why not? Because the same predispositions that make them good potential statesmen also make them ineligible for leadership positions. I think intelligent people have, at least subconsciously, some notion of this. That's why so many people thought that the "real president" was actually somebody like Dick Cheney or Karl Rove. Under Bion's framework, Cheney could have been considered the work group leader for the management of the state and Rove could have been considered the work group leader for politics and public relations. Bush, of course, was the assumption group leader.

There is another way to classify crowds and that's on the basis of how sophisticated their division of labor is. I think this is one of the most important ways to classify them. The simplest groups appear to have just a crowd leader and an undifferentiated crowd. However, the crowd loses some of its homogeneity when its members specialize in their work and exchange with other members to provide more efficiently for their common needs. As the group develops a more sophisticated division of labor the need arises for a permanent class of managers to coordinate the activities of the countless specialists. Here's why. It is most efficient for workers to specialize wholly in as few tasks as possible, but the more focused you become on just one or a few tasks, the less you know about the overall work to be performed. And yet you must have at least a general idea about all of the many processes that go into making a product in order to ensure that all of the parts form a coherent whole. So if you're making a car with other people and the only thing you know how to do is make tires, you won't be able to make the car by yourself, and you won't be able to make the car even if you got together with people who specialized in making brakes and steering wheels and the rest. A person is needed who specializes in coordinating the operations of other specialists, and while this sort of person is known by many names he is basically a manager. There are also managers of managers, all the way to the top manager, known in corporations as the CEO. Managers of managers coordinate coordinators. The top manager coordinates everyone working within an organization. The CEO may not know the details of how to make a steering wheel or conduct a public relations campaign, but he has a general idea of everything going on in the organization. He knows how to select the right subordinates, who know in turn how to select their subordinates, all the way down to the bottom of the hierarchy. Being an effective CEO requires delegating tasks intelligently, since there is no way that anyone could perform all of the tasks of a complex organization by himself.

Corporations are not the only organizations with a division of labor like this. All large organizations take the same basic form, whether it's a corporation or a military or a civil service or a non-profit organization.

A serious problem emerges for the crowd as its organization becomes more sophisticated. In the most primitive communities it is the custom to make decisions based on consensus and to oppose outspoken individuals who try to force their ways on everybody else. This is what is meant when hunter-gatherers are said to be egalitarian. Bion's study of groups is consistent with this: Bion says that group leaders must accommodate the expectations of their groups, and not the other way around. However, in a large organization the class of managers becomes indispensable to the functioning of the organization. The specialists below them are totally helpless without the organization, hence without the managers. This gives the managers a lot of power—enough power to compel obedience from the crowd even if the crowd doesn't particularly care to obey. But managers are rarely ever individualists, but form a crowd of their own, a crowd within a crowd, with distinct beliefs, behaviors, and interests. They become the master class of a subordinate group of workers. In a complex organization there is no escape from oligarchy; if one group of oligarchs is deposed another takes its place. That's the theme of my next chapter.

Chapter 7: The Iron Law of Oligarchy, or the Incompetence of the Masses

The Leader, the Oligarchy, and the Masses

Dreamers have sometimes imagined that society could exist without leaders and the led, but with everyone free and equal. The crowd psychologists argued that crowds cannot function without leaders, and the fact has been confirmed by experience, as for example when the police arrest the ringleaders of a mob and it immediately disintegrates into a disorganized mass. But although a crowd cannot function without leaders, nevertheless it can, when it is small and when the division of labor is not sophisticated, make and unmake its leaders and disregard orders which run contrary to their sentiments and beliefs. A common observation of hunter-gatherer groups is that they are, compared to us, egalitarian; they do not like "big men" who tell other people what to do, and they can usually resist such people. I think what crowds really do not like is individuals who are able and willing to bend the crowd to their will; although crowds must have leaders in order to function, they appear to prefer leaders who act as representatives or delegates rather than as despots who mold the crowd according to their own visions. Even pharaohs were resisted when they pressed too hard against convention. Akhenaten tried to convert the Egyptians to monotheism long before it became fashionable and was rebuffed. So I think Conway has the right idea, that questions of liberty revolve around how much power free individuals have relative to their crowds, and individual freedom and crowd freedom are always in opposition to one another. The power of the individual increases relative to the power of the crowd when the crowd becomes dependent upon qualities which only free individuals possess, such as when an organization is first being created or when the group's survival is at stake. It was the custom in ancient times for great men to make trouble within the state or between states in order to advance themselves, and when trouble occurred which they did not create, they took advantage of that too.

I think I should clarify something before I continue. There is a difference between the individuals who establish a group or lead it in times of peril and the managers who direct the specialists in an organization on a day-to-day basis. I touched on this when I talked about Whyte's organization men. As Whyte noted, the top bosses in organizations are not organization men themselves, and the organization men resist attempts by the top bosses to dominate them. The top bosses wish to reduce everyone below them to instruments of their wills. I think this pattern is common to all organizations with a sophisticated division of labor. Ancient Egypt had a top boss—the pharaoh—as well as organization men—the priesthood—as well as specialists—the workers. It is possible for a worker not to be a specialist, I suppose, but in a complex organization the two terms mean practically the same thing. Organization men resisting the dominance of hard-charging CEOs are playing out the same scenario that the Egyptian priesthood played out with the Pharaoh Akhenaten thousands of years ago. As for the specialists, or workers, they have always been and probably always will be helpless without leaders, but once they have leaders and the organization becomes more sophisticated in order to meet the demands of its environment, a class of managers is formed and the workers become hopelessly dependent on them. Power shifts to management. The power of management can only be overcome by exceptionally capable individuals, and this can usually only happen in exceptional circumstances. Management bows to "big men" like John D. Rockefeller, Andrew Carnegie, and Henry Ford when an organization is first created, as only free individuals can create organizations, as well as when the organization is in peril, as only free individuals can save it then. Examples of "big men" saving the organization in times of peril (which is sometimes, but not always, deliberately manufactured) include Alcibiades, Julius Caesar, the Founding Fathers of the United States, Abraham Lincoln, Napoleon Bonaparte, and Winston Churchill.

As I noted in the last chapter, crowds differ in how advanced their division of labor is. The more sophisticated it is, the more it can successfully undertake. But a crowd pays a price for this in terms of its freedom of action. This it sacrifices to a class of professional managers, which always emerge once the division of labor is advanced enough. The trouble, as I said before, is that a bunch of specialists can't coordinate their actions without the aid of managers. An old-fashioned craftsman could do every part of his job by himself; however, these were outcompeted by the big industrialists who hired managers to oversee workers who specialized in, perhaps, a single process of production, and had scanty knowledge of what other specialists did. The workers lost their independence, but in the long run their pay was better than what they could get as independent craftsmen. But it isn't just in economic life where the division of labor puts the crowd at the mercy of professional leaders. The same holds in political parties and in governmental bureaucracies as well.

The Iron Law of Economic Oligarchy

W.H. Mallock (1918), a British writer from the late Victorian and Edwardian eras, wrote a fascinating book called *the Limits of Pure Democracy* in which he establishes, I think conclusively, that industrial democracy as the socialists of his time conceived it was impossible. The socialists believed, correctly, that political democracy without economic democracy was a sham. Wealth and the control of the springs of economic life would be concentrated in the hands of an oligarchy who would use their power to lord it over everyone else. The solution, as the utopian socialists conceived it, was for everything to be owned in common, and for both the political and economic leaders of the community to be elected by popular vote. The sovereign power was Rousseau's general will, an entity whose properties were never clearly explained but which was apparently some kind of informed consensus based on the common interests of the community. Mallock writes about how some people actually did try to create utopian communities like this, but they all failed. Without a system of private property, and without entrepreneurial leaders, ordinary workers were totally helpless. Yet with a system of private property and entrepreneurial leaders, freedom and equality were illusions. Mallock says that although they were illusions, the alternative is a return to savagery, to living at the margins of subsistence, and therefore the industrial oligarchy should be obeyed. He says that the governmental oligarchy is indispensable in preserving the security and the property of its people, and therefore it should be obeyed as well. Hierarchy is the fate of civilized people.

Mallock talks about George Bernard Shaw's theory of socialism. Shaw was, at the time, one of Britain's most prominent socialists, and he disagreed with the idea that the profit motive was necessary for people to work; he said that the best workers, like Socrates, do their work without regard to whether they may profit from it. I would say that while that may be true for a handful of gifted people who prefer to work for fame or honor rather than money, and who have already had their basic needs provided for, for most people it isn't true. Profit is a stronger lure than fame and honor for the vast majority of people. Anyway, Shaw argues that compulsion can take the place of the profit motive. If people refuse to do the work assigned to them by the state, they can be forced to work. What I was thinking when I was reading this was that the Soviet Union matched that description pretty well, but it didn't turn out the way most socialists expected it to. It was no paradise where people could enjoy goods without having to work very hard for them, and where they could do interesting work rather than drudge work, and where nobody was exploited by elites. Mallock makes the argument that people might be forced by the state to do work which they are unsuited for, or which they despise, and that is clearly what had happened. Earlier in the book, Mallock makes other good arguments against socialism. He disagrees with Marx's contention that the capitalists do no useful work but merely collect the fruits of others' labor. Mallock says that it is the superior intellect and energy of the capitalist minority that enables industry to exist at all at a large scale, and without such talented people, everyone would be confined to the small-scale labor that characterized labor since ancient times, since that is the limit of what can be accomplished when workers direct themselves. The enormous increase of wealth during the Industrial Revolution was due mainly, he says, to the increasing division of labor. Specialized laborers could perform work more efficiently than generalists, and they could learn new techniques in their areas of expertise which would increase the efficiency of their labor still more. Specialized laborers require someone to coordinate and finance their efforts—the capitalists.

Mallock talks a bit about the industrialist Robert Owen's socialist community which he set up in America. This only worked well at the beginning, when Owen acted as a dictator to set the community up, and when he resumed his dictatorship at the request of the struggling members of his community (he did so twice). In-between the community floundered. The point Mallock is making is similar to that which Robert Michels made about political parties. Michels said that no matter how democratic a party is in its ideals, in order to be effective it must organize; and organization on a large scale means that a bureaucracy must be formed; but the formation of a bureaucracy results in the creation of two distinct classes: the leaders and the led. The leaders develop specialized leadership skills through experience in management while the led, lacking leadership abilities, become dependent on the leaders, and so the followers passively obey. Disgruntled members of the group are always rival oligarchs, or would-be oligarchs; the mass, again, is passive. Mallock is arguing that just as politics on a large scale requires leaders and led, industry also requires leaders and led (however, he says that in small, isolated communities, genuine democracy is both possible and common). "Industrial democracy" as it was conceived back then was just not likely to happen—and it still isn't. The fact that all socialist states established in the twentieth century resulted in the formation of the classes of leaders and led supports this hypothesis.

Mallock says that the Shakers had some success with socialism, but this was a small, self-selected group, and the members were required to be celibate. He says that in this they resembled the Franciscans. The successful utopian socialist sects he talks about were only socialist within the group; they conducted relations with the outside community along capitalist lines, investing in capitalist enterprises and hiring cheap laborers to work for them. Earlier in the book Mallock talks about how the Jesuits taught the natives of Paraguay how to make goods, which the Jesuits sold back in Europe for considerable profit. My understanding is that the Jesuits were organized like a socialist sect, so this is another example of successful socialism, but only within the group, and only with a division made between leaders and the led. Mallock says that families are successful examples of socialism, since each does work according to his ability but receives goods according to his needs; but it is difficult for this sentiment to expand to strangers as well as family members. And his examples suggest that while strangers have nevertheless in some cases managed to live in this way, it only happened under special conditions, like having careful selection of members and requiring celibacy.

Mallock says that the Owenite community ended with the reestablishment of private property, and similar groups met the same end. One of these communities was William Lane's New Australia which was established in Paraguay. The group took its slogans about equality seriously and so they saw no reason to follow the direction of their "equals"; they were unmanageable. Mallock talks about two embarrassing incidents involving the immigrants on the ship to New Australia. In one incident, the passengers insisted on having a say in how the ship should be navigated. In another incident, young men and women were "contemplating the moon" together on the ship's deck (in Mallock's words), and Lane, being a Puritan in temperament despite his atheism, demanded that they stop. They balked; Lane could not command them because he was their equal, they said. Lane asserted his right to command them on the grounds that the ship was owned by a company, and that the shareholders make decisions about the direction of its activities, and that he owned more shares than they did, and could therefore outvote them. After they arrived in New Australia, they put the incidents behind them and began establishing their community, and they did so with great excitement at first, and with great hope of things to come. Within twelve years most of them were starving and begging the communities they left for assistance getting back home. In the words of Mallock, "Lane himself disappeared as a ragged fugitive." Mallock writes that a common feature of demagogues like these is a sincere conviction in two contradictory beliefs: that all men are naturally equal and that they should be led by someone like themselves. Once the masses broke free from the chains of their old superiors, they could live freely and equally and abundantly.

Mallock continues along these lines, suggesting that not only would the community not have existed without Lane's initiative, but only as long as Lane acted as a dictator could the community function; but since he felt compelled to abide by the principle of equality, he had the directors of the group's economic activities chosen by the people themselves; the community was mismanaged and it ultimately failed. But nevertheless, Lane behaved at times as an autocrat. So at the slightest hint that the group was not entirely committed to his teetotaling principles, he called in the Paraguayan army to set them straight. He just did not assert his authority over the economic life of the group after he ceded that power to a democratic committee.

Mallock gives an early example of the problems that democratic decision-making caused. Before the main group of immigrants arrived at New Australia, a party was dispatched in order to get the area ready for their arrival. However, this group could not agree among themselves on where to pitch their tents; each had his own idea about what to do and none would assent to the leadership of anyone else. So they just pitched their tents on the nearest ground accessible into which they could drive a tent peg. But this spot was, of all the places they could have chosen, the one most exposed to rain. And it rained hard. The weather was so violent that their campsite was thrown into complete disarray.

But this incident was only the beginning. When Lane acted as an autocrat, people complained that their work was too hard, and that other people were being unfairly favored over them. So Lane set up a system whereby the people chose their own directors. It was trivially easy to get rid of them; all a dissatisfied person had to do was ring a bell to call a popular meeting and a new director would be chosen to take the old one's place. But the workers didn't respect each other any more than they respected their directors. Because property was owned in common, they didn't scruple about taking or wrecking the fruits of another's work. They didn't care for their tools or animals, either. They were so helpless that only one man bothered to make a home for himself which was better than the crude huts they hastily constructed when they first got there.

The situation only deteriorated from there. The group sold their animals, which were in such bad shape that they could only get the price of their skins. They proposed to Lane that they use their capital as wages and hire cheap native labor to harvest the resources of the forest. Lane agreed to the plan as the only way to secure the triumph of pure social democracy. He sent his brother John Lane to Melbourne to canvas for new members and new subscriptions, but he had little luck. People were not as interested in socialism as they were before, and among those who were, there were objections that Lane's group wanted to establish with the natives the industrial tyranny they were trying to escape from. John Lane argued that the principles of social democracy only applied to white men, and not to black or yellow men. But people weren't buying it. William Lane heard what happened and he turned on his followers, blaming them for everything that had gone wrong. They had not succeeded because they did not believe strongly enough in the group's mission. Lane would only care for the most committed followers; the rest he would abandon to their fates. The majority returned to Australia, says Mallock, "by the charity of the heartless rich," but some remained behind and became prosperous farmers with land that was granted to them as their own property.

As for William Lane, he and his small band of dedicated followers were able to secure a small tract of land from the Paraguayan government which they used to start their project over again. They still believed that their "each for all" policy would result in boundless wealth. But it didn't. They lived at the level of bare subsistence. But Lane was able to recruit some new followers from England. These happened to be prosperous people, to judge by Mallock's description of them. When the new followers were commingled with the old ones, the old ones sought to appropriate the nice things the new ones had, seeing as all property was held in common. The discord between the old and new followers was so great that Lane could not reconcile them. He never renounced his ideology, but admitted that it had some problems which he had not anticipated. He abandoned the project and sought a livelihood with a Melbourne newspaper.

I think Mallock is right in what he says, but it is nevertheless true (as he admits) that industrial capitalism robs workers of their independence even as it makes them richer. I get the impression that in our day most people don't mind that so much. Perhaps even in Mallock's day most did not mind. My suspicion is that the people who crave independence overestimate how much other people prefer it, and that they overestimate how much others dislike being told what to do. A lot of people want the burdens of decision-making lifted from them. They crave the security of routine. However, free spirits and people with dominant personalities are bound to chafe more than others under industrial discipline. But they can still become entrepreneurs if they want to, or do some other kind of self-employed work.

Mallock says that requiring equal incomes for everybody would greatly appeal to the idle and the jealous. An idle man would rest assured that the worst work paid as well as the best, while the jealous man would feel secure that whatever he got himself, no one better than him would get any more.

The idle and the jealous are very common, he says, and this is probably right. On the other hand, the number of truly great men is always small; even potentially great men are few. In a democracy consisting entirely of great men, lazy men, and jealous men, the great men would always be outvoted. I don't think promoting and paying people based on merit has a very large constituency. It's probably also true of honoring people based on merit. A common notion of justice is that what is due to each is what he contributed to the whole, so that a person who did little or no work, or did it poorly, would receive little or nothing, while someone who did much work, or did exceptional work, or did much exceptional work, would receive a great reward. I think a lot of people will assent to this upon hearing it because they have a high opinion of their own work, but in concrete instances, such as a superior worker being promoted ahead of them, or being granted a larger bonus, they would balk. They would in fact prefer that everyone be promoted without regard to merit, and be paid the same, at least compared to others who have been working in their organization for the same amount of time.

Honor is more an object of desire in aristocratic societies than democratic ones. However, the desire for honor is never absent even in a democracy. What exactly is honor? In the way it is being used here, it is a recognition by public opinion, or at least the opinion of the most eminent (which most of the time amounts to the same thing), that some people are superior to others in some respect. The best-known honors in democratic societies are awards like the Grammys and the Nobel prize. Wherever honors are at stake people can express envy just as well as they do when it comes to promotions.

Mallock says that the authority of the industrial oligarchy rests on the fact that unless the many submit to it, they will lose every chance of gaining what they are determined not to lose. Also, the authority of the governmental oligarchy rests on the fact that unless the many submit to it, simple industries will be paralyzed and higher ones will be rendered impossible, and the wealth, welfare, freedom, and the lives of all will be at the mercy of foreign armies whose leaders have succeeded in reducing the many to obedience.

Mallock says that no matter who is in charge, the power of the leaders is ultimately derived from certain exceptional capacities which are necessary to secure the wellbeing of the masses. If the masses do not submit, they will perish. If they cannot be brought around to this truth by reason, then they will learn it by harsh experience. Civilization depends upon the cooperation of unequals—of those who command and those who obey.

The Iron Law of Political Oligarchy

Another writer who was fascinated by the helplessness of the masses before their leaders within organized groups was Robert Michels, one of Max Weber's best students and an influential social scientist in his own right. Michels (1911/1915) developed the Iron Law of Oligarchy in his famous book, *Political Parties*. The law states that "who says organization, says oligarchy." That is, when a group originally forms and has a low level of organization, it may well be democratic; that is, the group can make and unmake its leaders and expect them to act according to the wishes of the group. However, the group is compelled to become more organized as it grows and as it meets with challenges; a class of permanent leaders is formed to regulate the group's day-to-day functions and to make important decisions when the group cannot all meet at the same place and the same time; but these leaders become indispensable to everyone else, as they are the only ones who understand how the organization works, and so the rank-and-file are compelled to obey them. The leaders are transformed from humble servants of the general will into oligarchs lording it over everyone else. The only way an oligarchy can be successfully challenged is by a rival oligarchy or by dissenters within its own ranks. But if the leaders join ranks the masses can never unseat them.

There are a number of reasons why Michels doubts that the masses will ever truly become their own sovereigns. One reason is that it is physically impossible for a large group of people—of groups of thousands, tens of thousands, or millions—to get together in a single location and deliberate on anything, and to do this whenever the need arises to make a decision about the direction of the group. Even the orators with the most powerful voices can't hope to have every member of the group hear him when it grows beyond a certain size. But if large groups cannot deliberate, then they cannot make decisions about the direction of the group. Representatives become necessary. But as he will say later, the representatives end up becoming an oligarchy.

Michels talks about how the representatives are transformed from executive organs of the general will into oligarchs. No matter how democratic the group's ideals are, day-to-day business and the preparation and carrying out the most important decisions must be left in the hands of individuals; it is just not practical, for the reasons discussed above, for the entire group to make these decisions. At first the chief is regarded as being the servant of the mass. Everyone is regarded as being absolutely equal. But this general conception of equality is gradually replaced by the equality among comrades belonging to the same organization, all of whose members enjoy the same rights. Everyone is supposed to have equal influence and an equal participation in the regulation of the common interests. Everyone is an elector and everyone is eligible to run for public office, and all offices are filled by election. The officials play a subordinate part as executive organs of the general will; they are always dependent upon the collectivity, and can be removed from office at any moment. The mass is omnipotent.

At first, the group tries to depart as little as possible from pure democracy by restraining the freedom of action of their representatives. Also, efforts are made so that any member may replace any other member; no one is allowed to become indispensable. But these efforts are only effective as long as the group does not grow too large. The larger it becomes, the more complicated the tasks of administration become. Then the delegates must have unusual capacities in order to carry out their duties, like a gift for oratory and a considerable amount of objective knowledge. It is no longer possible at this point to leave the election of delegates to blind chance, since there is a possibility that someone without the needed qualities could be chosen.

The old methods that allowed the masses to participate in party and trade-union administration were falling into disuse in Michels's time. The process by which the led was transformed into leader was being shortened and stereotyped, whereas in the past it was left to develop by the natural course of events. There were people in the labor movement who were saying that the leaders could not just be anyone chosen from among the rank and file; they had to be persons with superior educations in economic, technical, and commercial matters.

Michels talks about how the socialists founded leadership schools so that they could increase their supply of officials with "scientific culture." He says that the effect of this training is to create an elite of the working class, a caste of cadets composed of persons who aspire to command the proletarian rank and file. So, without anyone wishing it, there is a continuous enlargement of the gulf which divides the leaders from the masses.

Extensive organization results in technical specialization. Technical specialization renders necessary what is called expert leadership. Consequently the power of determination comes to be considered one of the specific attributes of leadership, and is concentrated in the hands of the leaders alone. So the leaders, who at first were nothing more than the executive organs of the general will, free themselves from the control of the mass. Michels says that this process happens in every organization that grows sufficiently large. All large organizations have a minority of people who direct and a majority of people who take direction. This minority may be termed an oligarchy.

Michels says that democracy declines and oligarchy ascends in an organization more and more as the organization grows in size and as it operates at a larger and larger scale, and as its division of labor becomes more and more sophisticated.

In order for an organization to make decisions affecting the whole and to execute them quickly, it must have a hierarchical structure. If the rank and file had to be consulted before any decision could be made, there would be an enormous loss of time and consequently of opportunities for action. The party also becomes incapable of acting in alliance with others. Prior to this Michels says that King Louis XIV's principles of government—promptness of decision, unity of command, and strictness of discipline—apply just as well to any organization existing today.

Over time, officeholders come to regard the retention of their offices as a moral right. They come to see the offices as their personal property. If an officeholder is refused reinstatement, he will threaten reprisals which will tend to sow confusion among his comrades, and the confusion will continue until he is victorious.

The threat of resignation is usually a machiavellian ploy by an officeholder to strengthen his hold upon his office. If a man has become indispensable to the organization, his bluff is called at the organization's peril. If they don't call his bluff, then they are inclined to behave more deferentially than before.

Michels gives some concrete examples of the blackmailing power of an indispensable man. In one case, King Frederick William IV of Prussia threatened to abdicate whenever liberal ideas were threatening to gain the upper hand against his romanticist conservatism in Prussian politics. His opponents were compelled to back down because if the king resigned, his office would go to Prince William of Prussia, an ultra-reactionary, which event was likely to incite an uprising among the lower classes. Otto von Bismarck also succeeded in making himself indispensable. Emperor William I could not rule the country by himself, and if he accepted the resignation of the "founder of the empire," it would have created all sorts of chaos in both domestic and foreign policy. So all Bismarck had to do to render the emperor obedient was to offer his resignation. Michels also gives the example of a Brazilian president who owed his position to the timely threat of resignation.

Michels gives examples from the socialist movement to show that the same principle holds in all parties. Then he says that the threats of resignation have a democratic air to them, but hardly conceal the dictatorial spirit of those who perform them. It seems on the surface that the leader is asking for a vote of confidence when in reality he is forcing them to acknowledge his indispensability and submit to his will.

Michels says that the vast majority of people do not have a lively interest for public affairs; mostly they prefer to attend to their private affairs. The minority who do have a lively interest in public affairs end up making the decisions for the group. The majority do not mind this, though; in fact they are delighted that someone is willing to take the trouble to look after their affairs. The need is accompanied by a genuine cult for the leaders, who are regarded as heroes.

Michels says that this tendency is manifest in the political parties of all countries, but that it varies from country to country in its intensity. So the Germans, more than other peoples, are susceptible to leadership by forceful individuals. This is a prescient commentary given the events to come in his day.

The indifference of the mass at normal times can make it difficult for the leaders to mobilize them even when some vital interest is at stake and the leaders have attempted to agitate them into action. The trouble is that the mass does not always understand fully the consequences of the matters which concern the leaders. When the mass lacks such understanding and the leaders make unexpected signals the mass does not respond. So it is incumbent upon the leaders educate the mass.

Michels says that the most striking proof of the organic weakness of the mass is furnished by the way in which they abandon the field of battle whenever they have been deprived of their leaders. After this, they are not capable of reorganizing themselves unless new leaders arise who are able to take their places. Many strikes and political agitations are defeated because the authorities have opportunely arrested the leaders. Michels says that it's not true, as some narrow-minded conservatives say, that popular movements are the wholly artificial creations of agitators, and that it suffices to stamp out agitators in order to stop a movement. The movements are natural, and the leaders take their place at the head of them generally by the force of circumstance and not by their own initiative. But nevertheless movements do collapse without their leaders.

Michels says that the leaders of organizations do an incredible amount of work on behalf of the mass. They do gain power and honors and offices, and they do become more and more indispensable, but they must be continually receptive to the demands of others, and can't slacken in this even when their health demands it. Without an exceptionally strong constitution this overwork can lead to an early death. Michels says that the mass is genuinely grateful for the work that their leaders do on their behalf, and this gratitude can become hero worship.

He says, a bit later, that in a democracy the born leaders are the orators and the journalists, since words have a powerful suggestive influence on the mass. The mass is also impressed by celebrities. If a person has obtained fame, they consider him to be suited for a position of leadership regardless of his talents or experience in leading a political movement. People who attain leadership positions from fame earned elsewhere come into conflict with men who have risen up from the party ranks. Michels says that the leaders who attained fame elsewhere tend to lose out, in time, to the ones who have risen through the ranks.

The leaders of the latter sort have a better understanding of how to lead a political movement. They take greater care to preserve the forms of democracy, which are dear to the mass, while in fact ruling over it as oligarchs.

Michels says that at the beginning, members of the organization may volunteer their time and efforts just on the days on which they get together for meetings. But as the organization grows it becomes necessary for there to be permanent leaders; dilettantism gives way to professionalism. But the professional leaders become distant from the rank and file in many ways, above all in terms of their knowledge and understanding. The gulf between leaders and led grows until the leaders lose all true sense of solidarity with the class from which they were sprung. And since the rank and file are absorbed in their daily routines, the leaders alone have access to the knowledge of how to work the machinery of organization. This makes them more indispensable and thus harder to remove from office, which is incompatible with democracy. Should the rank and file challenge the leaders, the leaders know how to operate the organization's machinery so as to render resistance ineffective. If the rank and file try to replace the leaders, they will find this difficult, because the current leaders acquired their expertise through long experience; it would take time for new leaders to form, and in the meantime the organization still has to be run. The mass cannot get rid of its leaders without harming its own interests.

Michels summarizes his arguments by saying that the democratic masses are compelled to submit to a restriction of their own wills when they are forced to give their leaders an authority which is in the long run destructive to the very principle of democracy. The leader's power lies in his indispensability. The incompetence of the mass in political matters renders them dependent upon the leaders, and helps justify the power of the leaders. The free election of leaders presupposes that the mass is capable of recognizing and appreciating the competence of the leaders, which they are not.

Democracy ends by undergoing a transformation into a government by the best—into an aristocracy. Michels asks that, granted the superiority of the leaders to the mass, why should they not regard it as their duty as well as their right to lead, and "not merely as representatives of their own party, but as individuals proudly conscious of their own personal value?"

Michels says that short terms of office can prevent the leaders from becoming too indispensable, and he says that in this regard, the United States has the best protections of democracy. The American voters were called upon, in his day, to exercise their function, on average, 22 times a year (this sounds a bit high to me but whatever the case, the basic point is sound). I would imagine that this would also make political leaders less competent than those who held office more or less permanently. This does appear to have been the result. But in the other cases Michels talks about (with the socialist parties of Europe) even when an official has to be periodically reelected, the same officials tend to remain in office as long as they have not done something egregiously wrong. Michels thinks this is due to the gratitude of the mass. They don't wish to oust someone who has done an incredible amount of good for them.

Michels says there are good reasons for keeping officials in office for extended durations. One is so that they can acquire expertise. Another reason is because, if an official believes his hold upon his office to be insecure, he will not feel inclined to exert himself to the fullest. Officials become irresponsible. When terms are short, they tend to think primarily of getting the most out of the office that they can before getting kicked out. There is complete disorder in administration as a result of this, and because there is a confusion of orders and regulations when there is a rapid succession of leaders. It is also easy in the general disorder for the guilty to shift responsibility onto the shoulders of others. "Rotation in office" prevents the formation of a bureaucratic caste, but there are so many other problems that are created as a result. Michels says that a great advantage of monarchy is that the hereditary prince has an eye to the interest of his posterity and so he has an objective and permanent interest in his position; he will almost always abstain from policies which would hopelessly impair the vital energies of the country.

There is another problem with frequent rotation in office. That is that relationships between different organizations demand a certain degree of personal and tactical continuity; without such continuity the political authority of the organization would be impaired. This is as true for political parties as it is for states. Michels says that England has long been regarded as an untrustworthy ally in European politics because no other country has been able to confide in agreements concluded with it, and this is because the foreign policy of the government depends upon which party is in power, and party changes occur with considerable rapidity. A party that changes its leaders too often has the same problem—it may find it difficult to form alliances at an opportune moment. These problems are due to the recognized right of the sovereign mass to take part in the management of its own affairs.

It seems to me that the spread of democracy in the Middle East and its threatened outbreak in other parts of the world might not turn out as well as a lot of people think. A dictator or king might not keep his word with foreign countries, but the frequent changes in leadership which democracy demands mean that it is far less likely that democratic leaders will keep their word (or rather, someone else's word). If the monarchy in Jordan fell, for example, the country's peace treaty with Israel would be less secure than it was before, just as the peace treaty between Egypt and Israel became less secure after the fall of Hosni Mubarak. Current leaders might agree to peace, but they can be rotated out of office and replaced by someone spoiling for a fight. All it takes is a change in the public mood. The people have a limited understanding of politics and think little of the future consequences of present actions. They are strongly inclined to hostility toward out-groups. They are moved more readily by appeals to emotion—hence to demagogy—than to appeals to reason. You might reason with a dictator or king and make deals with him to mutual long-term advantage. You cannot reason with a crowd. Democratic leaders might be reasonable persons themselves, but if they are really democratic leaders then their freedom of action is constrained by the mass.

Michels says that once the leaders have become secure in their positions, they try to get the power to select their successors. This opens the door to nepotism. So it may happen that a democracy becomes a plebiscitary dictatorship, after which it becomes a hereditary monarchy.

A little later on, he talks about the finances of political parties. Members who are economically dependent upon the party tend to remain with it even after their zeal for the cause has slackened. Also, he talks about how the workingmen were stingy, at least originally, when it came to paying employees of the party. They took particular care not to pay the intellectuals any more than the laborers. The stinginess was justified on the grounds that a comrade who was not paid a high salary was more likely to work simply for the good of the cause, but this turned out to be inefficacious in fact. Michels says that idealism alone is, for the majority of men, an inadequate incentive for the fulfillment of duty; enthusiasm is not an article which can be kept long in store. Men might stake their bodies and lives for a moment, or even in some months in succession, on behalf of a great idea; but they often prove incapable of permanent work in the service of the same idea even when the sacrifices demanded are comparatively trifling. As a general rule, it is best to pay people adequately. If the leaders are paid poorly they may become corrupt or demoralized. A poorly-paid leader might betray the party for gain, whereas one who finds in his occupation a safe and sufficient income is less likely to do so.

The party leaders who control the finances can put economic pressure on people both inside and outside the party in order to control them. Rivals and dissatisfied members of the rank and file can be shut out from sources of income within the party.

Businesses who are dependent upon the patronage of the working class can be boycotted if they prove unfriendly to the cause.

Michels says that when the masses oppose the leaders, the leaders tend to close ranks to defend their prerogatives as a class. And as long as they remain united, they are always victorious. Even when the masses become angry with their leaders, and vent their rage publicly, nevertheless the leaders remain in power. Sometimes the leaders feign acquiescence to the will of the mass but this is not sincere; it is meant to prevent the alienation of the mass from the leaders and the formation of a new elite which could displace them. When revolts occur, they occur at the urging of rival oligarchs who wish to use the mass to supplant the current leaders.

Michels elaborates on this. He says that there is always mistrust between the old leaders who currently hold command and the new leaders who wish to attain command. The old leaders mistrust above all others those who aspire to command their own organizations. They are wary of newcomers, who they do not regard as their eventual heirs but as successors who are ready to supplant them without waiting for a natural death. Michels says this is a bit like the conflict that always exists between the old rich and the new rich. In any event, the new leaders declare war on the old leaders ostensibly on the basis of eternal principle, but in reality they see this as the best way of forcing their way into the circle of chiefs. They present themselves as theoretical adversaries at meetings and "talk big" so as to intimidate the old leaders into parting with a share of their privileges. Often enough the old leaders stand their ground, in which case the new leaders give up the struggle and instead accept the tutelage of their superiors, hoping by a different route to obtain what they desire.

Michels says that the struggle between the old leaders and the new leaders constitutes a perpetual menace to freedom of speech and thought. The old leaders wish to control as strictly as possible the freedom of speech of those of their colleagues from whom they differ. They often force colleagues whom they suspect of rebellious inclinations to abandon publishing independent journals, and to publish all their articles in the official organs controlled by the leaders of the majority in the party.

Michels says that in this struggle, the old leaders can usually count on the support of the mass. The mass instinctively distrusts newcomers who have not been openly protected or introduced into the party by the old leaders. The newcomer must thus submit to a period of quarantine if he does not want to be exposed to the most violent attacks. Michels says that in the German labor movement, not only new members but outsiders like authors who are independent of the party machine rarely succeed in making their influence felt. But in Italy, the management of the Socialist Party is entrusted to young men and in France it is entrusted to free publicists. The Germans accord great respect for age.

Michels says the struggle between old and new leaders often assumes the aspects of a struggle between responsible and irresponsible persons. Those who do not currently hold power are free from the grave responsibilities of those who do hold power, and so they have a tactical advantage.

But the leaders can use certain underhanded methods in their defense. They can claim that the new leaders are irresponsible, and incompetent, and that they, the old leaders, are both responsible and competent; and they demand the immediate submission even of merely discontented comrades. The old leaders also claim that their understandings are superior to those of the mass, and that the mass should not be permitted to thrust unworthy colleagues upon them, and so the old leaders assume the right to determine who can and cannot join the inner circle.

The old leaders assume leadership if they can of all emerging movements before a new elite emerges from them that might challenge them. The old leaders can co-opt already-existing competition by, for example, giving them positions and honors as subordinates in the organization.

When the new leaders succeed in forcing their way into the inner circle, it is not usually the case that the new group replaces the old group; rather there is a merger of the two. If they are irreconcilable then the new leaders may form a separate organization.

Michels says that groups in the opposition are the ones who argue in favor of freedom of expression against the tyranny of the existing leaders, but once the new leaders get control they turn out to be just like the old leaders. The revolutionaries of today become the reactionaries of tomorrow.

According to Michels, in a democracy every private is considered to have a general's baton in his knapsack. One of the corollaries of Michels's theory, though, is that very few people are capable of running any organization. So if you picked an employee at random from a corporation and put him in charge of it, the odds are that he would fail miserably. If you kept picking employees at random as each CEO failed, then you would have to run through a lot of employees before you found one who could do the job. You might not find one at all; some that might have the potential to lead lack the expertise because they are nowhere near the positions of ultimate responsibility and never have been. There is a big difference between managing a small team and managing a company with tens or hundreds of thousands or perhaps even (like Walmart) millions of employees. And my suspicion is that it is not merely a lack of leadership experience that renders people incapable of leadership but the many years of serving as an employee—as a subordinate rather than a leader; as a person who takes decisions but does not make them, at least any really important ones. A lot of the best CEOs seem to be the ones who started with small companies and grew them into large ones. John D. Rockefeller, Andrew Carnegie, Henry Ford, Sam Walton, and Steve Jobs all fit this description.

Michels talks about how bureaucracy comes into existence, and what its purpose is, and whose interests it serves. He says that the organization of the state requires a numerous and complicated bureaucracy in order to function. The politically dominant classes use the state bureaucracy to secure their domination and to retain control over the levers of power. The instinct of self-preservation leads the modern state to assemble and to attach to itself the greatest possible number of interests, and the need for the organism of the state increases as discontent with the social order among the populace increases. But even though the state is eager to secure defenders through its patronage, the demand for such positions outstrips the supply. This is because of the precarious economic positions of the middle class in modern capitalism. Middle class people wish to secure for their sons employment which is protected from the competition of the market. The state provides that employment. The intellectual proletariat is created from the fact that there are not enough positions for these people. Sometimes the state is forced to hire them in large numbers in order to transform dangerous opponents of the social order into stalwart defenders of it.

Michels says that there are two classes of intellectuals. One class is those who have succeeded in securing a post within the state, and the other class is those who tried to obtain a post but could not. The first class of intellectuals behaves as an army of slaves who are always ready to undertake the defense of the state which provides them with bread. The second class of intellectuals is made up of implacable enemies of the established order. They lead the bourgeois opposition to the state and in part they also assume the leadership of the revolutionary parties of the proletariat. Although the bureaucracy does not expand fast enough to meet the demand for positions, nevertheless it grows continuously. And as it grows, it becomes less and less compatible with the general welfare. But it is essential as a means of buying off the opposition to the established order.

Michels says that political parties operate much the same way. He then talks about how, when the scope for action among the socialists was limited, they cared much more about refining and adhering to socialist doctrine. However, once they were free to organize and agitate, their organizations became ends in themselves almost. The leaders concerned themselves more and more with the day-to-day maintenance of their bureaucracies; they didn't have much time for philosophical matters. They held little regard for those who did care about philosophical matters. Michels says that specialization is to blame for this. The technical specialists began to impugn the competence and even the good faith of socialists who wished to advance socialism in some other manner than that which they were familiar with in their narrow specialties.

Michels says that bureaucracy is the sworn enemy of all individual liberty, and of all bold initiative in matters of internal policy. It tends to corrupt character; it makes employees subservient to superiors and haughty toward inferiors; it turns people into place hunters. He says that the more a bureaucracy is distinguished by its zeal, sense of duty, and devotion, the more it becomes petty, narrow, rigid, and illiberal.

Michels talks about the movements for centralizing power into fewer hands as well as those for decentralizing power into many hands. A single charismatic leader might try to take charge of the whole movement like Karl Marx attempted to do and create a kind of monarchy. Marx, however, was thwarted by other oligarchs. Leaders of local oligarchies tend to prefer having the top position in a local group to being second place in a larger group, and so they demand more local autonomy—greater decentralization of power. They use slogans that sound like they are fighting for freedom but if they achieve their goal the people subject to them are no more free than before.

Michels says that the leaders are changed once they have obtained positions of power. They come to crave power for its own sake; they enjoy the exercise of it. So psychological factors also contribute to the transformation of a democratic group into an oligarchy. There are other reasons why the leaders are reluctant to relinquish power. One is that it may be difficult for them to return to their old careers even if they wanted to (which usually they don't, after having attained preeminence). A manual worker will fall out of practice after years in professional politics. A scientist will not have the time to attend to his scientific work after he has become engaged in political affairs and will find it hard to go back. A barrister might be able to return to his profession, however, since political advocacy and legal work are not so different. So many of the leaders are financially dependent upon their positions. They may have families to support. It sometimes happens that the leaders are idealists when they join the party and become leaders, but they have doubts later on, and yet they cannot back out. So out of necessity they become opportunists.

Michels says that the party organization which was formed as a means to the end of proletarian victory over bourgeois society ends up becoming an end in itself. The party leaders stop caring about fulfilling the party's revolutionary goals and instead focus on getting the largest number of members possible, and the largest number of votes possible within the parliamentary system. They avoid trouble with the law; if a member's methods get him into trouble with the police they do not defend him. The party has become conservative, and resembles any other bourgeois party except for its revolutionary rhetoric, which is never meant to be taken seriously.

Michels says that the majority of socialist schools believe that in the future it will be possible to attain a genuinely democratic social order, while adherents of aristocratic political views believe that a socialist order, while dangerous to society, is at least possible. But among the scientifically-minded, led in Italy by Gaetano Mosca, a new belief was emerging that it was not possible for any highly developed social order to exist without a politically dominant class, which is always necessarily a minority. So this scientific group denied that democracy was possible at all (at least in large groups). They thought all the slogans of democracy to be a bunch of cant; the "god of democracy" was "the creation of a childlike mythopoeic faculty"; phrases such as "state, civil rights, popular representation, [and] nation" were descriptive of mere legal principle and did not correspond to any actually existing fact. The eternal struggles between aristocracy and democracy which are recorded in history are really nothing more than the struggles between an old minority clinging to power and a new minority which seeks to displace it as the dominant class. These battles have their cause ultimately in economic antagonisms.

After this Michels talks about Pareto's theory of the circulation of the elites. Pareto was another member of the scientific group. According to Michels, Hippolyte Taine was an influence on this current of thought. Taine is not very well known today, but he was well known in the late nineteenth century; his histories of the French Revolution and the old regime were highly influential.

Michels says that the state is always the organization of a minority. Even when the discontent of the masses culminates in the overthrow of the bourgeoisie, it still does not rid itself of the need for masters; a new organized minority springs from the mass which raises itself to the rank of a governing class. So the majority of human beings exist in a condition of eternal tutelage, and are predestined by tragic necessity to submit to the dominion of a small minority, and must be content to constitute the pedestal of an oligarchy.

The social revolution would not effect any real modification of the internal structure of the mass. The socialists might conquer, but not socialism, which would perish in the moment of its adherents' triumph. Michels is tempted to speak of this process as a tragicomedy in which the masses are content to devote all their energies to effecting a change of masters. Even the purest of idealists is unable to resist the corruption which the exercise of power effects in people.

The views of Robert Michels and Wilfred Bion appear at first sight to be in conflict. Michels argues that the group is more or less at the mercy of the leaders, owing to the incompetence of the former and indispensability of the latter, but Bion argues that the leaders are more or less at the mercy of the group, because the group will not accept as its leaders anyone who does not play his proper role as a leader. For Michels, it is the leaders who have the power. For Bion, it is the group that has the power. But Michels does seem to have been in agreement with Bion about democratic groups—actually democratic groups, and not nominally democratic ones. It is only when a group develops a sophisticated organization that power shifts from the group to the leaders. But I don't think any leader of any country in our day—or any day—could safely ignore public opinion. Perhaps it is the case that power always remains in the hands of organized groups, and the public is always dependent on these, but public sentiment may shift in favor of one candidate or another from among the leaders. The public chooses whoever plays out his role the best. If another organized group—like a revolutionary party—exists, then the people may shift their allegiance away from the ruling group to it if it loses faith in the established order.

Chapter 8: The Ruling Class and the Struggle for Dominance

The Ruling Class

Gaetano Mosca (1896/1939) argues in *the Ruling Class* that there is never one particular person, like a king, who governs a given society; rather, there is always a small group of people, organized and distinct from the mass, who govern. There may be a clearly identifiable leader, but he is the representative of the governing group and derives his power from it; he is never independent of it. The character of a society is derived chiefly from its governing group, its ruling class, and not from the people at large. The mass is disorganized and is incapable of asserting itself without leaders.

One of Mosca's key concepts is that of social forces, which are any human activity or perquisite that has a social significance. Among these are money, land, military prowess, religion, education, manual labor, and science. A group is said to rule when it is able to control the social forces that, at the given moment in society, are essential to the possession and retention of power. The author of the introduction coins the term "Mosca's Law" to give a name to Mosca's contention that "type and level of civilization vary as ruling classes vary." Ruling classes vary in the number and grade of social forces which they control, tolerate, stimulate, or create. The internal stability of a regime depends upon the ratio between the number and strength of the social forces that it controls or conciliates and the number and strength of the social forces that it fails to represent and has against it. Unfortunately, some successful regimes end up creating social forces which they are unable to control, and which turn against them. Social forces regularly manifest themselves in aspirations to power. Soldiers, the rich, the priests, the scientists, labor, and public officeholders all want to rule, and each has in its possession one of the social forces.

Another key concept in Mosca's theory is juridical defense, which is Montesquieu's theory of the balance of powers within a government applied instead to social forces. When one social force is able to dominate, the number of active social forces is reduced, and the level of civilization drops. Everyone is forced to believe, or pretend to believe, in the political formulas (myths justifying power relationships) which the wielders of the dominant social force hold sacred. This is tyranny. But when there are a number of social forces counterbalancing each other, then a large number of social forces can exist within the same society, and the level of civilization is said to be high. Everyone can pretty much do as he pleases, have his say, and realize his full potentialities.

Mosca thinks that this perfect balance is attained at times and in peoples where it has become law. The social forces are not checked by force applied on a case by case basis but by habit, custom, acquiescence, morals, institution, and constitution. Mosca's word for this is juridical defense, which amounts to government by law with due process.

If ruling classes can be appraised by noting the number and grade of social forces which they recognize, the governments by which they rule can be appraised by the grade of juridical defense which they provide.

A point that Mosca makes is that ruling classes rarely rule entirely by force; they feel compelled to justify their rule in terms which will allow the masses to believe that the existing order is the way things ought to be. These broadly accepted justifications of power relationships are called political formulas, and they have analogies in similar writers: Pareto had his derivations, for example, and Sorel had his myths. An example that Mosca gives is the divine right of kings. The masses of the Middle Ages were deeply religious, and so the ruling class justified its power as being derived from the sovereign, who in turn reigned by the grace of God. Although it may be easy for us to identify this as a political formula, back then very few people thought about it in such an analytical matter; it was simply taken for granted; it was the way the universe worked. I'm sure we have political formulas in our day as well, although very few of us recognize them as such. Mosca thinks that the will of the voters is a political formula in the United States, just as the political formula for the Roman Empire was that the emperor ruled by the will of the people. Mosca says that political formulas are not mere quackeries used to dupe the masses into accepting their subordination; they answer a real need in man's social nature of governing and knowing that one is governed not on the basis of mere intellectual or material force, but on the basis of a moral principle.

Mosca dislikes the idea of universal suffrage, and he attempts to undermine its theoretical foundations. Mainly, he means to prove that representatives are not the mouthpieces of the majority of electors. Mosca contends that just as in every other form of government, in a democracy with universal suffrage an organized minority imposes its will upon the majority. The voters do not elect their leaders; the leaders have themselves elected by the voters; or rather the leaders have their friends have the voters elect them. At first sight it might sound like Mosca is playing games with language, but he isn't. The trouble, says Mosca, is that people do not actually vote for their ideal candidates, nor, practically, could they. If everyone voted for the people they really liked best, then the votes would be so scattered that no candidate would have anywhere close to a majority of the votes. In order for the choices of so many people to coincide, the number of candidates for consideration for office must be reduced to two or three people who have some chance of succeeding. By what process is the number of candidates reduced? By the decisions made by organized minorities. But although the voters are limited in their ability to choose their representatives, nevertheless their ability to choose among two or three people chosen by an oligarchy obliges the candidates to appeal to sentiments of the crowd in order to tip the scales in their favor. So the candidates are responsive to the common herd.

Mosca says that even though representatives are accountable to public opinion, the same is true even of the most despotic governments. But Mosca says that "wariness of giving offense will be much greater when every single representative, whose vote may be useful or necessary to the executive branch of government, knows that the discontent of the masses may at almost any moment bring about the triumph of a rival." Mosca has some more criticisms in addition to this; basically, he sees the wheeling and dealing of the organized minorities in a democracy with universal suffrage as corrupt.

Mosca says that the contention that truth must always win out over falsehood is mistaken. Some falsehoods, like the great religions, satisfy real needs and so they are broadly accepted despite their falsity. It is also false that persecution does not work. It can work, and has worked, when it has been swift, merciless, and unwavering. He gives the examples of the successful spreading of Christianity among the Saxons by Charlemagne's persecutions, the eradication of Buddhism in India (its motherland) by persecution, the near extermination of Christianity in Japan by persecution, and the wiping out of Mazdaism from the Persia of the Sassanids; and there are many more than these.

Mosca says that the tendency of religious and political sects is to draw attention to the moral failings of their enemies while holding themselves blameless. But all of them, to varying degrees, are guilty of wrongdoing. As long as a person does not come into contact with other men, and especially if he makes no attempt to guide them, he can remain blameless. But when you have dealings with other men you are obliged to exploit their springs of conduct, including taking advantage of their weaknesses, or else you will be beaten by someone who is less scrupulous. Mosca quotes Cosimo dei Medici, "the father of his country," as saying that "states are not run with prayer books." But, Mosca says, a ruler who appeals only to the baser sentiments of his subjects is not likely to be successful. And with a sufficient display of energy, self-sacrifice, restless activity, patience, and, when necessary, superior technical skill, a man can lead without having to exploit baser sentiments so much. But men with such a combination of qualities are rare.

Mosca goes on to talk about how the methods of gulling the masses appear to be similar with every sect. They all have a declamatory style that excites crowds. They have rituals and displays of pomp to strike the fancy. They exploit the vain by creating ranks, offices, and distinctions. They exploit the simple, the ingenuous, and those eager for self-sacrifice or for publicity in order to create martyrs, and martyrs are exploited to strengthen the faith. They create myths of great men, or men with unblemished integrity, in order to give luster to their group and bring wealth and power to it for the sly ones to use. Also, they excuse every sort of wrongdoing as long as their members remain loyal.

Mosca goes on to talk about the Jesuits, and about their sectarian spirit and their dissimulation, artifice, and stratagem. But they were not so different from other religious and political sects. The principle that the end justifies the means is common to all of them, and they all esteem as great only those who fight in their cause, and they all remain silent on the merits of outsiders, and they all hold to the form and letter of their word while violating it in substance, and they all know how to distort a recital of facts to their advantage, and they all know how to find simple, timid souls and how to capture their loyalty and win their assistance and contributions to the cause. Earlier in the book Mosca talks about other dirty tricks. For example, he talks about how Mohammad hinted, in the presence of a zealot, that he was displeased with someone, after which the zealot killed the man, and Mohammad was able to say, in all honesty, that he never ordered the man to be killed. And Mohammad always seemed to have new revelations ready to justify whatever it was he wanted to do. There were other leaders of religious sects who manipulated people to their advantage. What I wonder about is how Mosca learned about all these dirty tricks. Pareto, another Italian, was not unfamiliar with them, either. I suppose it's a tradition in Italy. Renaissance Italy was glorious, but its rulers knew every dirty trick most people could imagine and a lot more of them that most people couldn't, and they put them into practice without scruple.

A point that Mosca makes on multiple occasions is that the people who rise in the world often do so through unscrupulous or otherwise disreputable means. Over time, people forget the base origins of aristocratic families and the means by which they forced their way to the top. Established families tend to have more refined manners than the newly rich because the members of the former never had to struggle to get to the top; they were born there.

Mosca doubts that philosophers would make the best rulers. Nor does he think that the best rulers are necessarily the best men, either in terms of morals or intellectual capacity. The trouble with having philosophers rule is that philosophers seem to prefer neither to command nor to obey; wisdom seems to deter people from wanting to obtain power more than it compels them to seize it. The best rulers are simply those who are the best at commanding men.

Mosca talks about how, until the late nineteenth and early twentieth centuries, it was the norm among European militaries to draw their officers exclusively from the upper classes while the enlisted men were drawn exclusively from the lower classes. The upper classes had far better educations and habits of leadership than the lower classes, and so the enlisted men naturally deferred to their officers. This also made it possible for the upper classes to entrust arms to the lower classes without fearing that the lower classes would use them to rebel. Mosca says that this arrangement was ensured in Britain and Germany by the practice of selling commissions, which only the wealthy could afford; the practice continued in Britain until 1871 and in Germany until 1914.

A point that Mosca brings up is that, unlike people who apply the results of science to practical problems, scientists themselves rarely profit from their work. He thought that it would be wise for a society for have some way of recognizing or compensating scientists so as to encourage an activity which benefits the whole community.

The Circulation of the Elites

Vilfredo Pareto writes in the same tradition as Michels and Mosca; he assumes that it is the elites in a society who determine its overall form, and that the masses are passive without leadership. Pareto first achieved fame as an economist, but he began writing sociological works in order to explain behavior which was not rational the way the economists of his day assumed economic behavior to be rational. Pareto argues in his works that the greater part of human actions have their origin not in logical reasoning but in sentiment, although people usually come up with rationalizations for their non-logical behavior. People deceive themselves into believing that they are really motivated by the causes which their imaginations have invented despite the fact that these are rarely the true causes. Pareto (1901/1991) says in his book *the Rise and Fall of Elites* that people who deceive others begin by deceiving themselves, and in this his views are in accord with those of modern evolutionary theorists like Robert Trivers.

Pareto's main contribution to the study of elites is his theory of the circulation of the elites, which describes how elites rise and fall and replenish their ranks. According to Pareto, it is the first two of the six main human sentiments he identifies that are responsible for the rise and fall of elites: the instinct for combination and the instinct for preservation. Pareto (1916/1935) describes these sentiments (or residues, as he likes to call them) and their many subclasses in his *magnum opus, the Mind and Society*. Basically, the instinct for combination is the tendency to invent and embark on adventures, and the instinct for preservation is the tendency to consolidate and make secure. The other sentiments Pareto doesn't talk about as much, but I will list them here. The third class is the need for expressing sentiments through external action and includes such things as religious and patriotic ceremonies. The fourth class of sentiments is the social instinct, which includes phenomena such as self-sacrifice for the sake of family and community and concepts such as the hierarchical arrangement of societies. The fifth class is the quality in a society that stresses individual integrity and the integrity of the individual's possessions and appurtenances. The sixth and last class is the sex instinct, or the tendency to view social events in sexual terms.

Why did Pareto come up with a weird name like "residues" for the human sentiments? Because they are what is left over from human actions when they are stripped of their rationalizations. Pareto's weird name for rationalizations is "derivations," and he talks about these extensively in *the Mind and Society*. Good examples of derivations are things like "democracy," "equality," "natural law," "right reason," "social justice," and "solidarity." These were all a bunch of cant, as Pareto saw it. But if you looked below the surface of people's speech habits you could discover the sentiments that really motivated them.

One sentiment or the other of the first two sentiments may be predominant in a given person or class of people. Those in whom the first sentiment is predominant can be called innovators, and those in whom the second sentiment is predominant can be called consolidators. Pareto divides elites into economic and political elites, and into those whose dominant residue is combination and those whose dominant residue is preservation. Economic elites in whom combination is dominant are termed speculators; those in whom preservation is dominant are called rentiers. Political elites in whom combination is dominant are termed foxes; those in whom preservation is dominant are called lions. Pareto attempts to show that history is mainly about the replacement of one elite by another—and it is always, he says, the replacement of those predominantly of the first residue with those of the second, or *vice versa*. According to Pareto, the history of man is the history of the continuous replacement of elites. His philosophy is summed up in his phrase, "history is the graveyard of aristocracies."

Pareto argues that an elite needs, at different times, both the ability to innovate and the ability to consolidate. When an elite is lacking in one or the other ability, it becomes unable to perform its function as an elite, and it may be displaced by a new elite emerging from the mass or from a conquering elite from outside the state. Innovation allows an elite to persuade, cajole, threaten, and manipulate friends and foes to solve problems. Conservative tendencies enable an elite to provide security and stability, and to move friends and opponents with forceful coercion when conscience, faith, and normal social pressures fail. Pareto emphasizes in his work the fact that the ability and willingness to use force is often lacking in innovative elites, and this can be a serious problem; a small band of ruffians is all it takes to seize the state if they aren't checked by force. This is actually what happened when Pareto's old student, Benito Mussolini, marched his Blackshirts on Rome. However, when an elite is faced with changing circumstances it must innovate or be swept away. Revolutions occur when people with innovative instincts are blackballed from entering the elite when their talents are necessary, or when people with conservative instincts are blackballed from entering the elite when *their* talents are necessary. Revolution can be avoided by open recruitment into the elite. Pareto says that the masses in all times and places tend to be conservative, while the makeup of the elite varies.

Pareto writes in *the Rise and Fall of Elites* that when a new elite seeks to take the place of an old one that it doesn't admit this frankly and openly but "assumes the leadership of all the oppressed, declares that it will pursue not its own good but the good of the many; and it goes to battle, not for the rights of a restricted class but for the right of almost the entire citizenry." Pareto doesn't deny that the revolutionaries might believe what they say; however, their promises are never kept. Once they obtain power they monopolize the spoils and become the new elite. At best they offer some formal concessions to the masses who have empowered them, but the masses have done little else but effect a change in masters.

Pareto thinks that humanitarian sentiments are a sign that an elite has lost its willingness to defend its position by force and that it is in danger of being displaced. He almost certainly has Taine's account of the French Revolution in mind here. According to Taine, the French aristocracy had imbibed all sorts of humanitarian ideas, and they acted as accomplices in their own dispossession.

The Evolutionary Psychology of Dominance

Dominance hierarchies are created by competition—more specifically, by competition among males for sexual access to females—and all human societies have dominance hierarchies. Very few sociologists of our day have attempted to ground their discipline in biology and behavioral science, but I did, by chance, find out about a few. Joseph Lopreato and his former student Timothy Crippen (2001) are among these, and I think they did a good job of this in their book *Crisis in Sociology: the Need for Darwin*. I can tell that the authors were strongly influenced by the Italian elitist school of sociology, that is, by Michels, Mosca, and Pareto. (I should note that Mallock was also influenced by Michels.)

This is what Joseph Lopreato and Timothy Crippen say about dominance behaviors and their relationship to self-deception in *Crisis in Sociology: the Need for Darwin*:

> The drive to enhance one's rank in the dominance order—the "climbing maneuver" (Lopreato 1984: 110-20) or the "sentiment of equality in inferiors" (Pareto 1916: sections 1220-1228)—is so powerful a force in the human brain that people have evolved to deceive themselves as well as others about its urgency. It is always more acceptable, and hence more effective, to seek a selfish aim by cloaking one's motives in the garb of the collective good. Deception of others is all the more effective when deceivers are taken in by their own deceit (e.g., Trivers 1971; Trilling 1972; Wright 1994: chap

12). The failure to understand these mechanisms of the mind has led to numerous errors in sociology. Deceived by the revolutionaries' sophistries of collective interest, we still think of sociopolitical revolutions, for example, as phenomena of *massive collective action* executed for the good of the group. In fact, as the aftermath of one revolution after another has shown, what once appeared to be collective action was after all a *mere summation of individual actions* whose results would profit mostly, or exclusively, only the few (Lopreato 1984: 117). Little wonder, then, that some scholars have perceived the dynamics of social status in the very nature of human language. As is predictable from sexual selection, the concern for rank is far more obvious among males than among females—more marked in the exploitative, philandering sex than in the more monogamous one (e.g., Tannen 1990). (p. 233)

The authors also talk about the physiology of dominance (p. 235-237). They say that competitive behavior is mediated by the testosterone, which of course exists in the greatest abundance in males. Modern research reveals strong links between testosterone and aggression. Men with high levels of testosterone are more likely than men with more moderate levels of testosterone to marry and more likely to divorce. If married, they are more likely to have marital difficulties, to use violence, to avoid spousal interaction, and to have extramarital partners. Aggression and dominance behaviors may be adaptive in terms of securing resources and status, but if unchecked they may have opposite effects in situations that require close cooperation.

The authors cite one study in which tennis players who won decisive matches experienced a rise in testosterone levels, while the reverse was true for losers. There was no rise in players who barely escaped defeat. According to another study, shortly after graduation medical students were already recording their rise in status by experiencing a significant rise in their testosterone levels. The conclusion of the authors of that study was that "there appears to be a reciprocal relationship between circulating testosterone and dominance behavior." Lopreato and Crippen add that this makes sense, given that hormones elicit given behaviors, and these in turn react on hormones, modifying their expression.

Here is the authors' summary of their discussion of dominance behavior and social stratification:

1. In any social system, desirable resources are always scarce, or so they are defined.

2. Competition for resources is a universal aspect of human existence.

3. Some individuals succeed better than others in the competition for a variety of causes, including the fact that human beings are unequally endowed with the innate traits needed to compete with success.

4. In any dominance order there is a degree of status inheritance and favoritism.

5. In different degrees, people are power-seeking animals whose hunger for power increases in direct proportion with the power already commanded.

6. Success in the competition is at times a result of sheer merit, but more frequently it is a function of manipulating rules to one's own advantage.

7. Successful, that is, dominant, males are especially attractive to females, with the result that—in one way or another—they achieve greater than average reproductive success; and women continue to manifest their tendency toward hypergynous mating.

8. Men's tendency to exploit women in varying ways is only

partially subject to cultural mitigation.

9. Destratification efforts do not succeed.

10. Class or collective movements are only apparently driven by collective interests.

11. Whatever the political form of a social system, power is concentrated in the hands of a few: the oligarchs.

12. Oligarchies are ever subject to challenges, often successful, from elements who covet power for selfish reasons but make appeals to collective interests.

13. Oligarchies seek to defend themselves with a variety of coercive and other techniques, including especially the cooptation of potential challengers.

14. The most successful challenges to established dominant groups derive from those who are in close proximity to the top.

15. Social systems, however rigidly stratified, feature a continuous flow of personnel from one stratum to another.

16. Dominance orders most of the time have the support of the populace because, among other reasons, they (a) bespeak opportunities for future success; (b) maintain a tolerable degree of internal order; (c) provide some direction for future development; and (d) organize the defense against really of potentially hostile social systems. (p. 244-245)

Most of the sociological phenomena that we observe can ultimately be traced back to sexual selection. According to Charles Darwin, sexual selection "depends, not on a struggle for existence, but on a struggle between the males for possession of the females; the result is not death to the unsuccessful competitor, but few or no offspring." It is well-established both empirically and theoretically that women prefer men who have high status in a dominance hierarchy or who are resource-rich. Why? Because such men are better able to provide for their offspring. Poor, low-status men are poor choices as mates because they are less able than other men to provide for their offspring; they might not be able to provide for them at all. In fact, this was the case during parts of China's history; some men were so poor, according to Lopreato and Crippen, that they barely had enough money to castrate themselves so that they could earn a living as eunuchs in harems. So, then, it is to a man's advantage in his reproductive rivalry with other men to rise in status or become rich, or both, and it is to a woman's advantage to mate with these men.

What about men? Men prefer women who are young and attractive. They don't care as much as women do about the status or resources of their mates. Why do they have these preferences? It's because men prefer women who are fertile, and younger women are more fertile than older women. Women in their late teens and in their twenties are more fertile than women in their thirties, who are more fertile than women in their forties. Beyond that, menopause sets in and women cannot bear any more children. If there were any men among our ancestors who preferred old, infertile women to young, fertile ones, they would have died out long ago. What about attractiveness? Lopreato and Crippen don't talk much about this, but my understanding is that men prefer attractive women because attractiveness is a reliable signal of good health and fertility.

Sexual selection explains why men cheat with younger women, and why they divorce older women and remarry with much younger ones. But women are different when it comes to age differences; in fact, women prefer to marry men who are older than themselves; they not infrequently marry men who are two or three decades older than them. Sexual selection explains why: older men are more likely to have acquired status and resources than younger men. Most women will prefer to marry a forty-something doctor or lawyer or businessman than an 18-year-old guy who has just graduated from high school.

In their struggle for status and for material resources, men compete with other men. The winners gain access to the best— and to the most—women. Status, material resources, competitiveness, and reproductive success all go hand in hand for men—or they normally would. In the past, in many societies, the most successful men sired more children than less successful men. Lopreato and Crippen talk a bit about how contraception has changed that, but they don't dwell on it. Also, there are many other dysgenic pressures within industrial societies that they don't talk about.

The welfare state allows people who would otherwise be unable to support themselves, much less reproduce, to not only have children but to have more children than the abler and more ambitious members of society. Also, the need of most able people to delay marriage for education and job training means that they must delay reproduction until later in life. And their jobs frequently take up so much of their time that many decide to have few children or none at all. The fact that children are a net economic loss rather than a net economic gain for most people also discourages many of them from having children. Those supported by the welfare state, however, can reproduce at will and allow other people to bear the full cost of raising their children.

In any event, it is clear that the competition among males for status and resources is the product of the pressures of sexual selection. In order to defeat other men, men form alliances. The outcome of this competition is social stratification—dominance hierarchies. At the top of these hierarchies is a winning alliance— what sociologists call an oligarchy—and at the center of the oligarchy is what primatologists call the alpha male.

Lopreato and Crippen note that females play a key role in the politics of other primates, but they don't talk about their role in humans. In any event, the authors say that at the top of the status hierarchies in primates is the dominant males, with women and subdominant males occupying the second tier. At the bottom are the much more numerous non-dominant males.

In this struggle for preeminence, men not only form alliances but make use of coercion and deception. Because deception is easily detected when it is conscious, self-deception evolved. Deception is more likely to succeed when the deceiver believes his own deceptions.

So an incredible amount of sociological phenomena can be explained with Darwin's very simple theory of sexual selection. This is in contrast to modern academic sociology's failure to come up with a single theory or law explaining the vast amount of evidence they have accumulated over the years, according to Lopreato and Crippen. Much of this failure is due, as the authors say, to ideology, especially feminism. Feminists do not want to acknowledge the biological differences between men and women because they say that it reinforces stereotypes and justifies male domination of women. But whether or not that is the case has little to do with whether or not evolutionary and behavioral science are correct.

I should note that the authors do not deny that men have historically tried to dominate women; in fact, they did, and they did so in large part through their control over material resources. But, as the authors note, women themselves were complicit in this because of their preference for resource-rich men.

One way in which men tried to control women was by controlling their sexuality. Why did they do this? That, too, can be explained in terms of sexual selection. While women can know with certainty who the fathers of their children are, since they know who they are mating with, men can't always be sure; they can't watch their mates all the time. When men could control the sexuality of their women they could be surer that the children of their wives were also their own.

Our ancestors belonged to much smaller tribes than most people today do. My understanding is that "Us" rarely referred to more than a few hundred people. I don't believe we can ever feel entirely at home in "tribes" of tens or hundreds of millions, much less billions of people. In the absence of a serious threat, I suspect that larger groups disintegrate into smaller ones; empires break up into nation-states, nation-states break up into ethnic groups, ethnic groups break up into tribes, tribes break up into clans, and clans break up into nuclear families. As people are faced with larger and larger groups up enemies, they form larger and larger alliances in order to counter those enemy groups. But these alliances, I suspect, are largely formed out of necessity, and not because people are naturally more comfortable with belonging to or identifying with larger groups. Lopreato and Crippen have some evidence that supports these observations, but they don't put it exactly as I do, and they are more tentative about it than they are about other subjects.

Chapter 9: The Wisdom of Crowds?

After I had already finished writing most of this book I found out about and read *the Wisdom of Crowds* by James Surowiecki. Surowiecki's thesis appears, on the surface, to completely contradict mine, and those of the authors I cite. In Surowiecki's view, crowds are wiser than any individual is; or more exactly, they can be wiser than any individual when they meet certain conditions, which are diversity, independence, and decentralization, which I will explain in a moment; he doesn't deny that sometimes crowds make foolish decisions. Surowiecki talks about Gustave Le Bon's *the Crowd* in the beginning of his book, and he says that Le Bon got crowds exactly wrong. He also uses an anecdote about Sir Francis Galton to show that, apparently, crowd judgements are sometimes better than expert judgements.

I found Surowiecki's book to be informative, and it's helpful to have a dissenting voice among writers on crowd psychology; otherwise crowd psychologists could become a crowd themselves. However, I found the book to be misleading in some respects. Surowiecki seems to promise with his title and introduction a defense of the wisdom of crowds, but what he actually delivers is mainly a defense of the aggregations of individual opinions, which is not the same thing as a crowd.

One of Surowiecki's conditions for crowds making well-informed decisions is that a diversity of views must be permitted. Each individual may have some private information which, if pooled, could provide a better picture of reality than any one person could provide. Surowiecki admits the difficulty sometimes of meeting this condition. There are strong pressures to conform to a single view. His condition of independence refers to the fact that individuals in a group must be able to depart from the views of his peers and not just follow along. The decentralization condition requires that there not be a coercive hierarchy influencing the views of group members; these create disincentives for all of the information acquired at the lower levels to reach the top; it often pays not to tell the boss when something has gone wrong.

The trouble with the first two of Surowiecki's conditions is that any aggregate of individuals who fulfill them cannot, by definition, be a crowd. The crowd psychologists explicitly deny that a crowd can have a diversity of opinions. One of the defining features of crowds is their homogeneity. They maintain this by persecuting deviants, who could become the nuclei of rival crowds, and who in any event undermine the faith of the others by their example. In other words, they make it very risky for any individual to think independently of the group. Should an individual succeed anyway, the crowd would most likely break up into competing crowds. The trouble with the third condition is that the Iron Law of Oligarchy often requires groups to set up hierarchies, despite their sometimes being inefficient. Destratification efforts have not been successful.

Another problem I have with Surowiecki's thesis is the dichotomy that he implicitly creates between the views of opinion leaders—he calls them experts—and the views of the crowd. And yet, as the crowd psychologists, Lippmann, and Bernays have shown fairly conclusively, crowds get all of their opinions from opinion leaders. So the dichotomy is a false one. What wisdom the crowd has must first be the wisdom of the opinion leaders. It's true that the crowd may be following deceased opinion leaders, like Jesus or Moses or Mohammad, rather than the most eminent living opinion leaders, but nevertheless the crowd always follows opinion leaders.

Surowiecki gives another example as proof of his thesis. This example is about how a group of experts found a lost submarine. None of the experts knew where it was. Each had only some of the information necessary to discover it. When the information was aggregated a coherent idea was formed of where the submarine might be found. And this collective judgment, as Surowiecki calls it, was accurate: the submarine was found. But this is not the judgment of a crowd, as I have argued, but the aggregate of individual opinions—in fact, of individual expert opinions—and I do agree that the best judgments are often made from the rigorous aggregation of expert opinions.

Actually, despite the above example Surowiecki denies that the aggregate of expert opinions is superior to the judgment that a group with more varied levels of understanding could provide. In other words, if you had an aggregate of experts, and an aggregate of experts combined with ignoramuses, the second aggregate would produce better decisions. I wasn't quite convinced of this. Surowiecki cites an experiment that appears to show this but I remember thinking that it could have been that *crowds* of experts display inferior judgment to the *aggregates* of a mixed assortment of *individuals*. Crowd psychology acts upon experts just the same as everyone else and it distorts their judgments. But Gustave Le Bon said as much.

Surowiecki cites the gameshow *Who Wants to Be a Millionaire?* as support for his thesis. The contestant was supposed to answer questions given to him by the host, and if he didn't know the answer he could ask the audience or phone a friend—someone they thought was well-informed. Surowiecki equates the friend with the expert and the audience with the crowd. The friends did fairly well but the audience was right more of the time. But this is a specious argument. One problem with it is that the audience was not randomly chosen from the population at large. They were a self-selected group. Most of them probably watched the show regularly, and they must have been enthusiastic about it if they wanted to be in the audience themselves. I would be willing to bet that the audience on the show was much better informed than the average group and that its members were fonder than most of answering questions on *Who Wants to Be a Millionaire?* If so, it wouldn't be unreasonable to call them a group of experts. And the poll presented to the contestant was the aggregate of those expert opinions. It was not a consensus generated by groupthink. If this scenario is at all plausible, and I believe that it is, then the thesis of Le Bon and Mackay still stands.

Surowiecki talks about the Challenger explosion and how investors seemed to know which companies were responsible for it before it became public knowledge. Some experts thought there was insider trading going on. Surowiecki says that no evidence was found of that; he thinks that this is another example of the wisdom of crowds. I would have to know more about exactly what happened in order to give a good judgment, but it could be that investors just followed the advice of opinion leaders. Maybe the opinion leaders were not doing insider trading but were knowledgeable about how the companies involved were managed. What if one of the experts had been saying for years that Company X was being lackadaisical about its safety standards? Maybe investors weren't convinced originally; the company could plausibly deny it until the day something went wrong; but then something went wrong. Who was responsible for it? Perhaps the company who the top expert had been saying for years had lackadaisical safety standards. I don't know if it actually happened this way, but something like this could have happened. If it did, then it would be another case of the crowd following an opinion leader. It would be one person's judgment, or the judgment of a few people, and not the judgment of the crowd. Or it could be another case of the aggregation of expert opinions. The unknowledgeable could have followed the well-informed set. (Surowiecki thinks that the result was the aggregate of investor opinions, but he I don't think he refers to the investors as experts.)

Surowiecki talks about how Google search results make use of what he calls the wisdom of crowds. But it seems to me that it's really another case of the aggregation of expert opinion and the following of the experts by everybody else. If I understood this section correctly, the way Google works is that results get promoted to the top of the search rankings when a page is initially linked to by a small number of other pages, and other people follow these initial linkers by going to the original page; these readers might also link to the original page if they find it useful, and *their* readers might click on the link, find it useful, and then link to it themselves; and so on. So momentum is built up if a lot of people find a page useful, and it might become a top search result, or if they don't find it useful the momentum never builds, and it never becomes a top search result. But not all links generate the same amount of links. If Slashdot or an influential blogger links to your page then it will get a lot more hits and links than if an obscure site linked to it. So it seems to me that opinion leaders behave the same way with regard to search results as they do in other social phenomena.

Surowiecki talks about betting and how people get the odds of a competitor winning just about right. So if the bettors think that a horse has a twenty percent chance of winning a horse race this is usually about right. The size of the winnings in these bets depends on the perceived odds of a competitor winning. This does seem to be an impressive example of what the aggregation of individual opinions can do. I strongly suspect that people who bet on horse races have better information about horse races than the average person does, however. So this may be another case of the aggregation of expert opinion. The novices could have followed the well-informed set again.

Surowiecki talks about how the principle applies in the marketplace. If there is a diversity of entrepreneurs and investors then even projects which have slim chances of succeeding will be tried and presented to the crowd for judgment about which is best. Surowiecki talks about how this was done in the case of the automobile business. Many different kinds of cars were tried but only the best cars were selected by customers and only a small number of companies survived the winnowing of the marketplace.

Surowiecki assumes that the best decisions, the ones that best promote the well-being of the group, are ones based on accurate information. An interesting question is whether the best decisions from the point-of-view of a group might not be based on motivational falsehoods universally held. Falsehoods can be beneficial if they improve morale and maintain unity. Truths can be harmful if they demoralize and divide the group. Groups with high morale and unity tend to beat groups with low morale and unity, all else being equal. Of the authors I have cited, Trotter, Lippmann, and Ross make reasonable arguments along these lines. Lippmann argues that the unity of the group is so important in times of emergencies that one wrong opinion may be better than two right ones. If the unity of the group is shattered by disagreement the enemy could take advantage of it to achieve victory. So the best decisions, that is, the decisions that lead to the best outcomes for the group, sometimes require absurd uniformities of opinion.

Surowiecki talks about groupthink and the pressures toward conformity. He talks about the Asch conformity experiments. In those experiments the subjects were unwilling to voice their independent judgments because they didn't want to upset the conformity of the group. But when one of the experimenter's confederates said what they really thought other people felt free to say what they really thought. The rate of conformity plummeted. Surowiecki says that independence of thought is one of the most important elements in making good group decisions but it's also one of the hardest things to keep intact.

Next Surowiecki talks about social proof. This is the idea that if a lot of people believe something, there is probably a reason for it, and so people tend to believe it for that reason. This is different from believing something for fear of punishment.

Surowiecki talks about how people tend to be more risk-averse than perhaps they should be if they want to maximize their gains. So he talks about a strategy in football which appears to be good, and is consistent with a careful examination of the data, but which is rejected by most football teams because it goes against the conventional wisdom. Surowiecki says there is a difference between the wisdom of crowds and the conventional wisdom. I'm getting the impression that Surowiecki is disowning any crowd phenomena that don't fit his thesis that crowds are wise. So whether or not crowds are wise depends on how you define crowds. Anyway, he says the risk-aversion is due to the fact that most people find it better to fail in a small, conventional way than to fail in a big, public way—and parting from convention draws attention to what you're doing. This is called herding. It's the idea that there is safety in numbers. The phrase "you can't get fired for buying IBM" captures the spirit of the idea well.

Next Surowiecki talks about information cascades. The idea is that the information that people base their decisions on isn't perfect, so they see what others are doing and use that as a guide for their own behavior; only, it may be that everyone else is following initial bad information. Surowiecki gives the example of two restaurants, a Thai restaurant and and Indian restaurant: the Indian restaurant is objectively better, but the initial information that people get is that the Thai restaurant is better than the Indian restaurant, so that's where most people go. Then most people keep going to the Thai restaurant because it's so crowded. Surowiecki says that cascades are not an example of the wisdom of crowds because people are not relying on their private information but are just following a handful of others who have set a trend. Information cascades sound a lot like the imitative faculty that the crowd psychologists talk about.

The third key condition for making intelligent group decisions is decentralization. This appears to mean something like devolving decision-making down to the lowest practical level of the hierarchy rather than concentrating decision-making in the hands of a single person or a few people at the top. People who are face-to-face with a problem have better information about it than someone higher up in the hierarchy who only has a general idea about it. I think Surowiecki is using the division of labor as an example of this. He uses Linux as another example of decentralization. Linux is an open source operating system, which means that anyone with Internet access who knows how to code can work on it. People just work on what they want to work on and ignore the rest. Surowiecki says that there are no bosses ordering people to do things, and yet Linux has been able to become the most successful competitor to Microsoft Windows. It seems to me, though, that there are still leaders and the led, even if the leaders can't physically or financially or legally coerce anybody into doing anything. And I would imagine that peer pressure and other group influences act upon the individuals in open source movement. The advantage of decentralization is that the amount of useful information in the system increases, he says. Decentralized groups don't have to deal with bureaucratic politics like a centralized corporation does. A greater diversity of opinions is possible. With a greater diversity of opinions, eventually someone will emerge who will be able to solve the problems at hand.

I should note that open source people do display some stereotypical crowd behaviors. For example, there are the editor wars between users of vi and Emacs. There are also rivalries between users of different operating systems and between different programming languages. But nevertheless, I think the open source community allows the individual greater freedom than he might otherwise have. It is not too difficult for an individual to travel from group to group; the individual is not utterly dependent upon any one of them. This provides some relief from normal group pressures. But if your livelihood depends on the good will of the group, or rather its leaders, as it does in a corporation, then you are less free, and are more of a slave to group pressures.

Surowiecki thinks that markets and bee colonies work a lot like Linux does. He says these decentralized systems are akin to letting a thousand flowers bloom and then picking the best ones. It's wasteful, though, and he thinks corporations can't afford to do things this way.

Surowiecki says that in order for decentralization to improve the decision-making abilities of the group, there has to be some way of aggregating all of the information in the system. In the example with Galton, Galton was the one who was doing the aggregating of the information. In the Linux example, it is Linus Torvalds and a small number of other programmers who vet all changes made to the system. Maybe this is a consistent pattern in decentralized groups: the masses may provide the bulk of the raw material but it is the oligarchy in each case who select and aggregate that material. Anyway, Surowiecki says that paradoxically, aggregation, which is a form of centralization, appears to be necessary to the success of decentralization.

The problems I have been talking about so far only apply to what Surowiecki calls cognition problems, which have to do with getting information accurate enough and voluminous enough for making good decisions, and then making prudent decisions based on that information. The next kind of problem is coordination problems, and I agree with Surowiecki that crowds can be, in this regard, wiser than any individual could be. So markets make better decisions than central planners do, and ant colonies behave intelligently despite the fact that each ant is not very intelligent. Most coordination problems appear to be solved by having group members obey certain fixed rules. Sometimes these rules can go wrong. So sometimes ants follow each other around in a circle until they die. However, most of the time the rules work well. The more even-handed crowd psychologists would concede this point.

One example Surowiecki gives of intelligent collective decision-making is of a bar that is enjoyable when it is not crowded but unenjoyable when it is crowded. But if everyone thinks that everyone else is going to go to the bar on Friday night, then they might all stay home, so that no one goes to the bar on Friday night. What actually happens, though, is that just the right number of people show up. Just the right number of people stay home. Yet there was no centralized decision-maker who decided that that would happen.

Surowiecki says that people coordinate their activities with shared cultural references called Schelling points. He also talks about social norms and how they allow for intelligent group decisions. One example is the norm of allowing whoever comes first to take a seat. Waiting in line is another good example.

But following custom doesn't always lead to perfectly rational decisions, Surowiecki admits. He talks about how prices are very often determined by custom rather than by rational calculation, so movie tickets for a popular movie may cost the same as tickets for an unpopular one. He also talks about how people who are conducting transactions with others would rather take nothing than accept what they regard as an unfair offer. So they are punishing people for being unfair, but it is at some cost to themselves, since accepting any offer in the experiment is better than accepting nothing. He talks about how people are more inclined to cooperate with others if they have long-term relationships with them, but he doesn't think that's the only reason why people cooperate since in experiments like the ultimatum game there is only one exchange.

Surowiecki talks about how the Quakers became successful in business because they were trustworthy and reliable. He talks about cooperation problems, like paying taxes. It is costly for each individual to pay taxes but they pay for collective goods. If everyone stops paying taxes the public goods disappear. If some people can get away with not paying taxes then other people feel like suckers and don't want to contribute either, so it is important that everyone complies in situations like this. People are actually willing to pay in order to punish cheaters.

Surowiecki says that sometimes diversity of behavior can create coordination problems. This is the case in traffic jams. One car can slow down many other cars.

Surowiecki thinks that small groups make worse decisions than large groups do. Apparently the larger a group is the better its decisions are supposed to be. Boris Sidis said that the exact opposite was the case. Surowiecki is still defining crowds as the aggregate of individual opinions, though, and those aren't actually crowds as Sidis and the other crowd psychologists defined them. Large, diverse aggregates of individuals contain more information than small groups do. This is why Surowiecki says what he says.

Surowiecki talks about polarization in groups. This is the idea that discussion in groups without dissenters tends to produce a more extreme consensus than could have been predicted from the individual opinions of the members.

Surowiecki talks about how there are barriers to the spread of information in traditional corporations, and about how this makes for less-than-perfect decisions being made by the people at the top. There are also perverse incentives at times, such as when employees are rewarded for exceeding expectations; this can cause employees to work less efficiently than they could at times.

Surowiecki doubts the ability of individuals to make good decisions as compared with the group—at least under the special conditions he identifies. He cites the cases of the many failed CEOs once hailed as geniuses to support this claim. It's true that some CEOs perform better than others, but Surowiecki thinks this may be largely due to luck. The successful ones might have just been in the right place at the right time.

Surowiecki admits that sometimes democratic publics make ill-informed decisions. However, he repeats Churchill's argument that democracy is the least bad of government forms. But Winston Churchill should have known better, since democracy was actually something that England had only recently become acquainted with, and he was an aristocrat himself. Until well into the twentieth century England was an aristocracy. The country first rose to prominence in world affairs as a monarchy, reached its peak as an aristocracy, and then declined dramatically just as soon as it became democratic. Churchill probably liked democracy because democracy allowed him to become prime minister; people tend to like what is good for them.

I should note also that the Congress of Vienna which concluded the Napoleonic Wars and established a century of relative peace and unprecedented prosperity was presided over by royals and aristocrats, not representatives of the people. A century later, the Paris Peace Conference which concluded World War I led to another disastrous war before even a generation had passed. That peace conference was presided over by the representatives of the people—the ones who fought to make the world safe for democracy. So I think the merits of democratic government have been unduly exaggerated, and the merits of aristocratic and monarchical government have been unfairly played down.

I think my review of *the Wisdom of Crowds* might come across as harsher than I meant it to; I actually thought the book was pretty good except for the misleading terminology. But it appeared to contradict a major thesis of my book, and it seemed plausible on the surface that crowds could be wise, so I had to provide the strongest defense I could of my thesis. If I didn't think Surowiecki had a plausible case I would not have mentioned his book.

Chapter 10: The Crowd and Modern Technology

I had an aversion to much of modern technology before I was able to explain why. I prefer not using a cell phone. I don't use Facebook. I use Twitter to keep up with what is going on in the world but I don't send tweets myself. I don't send emails unless I have a really good reason to, and I don't like receiving or answering emails. I don't even bother with text messaging. I'm uncomfortable with the idea of having information about me stored on the Internet for anybody to see at anytime, perhaps many years from now. I don't like the idea that anyone anywhere can take pictures or videos of me, without my permission, and that these can end up on the Internet where they can spread uncontrollably and remain in the public consciousness for as long as I live—actually, longer than that, perhaps. A lot of the things on the Internet are going to stay there for as long as the Internet exists.

What's wrong with these technologies? They seem pretty fun, even empowering, to a lot of people. Here is the most serious problem, as I see it. The new technologies are destroying the traditional division made between public life and private life. What is public is for the judgment of the crowd; what is private is not for the judgment of the crowd. In a world where everything was public, the crowd would know everything about you, and yet the crowd is intolerant. How could individual liberty survive in such a world? It's not as if we can't predict what such a world might be like: for most of the time the human species has existed there was no such thing as a private sphere. Among savages, everything is the concern of the crowd. The group tyrannizes completely over the individual, and there is no escape except by dying. The individual has no choice but to believe what the group believes, and to do what the group does, and the group believes and does a lot of things that are ridiculous or barbaric. Free individuals can only exist when allowed ample privacy.

Civilization depends completely on free individuals because the crowd is incapable of any but the crudest thoughts; what thoughts it has were given to them by free individuals.

I think the new technologies have already affected the quality of our leaders. The only people who will become leaders in the future are people who can stand to have every aspect of their lives scrutinized in real-time by the entire world. Everything they do will be second-guessed by all sorts of people who will be in a position to punish them. Every mistake they ever made will be known to everyone who can use a search engine. People with eccentric views—or even just views that are not completely in accord with public sentiment—will have a hard time obtaining leadership positions. Everyone else will be accountable to the spineless, unprincipled, ill-educated conformists at the head of our institutions.

I just recalled an incident from earlier this year which may be a harbinger of what is to come (Hill 2013, March 21). The incident involved the firing of two people over a private joke that was made public. During a technology conference, a couple of guys made a joke that (apparently) could be taken to be demeaning to women. A woman there overheard them and didn't like their joke, so she took a picture of them, attached it to a critical comment, and tweeted it. The organizer of the conference saw the tweet and talked to the two men about it. Their employer got word of it and fired one of them. People were outraged over that, too. So the woman got threats and her company got denial of service attacks and bad publicity. Then the woman was fired from her company as well. Thousands "liked" the firing. How is a person supposed to react to the fact that such a thing could happen to him, too— that one of his private comments might be made public and a vindictive eavesdropper could cost him his job? It seems doubtful that he can ban other people from having mobile devices that can take such pictures. The things are ubiquitous, and the government probably is not going to ban them. Should a person have to conduct himself at all times as if he were in public? That would be a nightmare. It means that a person could never relax, but would always be under the unremitting scrutiny of public opinion. As I've been arguing throughout this book, public opinion is not fair and it is not reasonable. Now one false move could get a person lynched electronically by a mob. And there are a large and expanding number of groups with chips on their shoulders. So there are all sorts of people you can't offend publicly without getting fired. This incident reveals that sometimes there are angry groups on both sides of a controversy capable of bringing pressure to bear. The companies talked about in the article were crushed between two groups—feminists and free speech advocates. They caved in to both of them, between the two companies. What are you supposed to do in a situation like that? I don't see why you can't have incidents pitting any other kind of special interest group against any other group. In the past, peace could be maintained among all these groups by allowing people to say what they wanted in private as long as they made no objectionable remarks in public. What happens when there is no longer any such thing as "private," and everything is public?

But it's not just the decline of privacy that's a serious problem. The new technologies also consume enormous amounts of time. Some people receive hundreds of emails every day, and that's on top of all of the other communications they have to keep up with. But time spent keeping up with electronic communications is time not spent doing something else. A person could use that time to acquire new skills, read books, build a business, spend time with others in person, paint a picture, go outside and do things, and so on. Or he could just take a break from it all and gather his thoughts. This would allow him to think more intelligently about what he is doing right now and about what he wants to do in the future.

There is something less tangible that the new technologies are undermining, and that's peace of mind. Everyone who uses them cannot ever get away from the demands of other people. If people send you messages they generally expect an answer, and the more promptly you answer the better. You may be able to lock yourself away in a room so that other people can't find you or get to you in person, but they will still be able to email you or send you text messages or post on your Facebook wall. If you carry a cell phone they will call you. Do you ignore them?

I suppose I should say that you can ignore the electronic communications addressed to you, but most people can't do it without doing injury to their own interests. You might lose friends or alienate family members. You might be required to keep up with electronic communications for your work, in which case you might get fired or lose business by ignoring them. At best you will be thought to be a weirdo. So it used to be a privilege to be able to use cell phones and email; now it's an obligation. The same sort of thing happened with cars. Horseless carriages were amazing at first, until most people were able to buy them and owning one became almost an obligation. It's still possible to live well without owning a car, but much of the infrastructure built since the invention of the car has been built with its use in mind. Most people assume that you own one and their expectations of you are shaped by this fact.

I have been living for years without becoming ensnared by the new technologies, but I live like a hermit almost and most people don't want to live like hermits. I know that if I hadn't lived like this, though, that this book would not have been written. I've been spending most of my time reading and writing and thinking about things while avoiding crowds as well as I possibly could. I don't expect to always live like this, but I will need to think carefully about how I can use the new technologies without becoming their slave.

To be fair, the new technologies have also provided ways for the individual to cultivate himself. I have taken full advantage of these, in fact, and my work would be considerably more difficult without them. One of the greatest privileges of living in our age is being able to read almost any book you care to read online or on your Kindle. I use Google Books, the Gutenberg Project, the Internet Archive, and the Amazon Kindle store all the time. I can convert almost any book into a file that my Kindle will read aloud to me with its text-to-speech feature. I can listen to books and do something else at the same time. I like to play video and computer games while listening to books, and I'm able to follow them as well as if I were reading them manually and not exhaust myself while doing it. I can read hundreds of pages a day like this, so it's incredibly efficient. It's daunting for me to read books that are over 2000 pages long when I have to read them the old-fashioned way (I did this once), but listening to the books with my Kindle makes it easy. Another advantage is the ability of the individual to self-publish and market his books with greater ease than perhaps ever before. I'm self-publishing through Amazon's Kindle store and through Smashwords.

Almost anything you care to know about you can learn about on the Internet, and the information you're looking for can be found at speeds and in volumes that would astonish any previous generation. But the problem, as I have said, is that it is harder than before to secure the time and the privacy for cultivating yourself. Perhaps things will work themselves out in the future. Anyone who tried to predict a couple decades ago what life would be like today almost certainly would have been wrong.

The new technologies pose another threat to self-cultivation, though. I have always felt pressured by the groups I've interacted with to behave as they have come to expect me to behave. I don't think I'm the only one who has felt this way, but for most of us it's just a subconscious feeling; it's hard to articulate it. The trouble with the expectations of other people is that you can't grow as a person if you always remain the same. But it also seems to unsettle your relationships with others when you change, since they might be compelled to change in response to you. So an overweight girl might not seem like a threat to her female friends, but what if she loses a lot of weight and men start paying more attention to her? And what if she starts dressing to please men after dressing like a slob for years? Then she would really start to become a threat to her female friends. This is awkward and difficult. I wonder if a lot of people resist self-improvement because of social pressures like this. I can think of some other cases where there would be some awkwardness. What if a guy known all his life for being a dumb jock decided to become an intellectual? What if someone considered to be shy by his or her friends decided one day to become more outgoing? What if someone considered to be outgoing suddenly wished to spend more time alone? What if someone from a conservative religious family decided to become a rock star? What if someone considered by everyone he knew to be a total loser started an Internet company and became a millionaire or billionaire? So it seems to me that people want to put everyone they know into neat mental categories and they don't like it when they try to leave those categories, or when people are not able to fit neatly into categories which they have long been familiar with.

What does all of that have to do with modern technology? It seems to me like the world is becoming more and more like one big crowd. The way people perceive you in one area of the world is likely to be the same everywhere else because information travels nearly instantaneously. In the past, you could move to another place if you wanted to change who you were. If you were shy and wanted to become more outgoing you could move someplace else and your new circle of acquaintances would only know of the new, outgoing you; you could leave your shy self behind forever. This seems to me to be more difficult to do now. It's harder to change how people perceive you. If you seem to be a dork by your online presence, then everyone with access to the Internet perceives you to be a dork. If you try to change there are still traces of the old you left in cyberspace. So the way things used to be, you could abandon your dorky self forever; the way things are now, everyone will always know that you were once a dork. And changing becomes harder to do in the first place, since moving isn't the quick fix it once was.

Chapter 11: Escaping Plato's Cave

And now I will describe in a figure the enlightenment or unenlightenment of our nature:—Imagine human beings living in an underground den which is open towards the light; they have been there from childhood, having their necks and legs chained, and can only see into the den. At a distance there is a fire, and between the fire and the prisoners a raised way, and a low wall is built along the way, like the screen over which marionette players show their puppets. Behind the wall appear moving figures, who hold in their hands various works of art, and among them images of men and animals, wood and stone, and some of the passers-by are talking and others silent. "A strange parable," he said, "and strange captives." They are ourselves, I replied; and they see only the shadows of the images which the fire throws on the wall of the den; to these they give names, and if we add an echo which returns from the wall, the voices of the passengers will seem to proceed from the shadows. Suppose now that you suddenly turn them round and make them look with pain and grief to themselves at the real images; will they believe them to be real? Will not their eyes be dazzled, and will they not try to get away from the light to something which they are able to behold without blinking? And suppose further, that they are dragged up a steep and rugged ascent into the presence of the sun himself, will not their sight be darkened with the excess of light? Some time will pass before they get the habit of perceiving at all; and at first they will be able to perceive only shadows and reflections in the water; then they will recognize the moon and the stars, and will at length behold the sun in his own proper place as he is. Last of all they will conclude:—This is he who gives us the year and the seasons, and is the author of all that we see. How will they rejoice in passing from darkness to light! How worthless to them will seem the honours and glories of the den! But now imagine further, that they descend into their old habitations;—in that underground dwelling they will not see as well as their fellows, and will not be able to compete with them in the measurement of the shadows on the wall; there will be many jokes about the man who went on a visit to the sun and lost his eyes, and if they find anybody trying to set free and enlighten one of their number, they will put him to death, if they can catch him. Now the cave or den is the world of sight, the fire is the sun, the way upwards is the way to knowledge, and in the world of knowledge the idea of good is last seen and with difficulty, but when seen is inferred to be the author of good and right—parent of the lord of light in this world, and of truth and understanding in the other. He who attains to the beatific vision is always going upwards; he is unwilling to descend into political assemblies and courts of law; for his eyes are apt to blink at the images or shadows of images which they behold in them—he cannot enter into the ideas of those who have never in their lives understood the relation of the shadow to the substance. But blindness is of two kinds, and may be caused either by passing out of darkness into light or out of light into darkness, and a man of sense will distinguish between them, and will not laugh equally at both of them, but the blindness which arises from fulness of light he will deem blessed, and pity the other; or if he laugh at the puzzled soul looking at the sun, he will have more reason to laugh than the inhabitants of the den at those who descend from above. There is a further lesson taught by this parable of ours. Some persons fancy that instruction is like giving eyes to the blind, but we say that the faculty of sight was always there, and that the soul only requires to be turned round towards the light. And this is conversion; other virtues are almost like bodily habits, and may be acquired in the same manner, but intelligence has a diviner life, and is indestructible, turning either to good or evil according to the direction given. Did you never observe how the mind of a clever rogue peers out of his eyes, and the more clearly he sees, the more evil he does? Now if you take such an one, and cut away from him those leaden weights of pleasure and desire which bind his soul to earth, his intelligence will be turned round, and he will behold the truth as clearly as he now discerns his meaner ends. And have we not decided that our rulers must neither be so uneducated as to have no fixed rule of life, nor so over-educated as to be unwilling to leave their paradise for the business of the world? We must choose out therefore the natures who are most likely to ascend to the light and knowledge of the good; but we must not allow them to remain in the region of light; they must be forced down again among the captives in the den to partake of their labours and honours. 'Will they not think this a hardship?' You should remember that our purpose in framing the State was not that our citizens should do what they like, but that they should serve the State for the common good of all. May we not fairly say to our philosopher,—Friend, we do you no wrong; for in other States philosophy grows wild, and a wild plant owes nothing to the gardener, but you have been trained by us to be the rulers and kings of our hive, and therefore we must insist on your descending into the den. You must, each of you, take your turn, and become able to use your eyes in the dark, and with a little practice you will see far better than those who quarrel about the shadows, whose knowledge is a dream only, whilst yours is a waking reality. It may be that the saint or philosopher who is best fitted, may also be the least inclined to rule, but necessity is laid upon him, and he must no longer live in the heaven of ideas. And this will be the salvation of the State. For those who rule must not be those who are desirous to rule; and, if you can offer to our citizens a better life than that of rulers generally is, there will be a chance that the rich, not only in this world's goods, but in virtue and wisdom, may bear rule. And the only life which is better than the life of political ambition is that of philosophy, which is also the best preparation for the government of a State.

– Plato, *the Republic*, Book VII

An important issue to me, and I assume for many of my readers, is how a person can survive and thrive as a freely-thinking individual in an age dominated by crowds. Plato was perhaps the first crowd psychologist. His mentor and friend Socrates was put on trial for allegedly corrupting the youth and for not believing in the gods of the state, for which crimes he was found guilty and was sentenced to death. But Socrates appears to have been a wise and virtuous man, at least by the accounts of his friends (the playwright Aristophanes had a different opinion, though). Anyway, I suppose I should start with the meaning of Plato's Allegory of the Cave, and what bearing it has on the rest of his philosophy, and what it means for us.

I never really understood the dispute over whether Plato's forms were "really real" or not. It seems petty to me, and I think it's missing the most important points that Plato was trying to convey. William James (1890) writes in *the Principles of Psychology* that most of what we see is not raw sensation; most of what we see is actually interpretations made by the mind based on past experience. We do receive raw sensations as newborn infants, but never again after that. What happens is that our minds form mental categories for our sensations using the psychological laws of association—the laws of similarity, contrast, and contiguity. James says that once our minds have established certain mental categories it is hard for most people to change them. He talks about how certain Polynesian natives, upon seeing horses for the first time, called them pigs, because that was the category into which the horse fit best from the ones they had. He says that his child of two played for a week with the first orange given to him, calling it a "ball." The first whole eggs the child saw he called "potatoes." And James gives more examples besides these of what he is talking about. He says that it is difficult for most of us to come up with new categories as we experience new things, and the result is that we grow more and more enslaved to the stock conceptions with which we have become familiar. Objects which violate our established habits are not taken account of at all, or if we are forced by argument to admit their existence, twenty-four hours later the admission is as if it were never made and every trace of the unassimilable truth vanishes from our thought. Genius, says James, is little more than the faculty of perceiving in an unhabitual way. I think that Plato's theory of forms is really about forming new mental categories that better match the world that actually exists. The trouble is that nearly everyone else is still stuck with their stock conceptions even if you come up with ones that better describe the world. If you acquired new mental categories by philosophical inquiry and then tried to convey your ideas to other people you would be badly misunderstood. It would be like trying to explain to James's Polynesians that horses are not pigs but a completely different thing. Given the intolerance of crowds to new ways of thinking, naturally you would be resisted if you tried to enlighten people, even if you had the very best of intentions. You might even be accused of corrupting the youth and disbelieving in the gods of the state. At best they would think you were stupid because you were bad at classifying objects the way they did and awkward because you were bad at acting according to their categories, and they would not want you to influence others to be like you. I think this is what Plato is talking about in the Allegory of the Cave.

It hasn't escaped my notice that these categories are a lot like Walter Lippmann's stereotypes. I suspect that Lippmann developed his theory of them from what he learned from James, who was his teacher. So this is how stereotypes are formed. I will talk more about how they are created in the next chapter.

All of this is consistent with Thomas Kuhn's (1962/1996) theory of science advancing by successive paradigm shifts, which, as he says, are shifts not only in cognition but in perception as well. I've read his book, *the Structure of Scientific Revolutions*, and I'm in complete agreement with him. Kuhn thinks that scientists literally see the world in a different way after they have accepted a new scientific paradigm. What they see is informed largely by what they expect to see, and what they expect to see is determined by intellectual frameworks derived from past experience. By "paradigm," Kuhn is referring to a scientific theory, but he uses the term in a similar sense to the one people mean when they talk about world views. A paradigm is a systematic explanation of a large number of particular facts, and there can be more than one paradigm attempting to explain the same set of facts. Some paradigms account for the facts better than others do. But scientists do not immediately abandon a paradigm if they discover new facts which the theory cannot account for. There may be some way to account for them that they haven't considered yet. Possibly they made a mistake. If not, maybe if they wait it out someone will come up with a solution for the anomaly. But if the old paradigm is met with more and more new facts which it is unable to account for, then science will enter a period of crisis. Kuhn says that a scientist cannot simply abandon a problematic theory without offering another one to replace it, since that would mean abandoning science altogether. In any event, during a period of crisis, the old paradigm is open to attack, and new paradigms may form which account for the new facts better than the old theory. When this happens, a period of "revolutionary science" has begun. Once a new paradigm has gained wide acceptance by the scientific community, scientists return to what Kuhn calls "normal science"—that is, they return to refining the existing paradigm, rather than working to replace it with another one. There may be sciences which do not yet have any paradigm, but once they acquire one they enter a period of normal science. Kuhn thinks that it is after a science obtains a paradigm and enters normal science that it becomes a specialized profession. Before a paradigm is formed, writings on the field are addressed to a general educated audience, but after it is formed, scientists address themselves primarily to their own colleagues.

Kuhn talks about a figure which has since become famous as an example of the different ways in which we can perceive the same object: the figure can be perceived, alternatively, as a rabbit or as a duck—or it can be perceived as just its constituent lines. Kuhn thinks that a similar mental process is occurring in the minds of scientists when they see the world through one paradigm or another. I should mention that Kuhn is extrapolating from the work of the gestalt psychologists here. For whatever reason, not many people pay attention to their work today, but I think that it may still be important. The most important idea of the gestalt theorists is that the human mind sees and thinks in terms of their wholes rather than their constituent parts. So they would say that the duck-rabbit figure is a good example of this: we see either the rabbit or the duck first, not the lines. But we can train our minds to perceive the constituent lines. This appears to me to be consistent with James's account of perception.

An important point that Kuhn makes is that there is no criteria for what is really "scientific" apart from what the scientific community believes at any given time. And this does appear to be the case in fact, whether it should be or not. But what this suggests to me is that a crowd ultimately decides what is and is not "scientific." Scientists are subject to the same crowd influences as everyone else, though conscientious ones do their best to cope with their biases and think as rigorously as possible. I should point out here that thinking scientifically is not at all normal; it has been considered perverse by the standards of most people for most of human history. Religious and magical thinking come more naturally to our species.

When I was reading Lee Smolin's (2006) book, *the Trouble with Physics*, I was thinking that string theorists behaved *exactly* like a herd. Smolin says that string theorists are prone, far more than the other scientists he's met, to allow a handful of senior researchers to determine what they should believe and what they should work on. His complaint is not that the senior researchers are not good thinkers, but that so many of the other ones exhibit a herd mentality. This mentality extends to abusing critics and dissenters and spreading their theory like a messianic religion. I think I should quote him:

> The narrowness of the research agenda seems to be a result of the string community's huge regard for the views of a few individuals. String theorists are the only scientists I've ever met who typically want to know what the senior people in the field, such as Edward Witten, think before expressing their own views. Of course Witten thinks clearly and deeply, but the point is that it is not good for any field if any one person's views are taken too authoritatively. There is no scientist, not

even Newton or Einstein, who was not wrong on a substantial number of issues they had strong views about. Many times, in discussion after a conference talk or in conversation, if a controversial issue comes up, someone invariably asks, "Well, what does Ed think?" This used to drive me to distraction, and occasionally I would let it show: "Look, when I want to know what Ed thinks, I ask him. I'm asking you what *you* think because I'm interested in your opinion."

Noncommutative geometry is an example of a field that was ignored by string theorists until it was embraced by Witten. Alain Connes, its inventor, tells the following story:

> I went to Chicago in 1996 and gave a talk in the Physics Department. A well-known physicist was there, and he left the room before the talk was over. I didn't meet this physicist again until two years later, when I gave the same talk in the Dirac Forum in Rutherford Laboratory, near Oxford. The same physicist was attending, this time looking very open and convinced. When he gave his talk later, he mentioned my talk quite positively. This was amazing to me, because it was the same talk, and I had not forgotten his previous reaction. So on the way back to Oxford, I was sitting next to him in the bus, and I asked him, "How can it be that you attended the same talk in Chicago and you left before the end, and now you really liked it?" The guy was not a beginner—he was in his forties. His answer was "Witten was seen reading your book in the library in Princeton!"

It should be said that this attitude is fading, probably in response to the current uproar surrounding the landscape. Until last year, I had hardly ever encountered an expression of doubt from a string theorist. Now I sometimes hear from young people that there is a "crisis" in string theory. "We have lost our leaders," some of them will say. "Before this, it was always clear what the hot direction was, what people should be working on. Now there's no real guidance," or (to each other, nervously) "Is it true that Witten is no longer doing string theory?"

Another facet of string theory that many find disturbing is what can only be described as the messianic tendency of some of its practitioners, especially some younger ones. For them, string theory has become a religion. Those of us who publish papers questioning results or claims of string theorists regularly receive e-mails whose mildest form of abuse is "Are you kidding?" or "Is this a joke?" Discussions of string theory's "opponents" abound on Web sites and chat boards, where, even given the unbridled nature of such venues, the intelligence and competence of non-string theorists is questioned in remarkably unpleasant terms. It's hard not to conclude that at least some string theorists have begun to see themselves as crusaders rather than scientists. (p. 274-276)

Smolin thinks that the groupthink in string theory is worse than in other fields, and perhaps it is, but I think that crowd behavior is the norm in science just as it is the norm everywhere else. That is the conclusion I have drawn from my reading and from my experiences in college.

How Creativity Works

Sometimes great ideas can be found in the most unusual places. The great military theorist John Boyd (1987) wrote a remarkable paper about creativity—that is, about destroying old mental categories and building new ones from their constituent parts, and from sense experience—called "Destruction and Creation." Boyd talks in this about the same things that Plato, James, Lippmann, and Kuhn do. This is only part of Boyd's theory, though, which is about how to always win in every competitive situation, which includes but is not limited to war. Simply put, a winner is someone who can make good observations, adapt his thinking as his environment changes, and decide and act upon those changing ideas as quickly as possible. A person who shuts himself off from experience and is not able to adapt his thinking, or who is not able to decide and act quickly enough, is going to lose to someone who does a better job of these things. The whole theory is summarized in his OODA (observe, orient, decide, and act) Loop, which he describes in his briefings.

Boyd says in his "Destruction and Creation" paper that to comprehend and cope with our environment we develop mental patterns. As the universe changes our concepts must change so as to match the universe, otherwise we will not be able to survive on our own terms.

Boyd thinks that individuals have a sort of contractual relationship with the groups they belong to, and that the goal of individuals is to improve their capacity for independent action. I don't know if I agree with this if he means people generally, though it does seem to me to be true for an exceptional minority of people. The sort of people who think like this are the exceptional people Lippmann talks about who have broad interests and views, and who move in and out of groups and are not exclusive members of any of them.

Boyd talks about how concepts are created. He says that there are two ways to do it. One way is to start with a comprehensive whole and break it down into its particulars. Another way is to start with the particulars and build a comprehensive whole out of them. Deduction is the mental process by which we proceed from the general to the specific; induction is the mental process by which we proceed from the specific to the general. Boyd says that deduction is akin to analysis and induction is akin to synthesis. He also thinks that the differential calculus is related to the concepts of general-to-specific, deduction, and analysis, while the integral calculus is related to the concepts of specific-to-general, induction, and synthesis. I wouldn't worry about the math part; it isn't necessary for understanding the theory.

Boyd asks the reader to imagine a domain (a comprehensive whole) and its constituent elements or parts. He asks us to imagine another one of these, and another one. He says that we can imagine any number of domains and corresponding parts in this fashion. He doesn't give specific examples but I will for the sake of clarity. A domain could be something like pets, and its corresponding parts would be dogs, cats, birds, fish, hamsters, and so on. Another domain could be school subjects, and its corresponding parts would be history, mathematics, biology, literature, and so on. A third domain could be jobs, and its parts could be doctors, lawyers, factory workers, plumbers, soldiers, waiters, and so on. Another domain could be the human body, and the parts could be the arms, legs, internal organs, muscles, and so on. And you can come up with many more ideas in your experience that can be thought about in this way. Boyd asks the reader to pretend that the domains do not exist but only their constituent elements. So in our imagination we now have a bunch of particulars swimming in a sea of anarchy. We have uncertainty and disorder in place of meaning and order. Boyd calls this kind of unstructuring a destructive deduction.

Boyd says that we can construct new wholes from this great mass of parts. In order to do this we need to find some common qualities, attributes, or operations among some or many of the constituents swimming in the sea of anarchy. Boyd doesn't say so, but I very strongly suspect that the new wholes are formed by the laws of association, which I will talk about in detail later on. This putting together of parts to form wholes is induction or synthesis. It's possible to reconstruct the old wholes by putting together the old parts in the old ways, but you will not end up with a new idea. New ideas can only be formed when you create new combinations of ideas. Boyd says that creativity has to do with induction or synthesis or integration, and these inductions he calls creative inductions. He emphasizes that the unstructuring of old wholes is a necessary first step for the formation of new ideas. Without that unstructuring the bits and pieces are still tied together as meaning within unchallenged domains or concepts.

Boyd says that, recalling that we use these mental patterns to represent reality, it follows that the unstructuring and restructuring just shown reveals a way of changing our perceptions of reality. If we want our ideas to help us navigate reality it would be best if they were internally consistent and if they accurately reflected reality as it is—and if they changed to reflect changes in reality. And reality does change. Boyd says that the internal consistency of the ideas can be verified if we can trace our way back to the original constituents that were used in the creative induction. If we cannot reverse directions, the ideas and interactions do not go together in this way without contradiction. So they are not internally consistent. If our ideas are not internally consistent that doesn't necessarily mean that the entire structure should be thrown away. Instead, we should attempt to distinguish the ideas that seem to hold together in a coherent pattern of activity from those which don't. During this task we check for reversibility and we also check to see how which ideas match up with our observations of reality.

We take the ideas that pass this test together with any new ideas we obtained from destructive deductions and we again attempt to find some common qualities, attributes, or operations to re-create the concept, or to create a new concept. We check again for reversibility and match up with reality. We repeat this cycle of destruction and creation over and over again until we demonstrate internal consistency and match-up with reality.

Boyd says that when this orderly state is reached the concept becomes a coherent pattern of ideas and interactions that can be used to describe some aspect of observed reality. Alternative ideas and interactions which could expand, complete, or modify the concept have little or no appeal now. Effort is turned instead toward fine-tuning the ideas and interactions in order to improve generality and produce a more precise match between the concepts and reality. The concept and its internal workings are tested and compared over and over again in many different and subtle ways. At some point, ambiguities, uncertainties, anomalies, or apparent inconsistencies may emerge to stifle a more general and precise match-up of concept with observed reality. I should note that this sounds very much like what Thomas Kuhn was talking about with his idea of science alternating between periods of revolutionary science and normal science. In fact, Kuhn's book is in Boyd's bibliography.

In some of his sections Boyd talks about some ideas from logic, mathematics, and physics and he uses them to support his theory. Among these are Gödel's Incompleteness Theorem, the Heisenberg Uncertainty Principle, the concept of entropy, and the Second Law of Thermodynamics. You don't have to know about these things in order to grasp Boyd's theory and I won't talk about them here; Boyd's "Creation and Destruction" can be found with a simple online search if the reader is still curious about it. My judgment is that it's more likely to confuse than enlighten. The upshot of all of it is that if a person does not remain open to experience from the outside world, or if he doesn't bother to organize, and continuously reorganize, the elements of experience that are continually accruing in his mind, then his thoughts will become more and more disordered and he will become unable to make accurate predictions about reality, and he will be unable to act appropriately in it. If he is unable to act appropriately in the world then he will not be able to survive on his own terms, and perhaps he won't survive at all. That may sound overly dramatic, but remember that Boyd's talking about surviving on a battlefield.

But does it not follow from what I have said that if you change your mental categories like this that you will find yourself out of synch and perhaps out of favor with the crowd? In fact, Boyd had a difficult relationship with the military bureaucracy. Boyd's achievements were numerous, and many were incredible, and yet he still did not make general (his highest rank was colonel) and he was loathed by most of his superiors. Boyd was a fighter pilot, and he was known as "Forty Second Boyd" for his ability to defeat any opposing pilot in air combat maneuvering while starting from a disadvantageous position. He wrote an influential manual on air combat tactics. He developed the theory behind the highly successful F-15 and F-16 planes and he led the teams that designed them; without Boyd the Air Force might still have been using planes that were inferior to what the Soviets had at the time. Boyd was one of the leaders of the military reform movement after the Vietnam War. He also taught the Marines maneuver warfare, which made them, man for man, the most formidable of the military services. He also developed the strategy that won the first Gulf War. He and his acolytes fought corruption and inefficiency within the pentagon bureaucracy and they paid for it with their careers. So Boyd might have been the military's greatest hero of the post-World War II era, but few outside the military know his name. I argue that this was because of his intellectual deviance, the very thing that enabled his great accomplishments.

Creativity and Mental Illness

I should mention that mental illness ran in the Boyd family. According to Boyd's biographer, Robert Coram (2002), Boyd's older brother Bill displayed symptoms of schizophrenia and died at age 27 in a mental hospital. According to Bill's medical records, Bill's maternal grandmother and an uncle both had mental problems and he had a sister who was "nervous." The sister was probably Marion:

> The second incident was no less powerful. Even though by 1944 the Army was drafting men in their late 30s, Bill, John's older brother, was twenty-seven and still at home. Bill had tried jobs as an elevator operator, laborer, and security guard. He had quit or been fired from every job. He became depressed that he was not one of the hundreds of other young men from Erie who went away to the war. The family told everyone he could not serve because he had a heart murmur. The truth was something quite different.

> The illness that had been festering for years exploded on Saturday, April 1, 1944, when Bill, with no provocation, struck his mother. The next evening he became quite agitated

and jumped through a window, cutting his arm and hand so badly that he was taken to the hospital for stitches. Two people were required to hold him in bed and administer sedatives.

His medical records show that on Monday he said he had radar in his teeth. He told hospital workers, "I want to go to see the Pope. I'd turn Catholic if he could help me. I want to go by way of India." Later that day he complained of a terrible headache and said, "I want to see a doctor. I'm begging for mercy. You have me cornered." Various sedatives were administered and then he was admitted to Warren State Hospital, a mental institution east of Erie. He died there May 3 and was buried in a single plot in the Erie Cemetery. His death certificate says he died after a one-day bout with terminal bronchopneumonia brought on by acute catatonic excitement, and that the excitement was due to dementia praecox of more than four years' duration. In current parlance, Bill was schizophrenic.

Bill's medical records indicate that his maternal grandmother and an uncle both had mental problems and that there was a sister who was "nervous." Although she is not named, this sister was probably Marion.

After that, people from the mental institution asked Boyd's mother if anyone else in the family needed to be taken there because of mental illness. At the time, mental illness was heavily stigmatized, and she told her children not to tell anyone what really happened to Bill. If anyone asked, they were to say he died from pneumonia.

According to the psychologist Kay Jamison (1993) in her book, *Touched with Fire*, mental illness runs in the families of a lot of creative people. Jamison (1999) says in another book, *Night Falls Fast*, that most people who commit suicide are diagnosable with mental illnesses. Evidence like this makes me think that Wilfred

Trotter is right about what he says about mental illness, that people who prefer sense experience to herd suggestion experience great psychological distress, but they can also have better understandings of their environments and may be able to act more effectively within them. Maybe some people are not able to cope with the mental anguish or they are not able to order the sense experience into accurate models of the world; it just remains as irritants in the mind and it doesn't become anything more than that, and they just go mad. And maybe others are not as strongly affected by separation from the herd or else they are better able to process sense experience into models of reality. If it's really true that the ideas and habits which most people act in the world with are received from the surrounding herd, then if you somehow fall out of synch with them, it seems that you *must* use your intellect to order the elements of sense experience into mental models of the world, and you probably also have to develop your habits on your own initiative; otherwise you'll flounder about with no idea of what you're doing. Maybe to others you'll seem mad. Maybe that's what madness is.

So I'm wondering if what we think are genes for mental illnesses are really genes for mental illnesses, or if they are actually genes for creativity or unusual receptivity to sense experience, and the side effect of that is mental illness. Any ability that made a person's mental world different from those around him would tend to separate him from the herd, causing mental anguish. I don't know if anyone has proposed this theory, but it seems plausible to me. Another theory which is consistent with the facts and is more commonly believed is that the genes really are genes for mental illness but they have the side effect of improving creativity. So the arrow of causation points in the other direction. This seems to be the explanation that Jamison and most other experts accept. I like the other explanation because it fits better with the rest of my theory, but again, either explanation fits the facts.

In *Touched with Fire*, Jamison mainly talks about people who excelled in the arts. In the appendix of *Touched with Fire* she lists a number of writers, artists, and composers who probably lived with depression or manic-depression. Among these were Lord Byron, Samuel Taylor Coleridge, T.S. Eliot, Emily Dickinson, Victor Hugo, William Blake, Edgar Allen Poe, John Keats, Percy Bysshe Shelley, Lord Tennyson, Walt Whitman, Sylvia Plath, Ezra Pound, Charles Dickens, Joseph Conrad, Ralph Waldo Emerson, Mark Twain, Virginia Woolf, F. Scott Fitzgerald, William Faulkner, Ernest Hemingway, Hermann Hesse, Herman Melville, Leo Tolstoy, William James, Henry James, Vincent van Gogh, Edvard Munch, Irving Berlin, Noel Coward, and Robert Schumann.

This isn't all of the ones she lists, or even all the ones which most people will recognize, but it's a good sampling of famous names. She has icons showing who spent time in a mental institution, who attempted suicide, and who committed suicide. Those little icons are all over the place. I would guess that at least half of the people she lists had at least one icon next to their names, though there were not quite so many for the ones I picked. But among the people I listed, Eliot, Plath, Pound, Woolf, Fitzgerald, Faulkner, Hemingway, Hesse, van Gogh, Munch, Berlin, and Schumann all spent time in mental institutions, while Poe, Shelley, Conrad, Hesse, and Schumann attempted suicide, and Plath, Woolf, Hemingway, and van Gogh succeeded.

It's true that diagnoses given after a person has died are not infallible (the same can be said of the living), but enough is known about the lives of these famous creatives that it's possible to make some fairly good judgments about them. A writer who said in his memoirs that he had frequently contemplated suicide probably suffered from depression. A poet who spent years in a mental institution probably suffered from some kind of mental illness. If those who knew her said she was alternatively exuberant and depressed then she probably had bipolar (manic-depressive) disorder.

What is to Be Done

So it seems to me that if you are determined to think freely but rigorously that you will, if you can combine it with the right habits of observation, decision-making, and acting, be able to do amazing things. But it will probably pay to be aware of the behavior of crowds, and not to challenge them too overtly, but also not to give in to herd suggestion when it conflicts with experience. This is tough. But there are things that a person can do to make it easier. If you can surround yourself with other people who want to be like this, that will help tremendously. Life is difficult facing an intolerant crowd as an isolated individual. It's been done, though. Nietzsche, Kierkegaard, and Schopenhauer did it. But not everyone wants to live like a hermit. Nietzsche went mad. Boyd took a different approach; he surrounded himself with acolytes. Socrates had his own circle of friends. Jesus had his disciples. Steve Jobs had Apple; though it hurt him to be parted with it for a time, he learned a lot from his time apart from the company and was a better person when he returned to it.

Some people may say that it is cowardly not to confront the crowd head-on, but whether it's cowardly or not, it's imprudent. An individual has practically no chance of defeating a crowd in an open contest. But individuals are more intelligent than crowds and can outwit them. The only way for an individual to defeat a crowd or keep himself from being defeated or absorbed by it is to think and act more intelligently than a crowd can.

Plato didn't say that the freely-thinking individual should get even with the crowd for curbing his freedom. Plato also believed, correctly, that if you gave intellectual training to a rogue that he would only do more harm. In order for a person to be eligible to become a philosopher king he also had to master his bodily appetites; otherwise he would use his learning in their service. But if a person received both intellectual and character training he would not be inclined to struggle with the others of his community for control of the state. He probably would not want to rule. Plato says that he must be compelled to do so, because this is the only way for the state to be saved.

As for the education of the masses, they were to be fed an intellectual diet of Noble Lies. Their influences were to be strictly controlled to make them virtuous citizens. Plato was keenly aware of how, if the formation of people's minds and characters were left to chance, they would probably turn out badly. In Plato's day, people justified bad behavior by pointing out the example of badly-behaved gods. And it seems likely that bad examples did influence them to behave badly, if the crowd psychologists are correct. That meant that the poets had to be banished from the state. If Plato were alive today he'd demand control over what media he could control and he would, if he could, shut down the Internet. That's the only way to shield people from bad influences. The state would be totalitarian like North Korea. So the price of freedom of expression is that some of the things people say and do will influence others to behave badly.

Is a Platonic dictatorship a good idea? My understanding of things is that regimes are rarely created according to the whims of individuals, or even the whims of groups; what form a state ultimately takes is determined by factors that are hard for people to control, like technology, geography, climate, culture, and historical experience. When people try to create states based on abstract theories, as in the French and Russian Revolutions, things don't turn out as expected. So even if Platonic regimes were desirable in the abstract there is no guarantee that they could be practically implemented or that they would be as pleasant as promised.

People who criticize Plato for advocating totalitarianism usually misunderstand what the majority of people really want. Most people crave certainty over truth. The two are not the same thing. Being good at finding truth means being willing to revise your opinions as new evidence comes in, or as you mull over what you've already found out. It means renouncing absolute certainty. And while an individual or even an aristocracy can change opinions quickly, a great mass of people can never do that. It seems clear to me, from the evidence I've presented, that the majority of people much prefer their pleasing illusions to dispassionate, sometimes discomforting truth. So far, no skeptic has ever succeeded in getting the crowd to think rationally. The Socrateses of the world end up drinking hemlock. The Menckens of the world mock the crowd to no avail. The Dawkinses scold them in vain. The Platos may eulogize the victims of the crowd and make them heroes after-the-fact, but that does little good in a person's own lifetime. Also, as Lippmann argues, *everybody* thinks in terms of fictions, though some may be more realistic than others. There is just no other way to grasp a complex reality than to make use of them. Also, it is a fact that people tend to emulate their social superiors, for better or worse. But that implies that if people are to behave well then the leaders of a society must behave well. Their liberty, at least in public, must be constrained. Not everyone is eager to be constrained in this way. To remain free in their private lives the leaders can make use of fictional personas in public, but in that case they are not being entirely candid. Also, as I've argued in these pages, there is no avoiding hierarchy in a civilized society.

Given this state of affairs, which Plato understood very well, why not organize a regime hierarchically with Noble Lies and philosopher kings? If someone has to be in charge, why not have the wisest and most noble lead? There are others who could rule. The rich could rule, and so could the warriors, and so could the representatives of the people. But Plato rejects each of these alternatives as being the best possible regime. That's not to say that each of these groups does not have its place in an ideal society, but they should not rule. In Plato's ideal regime, the wise and virtuous rule, the warriors enforce the decrees of the rulers and defend against outside enemies, and the great mass of people are engaged in economic activity in order to provide for the needs of the society. Since how people behave is determined in large part by their beliefs and habits, and these are determined by environmental influences, it seems sensible to Plato to have them carefully molded from an early age, when people are most malleable.

Religions and myths have developed in, as far as I know, every society that has ever existed. This is when it is perfectly possible for people to defer judgment when they don't know something rather than making wild guesses. And religions and myths are not even the best guesses that could have been made at the time they were invented. They seem to be designed to appeal to people's hopes, and to allay their fears and help them cope with disappointments, and to allow for easier cooperation among the members of a group. Dispassionate truth is not valued for its own sake with the exception of doctrines meant for an elite minority. If religions and myths are noble lies, or at least noble self-deceptions, then the proof already exists, and in abundance, that a society can function well when most of the people within it believe them. So Plato's noble lies are not as pernicious as they might appear at first. But perhaps such myths are more effective when they are felt to be inspired rather than deliberately contrived.

In any event, if the masses are to believe noble lies, how do you ensure that the rulers don't believe them as well? That would impair their judgment. Or if they disbelieve them, how do you keep their opinions from circulating among the masses? The solution seems to be to have a class system like the one Plato proposes. But class circulation is unusually rapid in modern capitalist societies. Most of the rich are new rich, and it's uncommon for a family to remain in the elite for more than two or three generations before sinking back into the mass. So it's difficult to prevent ideas and habits from passing from one class to another. Also, the elites have little leisure to cultivate themselves, and they can't act independently of market pressures.

It seems to me like it would be easier to maintain an enlightened elite when the propertied classes are landed aristocrats. Landed aristocrats have the leisure and independence to cultivate themselves, while the masses lack these advantages; this is what maintains the intellectual barrier between the two classes. That's the way Western Europe was before the Industrial Revolution. People forget in our day that the Enlightenment was patronized by such elites—by aristocrats and monarchs, not the people or even the middle classes. The masses remained ignorant and superstitious, and perhaps that was for the best. But I don't think the old regime can ever come back; the conditions required for such a regime no longer exist.

It's also possible to maintain an enlightened elite if you have a slave society. The slaves work so that the masters have the leisure to cultivate themselves. That's the way it was in the Greco-Roman world. A slave master does not have to worry too much about market pressures. If he wants to spend most of his time reading and writing books and debating philosophical issues he can. He can mold his character and the character of his children according to some high ideal. Nevertheless, even if slavery did not repel most of us it is not competitive with modern capitalist economies. The economic system of the Northern United States was much more efficient than the economic system of the Southern United States, which was one of the major reasons why the North won.

Perhaps some day machines will be able to perform all economic functions for a society; human labor will become as obsolete as horse labor became after the invention of the automobile. But this would lead to a collapse of the market economy, or at least it seems like it would. If the machines are the ones doing all the work how will consumers acquire the money to consume with? Money is a medium for the exchange of goods and services, and yet in such an economy only the people who owned the machines and perhaps a small number of highly skilled scientists and engineers would have any goods to exchange. These people could exchange exclusively with themselves and leave everyone else out of the economic system completely. Economic power would be concentrated in a few hands. The robot-masters would become the new elite, and they wouldn't be accountable to anyone outside of their narrow circle. But they would either have to make concessions to the mass—provide bread and circuses in other words—or they would have to best them in combat. Historically, people have not responded well when machines put them out of work.

Anyway, I was thinking that perhaps such a class could become philosopher kings. As long as they controlled all the machines and didn't break ranks, they would be free from market pressures. They wouldn't have to work, but could spend their time and efforts cultivating themselves, just like landed aristocrats or slave masters. If they could create sophisticated robot armies they would have so much leverage against the mass that they could reorder their society however they chose to. If technology were sophisticated enough, it might even be possible to make constants like geography, climate, and culture into variables. Things that are currently impracticable could become practicable. This is a long-shot I suppose, but it's not impossible.

Chapter 12: The Origins of Ideas and Behavior

I thought it would be a good idea to include a chapter in my book on where ideas and behavior come from. I think a book on crowd psychology could be written without addressing this, and in fact most of the books I talk about were; Tarde is the major exception with his theory of the imitation of invention. I touched on the subject a bit in my chapter on the mental mechanisms of the crowd, and in the last chapter, but did not go into it in depth. The reason why this subject is so important is because the only ideas and behaviors crowds have which are not strictly instinctive are those formed by the processes discussed in the present chapter. The categories I talked about in the last chapter are formed by them. Remember, it is through those categories that we perceive and understand and act upon the world.

I think that the associationist psychology is basically right. There are many different formulations of it, but the best one that I've come across is the one William James (1890) gives in *the Principles of Psychology*. The psychological laws of association, which are responsible for all of the ideas we have, are derived from the Law of Habit. All behaviors are products of the Law of Habit, and in their case sensory processes are being associated with motor processes instead of there being an association of two ideas. According to James, there is only one elementary law of association and that's the law of association by contiguity; association by similarity and contrast are derivative of it.

I want to reemphasize here my agreement with Gabriel Tarde's basic idea—that ideas and behaviors first emerge in individuals and are then spread by the laws of imitation (the best known law of imitation is that ideas spread from social superiors to social inferiors). I don't know if his version of associationist psychology is correct—it sounds plausible to me—but in any event William James's version is canon for me wherever there is disagreement between him and another thinker. James's system is just too good for me to part with without some very good reasons. I accept also that ideas and behaviors are spread through the medium of the subconscious mind, and Boris Sidis explains how that works. So I'm creating in my book an interlocking system of ideas based on the theories of these thinkers.

The Law of Habit

I should explain James's theory in greater detail. The Law of Habit is not just a psychological law but a physical one. It's also the basis for most of James's system of psychology. I don't know if all phenomena of the mind can be derived from it, but James comes close to doing it. James was familiar with, as far as I can tell, almost every important book written about the subject of psychology up until his day. He took the very best of what he learned and worked it into as coherent a system as he could; what seemed to him to be dubious he discarded or was agnostic about.

James says that even dead matter exhibits habits; that's what he means when he says that the Law of Habit is a physical law. He quotes one writer as saying that the musical instruments of great masters really are superior instruments because of the impressions left upon them by the masters; the instruments themselves are in the habit of playing exceptionally well. James also says that people may become sick or injured because they have gotten in the habit of becoming sick or injured. This sounds strange, but it seems plausible from the examples he gives. Another example that I thought of is how well-worn baseball gloves seem to be easier to catch with than new gloves. The leather of the new gloves is stiff, and the ball seems to fall out more easily. When I was a kid I used some well-worn gloves that other people had and the ball seemed to stay caught a bit better than with my newer glove. It actually would not be that hard to run an experiment to see if well-worn gloves catch balls better than new gloves, or if the gloves used by great baseball players are better than the gloves used by everyone else. Just have the same person catch baseballs under the same conditions except that they are using different gloves, and make sure the sample size is large so that the differences can't be explained as being due to chance.

James discusses how the Law of Habit applies to the nervous system, how new habits are formed within it, in other words, and how this results in observable changes in behavior. He says that if we assume that changes in habit must be the result of the pressures of outward forces upon plastic materials, then the pressures which act upon the nervous system cannot be mechanical pressures or thermal changes to any of the forces to which all the other organs of the body are exposed. This is because the brain and spinal cord are shut up in bony boxes so that those influences cannot easily disturb them; they are also floated in fluid so that only the severest shocks can give them a concussion. The only way to influence the nervous system is through the blood or through the sensory nerve-roots. The hemispheric cortex is particularly susceptible to the infinitely attenuated currents flowing in from the latter channels. Once the currents get in, they have to get out, and the only things they can do to get out of the hemispheric cortex are to deepen old paths or create new ones. James says that "the whole plasticity of the brain sums itself up in two words when we call it an organ in which currents pouring in from the sense-organs make with extreme facility paths which do not easily disappear." A simple habit, like biting one's nails, is nothing but a reflex discharge of the sort just described; its anatomical substratum must be a path in the system. Complex habits are nothing but concatenated discharges in the nerve-centres, "due to the presence there of systems of reflex paths, so organized as to wake each other up successively—the impression produced by one muscular contraction serving as a stimulus to provoke the next, until a final impression inhibits the process and closes the chain."

So if I am understanding James correctly, habits start with objects in the environment acting upon a sense organ; at this point the sense organ sends a current through the nervous system to the brain, and then the current leaves the brain and travels through the nervous system to the muscles or to some gland. I assume that at the end of this is where the action occurs. So the sense organs are transmitting information from the environment to the brain, and the brain is processing it and sending instructions to the muscles and glands. The point James is making is that the habit is the pathway that the current travels from sense receptors through the nerves to the spinal cord and brain, and from there back through the nervous system to the muscles and glands. And it is the current itself that creates the pathway. A simple habit just has one of these pathways, while a complex habit has one habit triggering another habit, triggering another habit, and so on, until the final habit is executed. A good question is how a current can travel a path that does not exist. If a current is creating a path, then it seems to follow that the path cannot have previously existed. James admits the problem and attempts to resolve it.

James argues that nerve currents trace out pathways in the nervous system the same way all the other pathways in our experience do. A path once traversed by a nerve-current, he says, might be expected to be scooped out and made more permeable than before, and this process ought to repeat itself with each new passage of the current. Whatever obstructions hindered the current from forming a path at first would be swept away bit by bit until the current becomes a natural drainage-channel.

This seems plausible to me, considering how a similar process appears to have happened when the Colorado River formed the Grand Canyon. The Grand Canyon exists, and the Colorado River passes through it. But the Colorado River could not have passed through the Grand Canyon before the Grand Canyon existed, so how can it be that the Colorado River created the Grand Canyon? The answer appears to be that the Grand Canyon was not formed all at once, but a small pathway was carved out at first, and the river eroded the rest of the canyon away through continual passage through the original channel it created. James says that nerve currents work the same way.

James quotes the nineteenth century physiologist William Benjamin Carpenter as saying that it is easier for a growing organism (like a child) to develop new habits than it is for an adult. Habits in adults are relatively more fixed. The reason why is that organs tend to "grow to" the mode in which they are habitually exercised; examples include the way muscles grow larger the more they are exercised, and the way joints become more flexible through gymnastic performances. But the reconstructive activity through which organs grow is most pronounced in nervous tissue, and this is indicated by the enormous amount of blood it receives. Carpenter says that in other kinds of tissues, like those of the muscles, damaged tissue is replaced by tissues of a lower and less specialized type, while with nervous tissue damage tissue is replaced by normal tissue. Carpenter talks about the results of one experiment in which a spinal cord was divided but in time completely recovered its old functions. Carpenter says that all other nervous tissue is constantly being replaced by new tissue in the same fashion as it is "wasted" through use. He says that nervous activity is exceptionally abundant in childhood, and this accelerates the constant reconstruction of the nervous system which takes place in the course of building it. And it is this process which constructs the secondarily automatic modes of movement which characterize humans; the movements of animals are instinctive, but those instincts are replaced in us by the building of our nervous mechanisms in the fashion described above. Some of the habits we develop are common to our species except where physical disability prevents it, while others are specific to individuals. Special training is required for the latter to develop and that training is more effective the earlier it is begun. Habits acquired in childhood remain with the adult through normal nutritive processes and can be used again even after long inaction.

Carpenter says that the psychology of association is explained by the physiology of nutrition, as described above. Both express the fact that any sequence of mental action which has been frequently repeated tends to perpetuate itself, so that we find ourselves automatically prompted to think, feel, or do what we have been previously accustomed to think, feel, or do under similar circumstances, without any consciously formed purpose or anticipation of results. Carpenter says that the cerebrum is no exception to the rule that each part of the organism forms itself in accordance with the mode in which it is habitually used, and because of its incessant regeneration, this will be especially true of the nervous system. Every state of ideational consciousness left upon the cerebrum which is either habitually repeated or very strong will leave an organic impression upon it. The same state can be reproduced in the future in response to a suggestion fitted to excite it. Associations formed early in life are strong because they are formed during a period of rapid growth, in which the nervous system is being built by incessant regeneration in response to incessant nervous activity. When an organic modification has been fixed in the growing brain, it stays there like a scar until the end of one's life because it is continually reconstructed by nutritive processes. It becomes a normal part of the brain.

James says that "Dr. Carpenter's phrase that our nervous system grows to the modes in which it has been exercised expresses the philosophy of habit in a nutshell." James traces some of the practical applications of the principle to human life. The first result of it is that habit simplifies the movements required to achieve a given result, makes them more accurate and diminishes fatigue. James quotes Carpenter again about how the principle applies to the case of a piano player. When a person is first learning how to play the piano, he will not use his fingers alone, but his whole hand, his forearm, and perhaps even his entire body; he might even move his head as if he would press down the key with it, too. There may also be a contraction of the abdominal muscles. But the impulse is directed to the motion of the hand and the single finger (I assume the movement of the other parts are unintended consequences of this). The impulse is directed to the motion of the hand and single finger because the movement of the finger is the movement thought of and because its movement and that of the key are the movements we try to perceive, along with the results of the latter on the ear. (I think we might be able to infer that the things we pay attention to act as the chief stimuli to our actions. The things we pay less attention to we respond to more weakly and less often. And we might also be able to infer that what we think and will to do is what determines our actions. So if we think to do a certain thing, and direct our attention to the corresponding objects in the environment, and we manipulate those objects with our limbs and the muscles attached to them, and receive continual feedback through the sense organs about the objects attended to, we will be able to adjust our thoughts and our nerve currents and muscle movements to better manipulate the objects.) Carpenter says that the more often the process is repeated, the more easily the movement follows, on account of the increase in the permeability of the nerves engaged. Recall what James said about nerve currents carving out pathways by passing repeatedly through the same path. This is what Carpenter is referring to.

The more easily the movement occurs, says Carpenter, the slighter is the stimulus required to set it up, and the slighter the stimulus is, the more its effect is confined to the fingers alone. So an impulse which originally spread its effects over the whole body, or at least many of its movable parts, is gradually confined to a single definite organ, in which it effects the contraction of a few limited muscles. In this change the thoughts and perceptions which start the impulse acquire more and more intimate causal relations with a particular group of motor nerves. (This appears to be the reason why people are clumsy at first when they learn a new skill, and why they approximate bit by bit to the desired habits, and why people who are masters at the skill show no flaws which would be perceptible to a non-expert.)

Carpenter uses a simile to describe this process. He compares the nervous system to a drainage-system inclining on the whole to certain muscles, but with the escape there somewhat clogged. So normally, the greatest volume of water tends to pass through the drains that are the least clogged, but in the event of a sudden "flushing," the whole system of channels will be filled and water will overflow everywhere before it escapes. So if a piano player who has learned to confine his movements to his fingers becomes excited, he might move his head and trunk and other body parts as he plays, somewhat like he did before he learned to confined his movements to his fingers. (Why is it that some "drains"—that is, nervous pathways—are less "clogged" than others? Because some pathways are "de-clogged" by having "water"—nerve currents—continually passing through them, or passing through them with great force by a strong stimulus, or both. So nerve currents take the path of least resistance. The path of least resistance is decided by which pathways are most well-worn through use. We form habits by the carving out of these pathways by repeated actions.)

James says that man is born with a tendency to do more things than he has ready-made arrangements for in the nerve-centers. While most of the behaviors of animals are automatic, in man the number of them is so enormous that most of them must be the fruit of painful study. If practice did not make perfect, and if habit did not economize the expense of nervous and muscular energy, he would not be able to do much of anything.

James quotes the influential nineteenth century psychiatrist Henry Maudsley as saying that if an act did not become easier after being done several times, and that if the careful direction of consciousness were necessary to perform it on each occasion, that the whole activity of a lifetime might be confined to one or two deeds, and no progress could take place in development. A man might occupy himself all day with dressing or undressing himself; everything he did would be as difficult for him as it is for a child doing something for the first time.

James says that the next result of the philosophy of habit is that habit diminishes the conscious attention with which our acts are performed. So when we are first learning how to do something, we pause at each step to think about what we should do next, but after we have made a habit of it the sequence of steps executes, from start to finish, without us having to think about it. So few of us could say which pant leg we put on first when getting dressed, or which way a door swings, or in what order we brush our teeth or comb our hair, but we do the same things all the time without thinking about them. Sometimes we execute habits when it is not appropriate to execute them. One example of this that I can think of (James has his own examples) is when you are in the habit of driving a certain way to work every day, but then you have to drive someplace new which lies along a similar route; if you aren't paying conscious attention to what you're doing you might end up driving to work by accident.

After this James talks about the means by which a chain of actions is executed in a habit. It is the sensation occasioned by the muscular contraction just finished which triggers the next step. In contrast a strictly voluntary act has to be guided by idea, perception, and volition throughout from beginning to end. In habitual action, mere sensation is a sufficient guide to action and the upper regions of the brain and mind are comparatively free.

In habitual behaviors, the only thing the centers of idea or perception need to do is to send the signal to the lower centers to start the chain. This signal may be the thought of the first movement or it may be the thought of the last result. So an expert pianist is able to play a difficult piece of music just by looking at the notes. James says that the only difference between instinct and acquired aptitudes like these is that the latter are triggered by the will.

We are All Bundles of Habits

James talks about how habit is the most precious conservative agent of society. It alone, he says, keeps us all within the bounds of ordinance, and within our daily routines. It is the only reason why the poor do not rise up to overthrow the rich, and why people still do the hardest and most repulsive work, to name a couple effects of habit. It is the reason why we remain along the paths of life determined by nurture or by early choice even though the things we do might not suit us at all; there is nothing else we are suited for after we have grown up, and by that time it is too late to begin again. Habit also keeps social strata from mixing. By the age of thirty, in most cases our characters have been set and will not change significantly in the future. James thinks that on the whole this is for the best.

James says that the period between twenty and thirty is the critical one in the formation of intellectual and professional habits, while the period before twenty is for the fixing of personal habits like vocalization and pronunciation, gesture, motion, and address.

James doesn't think it's a good idea to leave your habits unsettled. He says that habits are just fine to have, but you should make your nervous system your ally instead of your enemy. You should avoid like the plague doing things which are harmful or useless to you, as you will get in the habit of doing them. You *should* get in the habit of doing things which are helpful for you. And the more useful things you can make a habit of the better off you will be, and the more the higher powers of the mind will be set free for their own proper work. If nothing is habitual for you, then you will be plagued by indecision and you will have to deliberate about every little thing that you do. James advises his readers, if they have not made habits of their daily routines, to set the matter right immediately.

James discusses the Scottish philosopher Alexander Bain's maxims on habit. The first maxim is that when you are forming a new habit, or leaving off an old one, you should take care to launch yourself with as strong and decided an initiative as possible. You should change your circumstances so that every thing that you do reinforces the new habit, and so that you will have no temptation to return to old habits. The second maxim is never to suffer an exception to occur until the new habit is securely rooted in your life. Each lapse undoes a lot of work you have done to build the habit. James says that it's imperative to secure success at the outset. Failure at first is likely to dampen the energy of all future attempts, whereas past experience of success nerves one to future vigor. He says also that in breaking bad habits, the best thing to do is to stop doing them immediately, but only as long as it is not so difficult that failure is sure to result, as this would discourage future attempts to break the habit.

James adds a third maxim to Bain's two maxims: "Seize the very first possible opportunity to act on every resolution you make, and on every emotional prompting you may experience in the direction of the habits you aspire to gain." This is because it is not in the moment of their forming, but in the moment of their producing motor effects, that resolves and aspirations communicate the new set of habits to the brain.

No matter how many maxims one may possess, and no matter how good one's sentiments may be, if a person has not taken advantage of every concrete opportunity to act then his character will remain entirely unaffected for the better. For this reason James cautions against excessive theater-going and novel-reading, and listening to music if you are not a performer yourself or musically gifted enough to understand music purely intellectually. The trouble is that you develop the bad habit of not acting upon your sentiments, even when they are good ones, when they arise. A person with good sentiments who never acts upon them will not develop good character.

James says that there are not simply particular lines of the discharge of nerve currents but also general forms of discharge. So as in the former examples, letting emotions evaporate gets us into the habit of allowing them to evaporate; and James postulates that flinching from effort will get us into the habit of flinching from effort, and it will undermine our ability to take efforts. And if we permit our attention to wander all the time, then we will lose our ability to focus attention. James says that effort and attention are in fact the same psychic act, and he will expand on this later in the book. James does not know what brain-processes effort and attention correspond to, though. But he does believe that they depend on brain-processes because they are subject to the law of habit, which is a material law. James's final maxim on habit relates to these habits of the will; it is to "[k]eep the faculty of effort alive in you by a little gratuitous exercise every day." In practice, this means doing something ascetic or heroic every day even though you do not need to do those things. It keeps you in the habit of undertaking ascetic or heroic actions just in case the need arises one day to make use of those habits. Everyone else may collapse in the face of difficulty but you will be prepared.

James says that we create hell on Earth for ourselves by habitually fashioning our characters in the wrong way. If the young knew that they were soon to become little more than walking bundles of habits, they would give more heed to their conduct while in the plastic state. Every good or bad deed that we do leaves its mark upon our characters, never to be erased. Even if no one is watching, even if there are no immediate consequences for the things you do, nevertheless your actions are forming habits which will shape your future actions. But there is a positive side to this. If a young person wishes to succeed in some arduous profession, he doesn't need to worry as long as keeps faithfully busy every hour of the working day. One day he will wake up to find himself one of the competent members of his generation. James thinks the fact that young people do not know this causes a tremendous amount of unnecessary discouragement and faint-heartedness.

All Ideas are Formed by the Laws of Association

As for the psychological laws of association, James says that both the analysis and the synthesis of ideas are necessary in order to improve our conceptions of things. This is is in exact agreement with Boyd's theory of learning.

James says that people can be timed on how fast it takes for one idea to call to mind another. The more quickly the association takes place the more expert we are at the task. So a person who speaks English as his mother tongue may make associations between spoken and written words very quickly while someone who speaks it as a second language will probably take longer to make the same associations.

James says that objects once experienced together tend to become associated in the imagination, so that when any one of them is thought of, the others are likely to be thought of also, in the same order of sequence or coexistence as before. This he calls the law of mental association by contiguity. James accounts for this phenomenon by the laws of habit articulated earlier in the book. Earlier he spoke of the association of sensory and motor processes with one another; with the law of association by contiguity ideational centers and their coupling paths are associated instead.

James says that were there no other factor interfering with the process, upon thinking of an idea the whole network of ideas associated with it would be recalled to mind at the same time. This is not necessarily a good thing since not all of the ideas associated with the original idea are of interest to us or to those we're talking to. James says that when recounting something, some people insist upon recounting every single detail, no matter how trivial; these people are lacking in the ability to confine the ideas they recall just to what is interesting to the hearers. James calls the bringing to mind of associated ideas redintegration.

James calls the recalling of every associated idea without interruption impartial redintegration, and he gives examples of this.

James says that ordinary thought does not follow the law of impartial redintegration. In no revival of a past experience are all the items of our thought equally operative in determining what the next thought shall be; some ingredient is prepotent over the rest. The items that are prepotent are those which appeal most to our interest. The law of interest, expressed in brain terms, is that some one brain-process is always prepotent above its concomitants in arousing action elsewhere. The kind of redintegration that is guided both by contiguity and by interest James calls ordinary, or mixed, association.

James talks now about association by similarity, which he says is made from impartial redintegration. He does not believe that simple ideas automatically call to mind similar ideas. So when you think of a shade of blue, it will not tend to recall to mind other shades of blue unless you have in mind some general purpose like naming the tint of some blue object. So what he seems to be saying is that there is no elementary law of association by similarity; rather, association by similarity is derivative of impartial redintegration, which is done because some things interest us more than other things. And recall that impartial redintegration is a skewing of associations made according to the law of association by contiguity, which according to James *is* an elementary law of association. So I don't think James would disagree if we said that association by similarity is derivative of association by contiguity.

James affirms a little later that he does believe association of coexistent or sequent impressions to be the one elementary law of association. He says that there were people in his day who insisted that association by similarity was not only an independent law but also that association by contiguity was derived from association by similarity; James rejects this.

Association by contrast is the third major agent of association. James says that although it has been held to be an independent agent, there were authors in his day who argued that it was reducible either to similarity or contiguity. James believes contrast to be explainable by the principles he has presented already. He appears to be suggesting that association by contrast is reducible to association by similarity, which is reducible in turn to association by contiguity. Contrast always presupposes genetic similarity, he says; it is only the extremes of a class which are contrasted, like black and white, not black and sour or white and prickly. Psychological machinery which is able to produce a similar at all should be able to produce the opposite similar as well as any intermediate term.

So to summarize, ideas are associated together in the mind because they occur at the same time or one right after the other. But ideas do not ordinarily recall each other without qualification; there is another filter besides contiguity, and that is interest. The process of association by contiguity without the filter of interest is impartial redintegration. The process of association by contiguity *with* the filter of interest is partial redintegration. Association by similarity is a product of this latter process. Association by contrast is a product of association by similarity. The physiological processes underlying the association of ideas are explained by the Law of Habit James talks about earlier in the book, only instead of sensations being associated with motor process, what is being associated is ideational centers and their coupling paths.

James says that the association of ideas explains all sorts of psychological phenomena, including memory, expectation, fancy, belief, judgment, reasoning, benevolence, conscientiousness, ambition, fear, love, and volition.

There is much more in James's book that is worth talking about, but what I'm interested in in this chapter is how ideas and behaviors are formed, so I will have to stop with this.

Chapter 13: A Plan for a Complete Theory of Human Nature

There is one last thing that I want to talk about before concluding my book, and that's how the ideas in this book fit in with human nature in general. I find it difficult sometimes to restrict my discussions to just one aspect of human nature, since no one aspect exists and functions in isolation from the rest. So I've talked about cognitive biases, sensation and perception, the laws of association, the Law of Habit, dominance hierarchies, evolutionary theory, politics, ethics, and a lot of other things, and yet these things don't immediately come to mind when most people think about the psychology of crowds. But all of these things are either the causes or the effects of crowd psychology, so I don't feel like I'm going "off-topic." But these causes and effects have their own causes and effects. A cause of a cause of crowd psychology is indirectly a cause of crowd psychology. An effect of an effect of crowd psychology is indirectly an effect of crowd psychology. And the same thing could be said about causes of causes of causes and effects of effects of effects. So I'm convinced that everything in the universe is related one way or another to every other thing. Even particle physics could be said, with reason, to be a cause of crowd psychology. But it would be impractical to write a book that discussed every remote cause and effect of a subject even if it weren't daunting. The most reasonable course seems to be to discuss fields that are immediate causes and effects and not go too far beyond that. I think I've succeeded with that in this book.

However, human nature is a broader subject than I've discussed in these pages, and I've given thought to aspects of it which I haven't talked about very much or at all. I think I would be doing a service to my readers to let them know where I'm coming from. Also, these ideas would be the basis of future books if I write any. If this book is successful then I probably will write more books.

So this book could perhaps become the first in a series on human nature. I haven't fully worked out my theory, but I have a general idea of what I want to say. Anyway, I'll explain it here briefly.

Let's assume again that crowds only have the ideas and behaviors which are spread to them after being originated by some innovative individual. Let's also assume that these ideas and behaviors are created by the laws of association and ultimately by the Law of Habit. Some behaviors, and I believe some ideas too, are strictly instinctive; that is, they don't have to be learned; we are born with them. I'll set those aside for now though. This leaves us with the question of why we learn the particular ideas and behaviors that we do. Why did those innovative individuals develop the ideas and behaviors that they did, and not some other ones? Why did the ones that spread happen to spread and not some other ones? Why do such behaviors as walking around on one's hands never catch on?

Our Needs Determine our Thoughts

Yes, people follow others in their communities who are successful, or who appear to be so. Successful at what? Acquiring socially prominent positions and abundant resources, mostly. But that doesn't seem to be everything. My suspicion is that people follow, not just social superiors, but people who have succeeded at satisfying some physiological need which leader and led share alike. I conceive of physiological needs in a comprehensive way, including everything in Abraham Maslow's (1943) hierarchy of needs—that is, basic physiological needs (the need for food and water, for example), safety needs, the need for love and belonging, the need for esteem, and the need for self-actualization. So a socially prominent person (who has satisfied the need for esteem) may follow someone who is less socially prominent if that person is better able to satisfy some physiological need which both share. If Bob is the CEO of a large corporation and Jack is a fitness guru, and Bob wishes to get fit, he will defer to Jack. If Jack changes careers and wishes to work at Bob's company, then Jack would be deferring to Bob.

The physiology of needs is, like crowd psychology, one of the most central sciences there is. Chemistry is sometimes called the central science among the natural sciences because it links so many other disciplines to each other. Chemistry is caused by physics and is the cause of biology. Physiology is one of the most important branches of biology and it is the scientific study of the vital functions of organisms; it is about the processes that keep us alive, in good health, and reproductively fit.

I have a very strong suspicion that what ideas we have and what behaviors we learn are ultimately dependent upon our physiological needs. William James disagrees with the associationist psychologists on an important point, and that is whether or not people are the will-less products of sense experience. James denies this, arguing that attention determines what will ultimately become the contents of our minds, and it is those contents which are molded by the laws of association into complex ideas. There are millions of things in our environments which we could attend to but do not, and therefore the overwhelming majority of what is around us does not determine what we think. What commands our attention? What is interesting to us, says James. James talks a bit more about what it means for something to be interesting, but what I was thinking when I was reading the book is—what if what determines what is interesting, and what therefore commands our attention, is physiological needs? One physiological need is the need for food. Is it not true that when people are hungry that their attention turns to the subject of food? The same holds for thirst: the attentions of thirsty people are directed towards water. The attentions of people who are freezing are directed toward warmth, and the attentions of people who are overheated is directed towards cool things—things like air-conditioned rooms, cold drinks, and possibly ice cream. Another physiological need is the need for a mate. Pretty much everyone thinks about this subject pretty much every day. In other words, our attention is drawn to it. And it seems clear that our attentions are not turned so much to things which we have in abundance, so that we don't think so much about food or water when we are satiated. So what I'm saying is that our mental worlds are determined ultimately by our physiological needs.

I'm not the only one to have argued for something like this. The evolutionary biologist Jakob von Uexküll (1934/2010) argued that organisms may have different mental environments even if they share the same physical environment, and it is the mental environments which they are reacting to. So he is in agreement with Lippmann, though the two probably didn't know of each other's work. Uexküll argued that the mental environments of organisms were determined by the organism's needs; so they are determined by the need for food, water, and shelter, by the need to protect themselves against potential threats, and by the need for points of reference for navigation. Since different organisms have different needs and different ways of sensing and perceiving the world, their mental worlds are bound to differ.

Our Needs Determine our Behaviors

The behaviorist Clark Hull (1943) had an interesting theory about how physiological needs motivated behavior, and it meshes well with what I have said so far. Hull says in *the Principles of Behavior* that the behavior of an organism is dependent upon its relationship with its environment, with which it constantly interacts. There are two kinds of environment: internal and external. The internal environment is essentially the physiology of the organism, while the external environment is subdivided into inanimate objects and other organisms (the latter of which includes mates and other conspecifics). Hull is in agreement with Darwin that the structure and function of organisms, including their behavior, serves to enable the survival and reproduction of the organism. Survival and reproduction depend upon the satisfaction of physiological needs; it is because the behavior of organisms serves to satisfy those needs that it has survival and reproductive value. The organism receives information about its environment from its sense organs, which is communicated to the brain through the nervous system; the brain sends messages back through the nervous system to the muscles and glands, which cause the organ to act so as to satisfy physiological needs. The organism sometimes fails, but when it is successful in satisfying those needs, its ability to survive and reproduce is improved.

All of what I've said so far about physiology, ideas, and behavior accords with what is known in stress physiology. When people experience stress what they are really experiencing is tension or pain due to their inability to satisfy physiological needs. When the needs are met, the stress is reduced. The body mobilizes its resources in order to maintain homeostasis, which is a state in which the life functions of the body are able to be performed most efficiently. If the internal environment of the body is too acidic, too basic, too hot, too cold, or is starved for nutrients, then those functions will break down and the body might suffer permanent damage or even die. So this is the ultimate reason for our behavior, and even for the mental pseudo-environments which we take to be the "real world" and respond to every waking moment of our lives.

So I'm saying that the ideas and behaviors that tend to spread are those which seem to us to be the most effective at satisfying our physiological needs. We follow people who have the same immediate needs as us and who have achieved the greatest successes at satisfying them. The need for social status (which would fall under Maslow's need for esteem) is a real physiological need. So I'm arguing that Tarde's law of imitation regarding the imitation of superiors by inferiors is a special case of a more general law.

This theory I'm developing from the ideas of the thinkers I've mentioned is consistent with Edward Bernays's theory and practice of propaganda. Recall that according to Bernays that you have to appeal to certain basic instincts which people have in order to influence them—things like the need for shelter and the need for good health. Advertising experts, public relations people, and salesmen all appeal to these basic instincts. Don't believe me; pay attention next time you see an advertisement and think about what they're doing. I was thinking that you could use Maslow's hierarchy of needs just as well as William McDougall's basic instinct theory in appealing to customers. I prefer using Maslow's theory because it works very well with the rest of my system.

Economics is Derived from Human Physiology (and Crowd Psychology)

Someone might say that the study of the physiology of human needs has to potential to revolutionize the study of economics, but actually it has already done so. The revolution was called the Marginal Revolution, and it happened in the latter part of the nineteenth century. Marginal utility theory, which is canon among economists on the question of why things have value (are "worth" something), is derivable (in fact, was derived) from the science of human physiology. Before the Marginal Revolution, economists believed (like Smith, Ricardo, and Marx) that things had value because of the amount of labor put into making them, or else they believed (like Henry George) that things derived their value ultimately from the resources of the land with which they were produced. This is one of the central questions of economics because what a thing is "worth," or at least believed to be "worth," determines what people will pay for it, and what they will sell it for. The marginal utility theorists, William Stanley Jevons, Carl Menger, and Leon Walras, all proposed the theory independently of each other. Their idea was that things had value because people believed them to have value, and that the more people became satiated with a good the less they were willing to spend on it. Once satiated with one good people preferred to spend money satisfying other needs. So you can see how marginal utility theory works very well with Maslow's hierarchy of needs, and with the other theories I'm discussing here.

I should note that according to Maslow, more basic needs must be satisfied before we are inclined to satisfy higher level needs. So we strive to satisfy the needs of food and water before we try to satisfy the needs for belonging or esteem. Marginal utility theory would seem to predict this sort of behavior as well. According to marginal utility theory, we purchase less and less of a good as we become satiated with it. But that doesn't mean we stop buying things; we buy something else instead. So if we have only enough money for either food or books, we will buy the food and skip the books. But if we have enough to buy both the food and the books we might be inclined to buy the books after we've bought enough food. I'll discuss marginal utility in greater detail and that will show how well the two theories support each other.

William Stanley Jevons (1871) says in his *Theory of Political Economy* that he was influenced by an obscure author named Richard Jennings who sought to prove in his book, *the Natural Elements of Political Economy*, that political economy (that is, economics) is dependent upon physiological laws. Jevons says that economists didn't pay much attention to the book, but he thinks it's important. Jevons cites Jennings to show that the law of marginal utility is no novelty, but is carefully deduced from established principles:

> The writer, however, who appears to me to have most clearly appreciated the nature and importance of the law of utility, is Mr. Richard Jennings, who, in 1855, published a small book called "The Natural Elements of Political Economy". This work treats of the physical groundwork of Economy, showing its dependence on physiological laws. It appears to me to display a great insight into the real basis of Economy; yet I am not aware that economists have bestowed the slightest attention on Mr. Jennings' views. I take the liberty, therefore, of giving a full extract from his remarks on the nature of utility. It will thus be seen that the law, as I state it, is no novelty, and that it is only careful deduction from principles in our possession that is needed to give us a correct Theory of Economy.

'To turn the relative effect of commodities, in producing sensations, to those which are absolute, or dependent only on the quantity of each commodity, it is but too well known to every condition of men, that the degree of each sensation which is produced, is by no means commensurate with the quantity of the commodity applied to the senses. These effects require to be closely observed, because they are the foundation of the changes of money price, which valuable objects command in times of varied scarcity and abundance; we shall therefore direct our attention to them for the purpose of ascertaining the nature of the law according to which the sensations that attend on consumption vary in degree with changes in the quantity of the commodity consumed.

'We may gaze upon an object until we can no longer discern it, listen until we can no longer hear, smell until the sense of odour is exhausted, taste until the object becomes nauseous, and touch until it becomes painful; we may consume food until we are fully satisfied, and use stimulants until more would cause pain. On the other hand, the same object offered to the special senses for a moderate duration of time, and the same food or stimulants consumed when we are exhausted or weary, may convey much gratification. If the whole quantity of the commodity consumed during the interval of these two states of sensation, the state of satiety and the state of inanition, be conceived to be divided into a number of equal parts, each marked with its proper degrees of sensation, the question to be determined will be, what relation does the difference in the degrees of the sensation bear to the difference in the quantities of the commodity? First, with respect to commodities feelings show that the degrees of satisfaction do not proceed *pari passu* with the quantities consumed; they do not advance equally with each instalment of the commodity offered to the senses, and then suddenly stop; but diminish gradually until they ultimately disappear, and further instalments can produce no further satisfaction. In this progressive scale the increments of sensation resulting from equal increments of the commodity are obviously less and less at each step,—each degree of sensation is less than the preceding degree. Placing ourselves at that middle point of sensation, the *juste milieu*, the *aurea mediocritas*, the *aptarov fierpov* of sages, which is the most usual status of the mass of mankind, and which, therefore, is the best position that can be chosen for measuring deviations from the usual amount we may say that the law which expresses the relation of degrees of sensation to quantities of commodities is of this character: if the average or temperate quantity of commodities be increased, the satisfaction derived is increased in a less degree, and ultimately ceases to be increased at all; if the average or temperate quantity be diminished, the loss of more and more satisfaction will continually ensure, and the detriment thence arising will ultimately become exceedingly great'. (p. 59-62)

Carl Menger, who was also the founder of Austrian economics, framed his theory a bit differently from Jevons. Jevons was fond of utilitarianism, which I am wary of. It seems to me to be good enough for an economist to state that goods satisfy needs without attaching to that observation the ethical doctrine that it is a good thing that this is so, and that the more people who are satisfied this way the better. Utilitarianism strikes me as a kind of secular faith. By that I mean, if I said that maximizing the happiness or pleasure of the few was more ethical than maximizing the happiness or pleasure of the greatest number, how could the utilitarians and I ever resolve our disagreement? Or what if I agreed with the more ascetic faiths that in fact, it is sinful to maximize pleasure and holy to abstain from pleasure? The utilitarian doctrine is taken on faith just like so many other ethical doctrines. It isn't science. Menger (1871) frames his theory in terms of needs instead of in terms of the doctrine of utility, and for that reason I prefer Menger's. Menger formulates his theory in his *Principles of Economics*.

I think I should quote Menger's definition of what constitutes a good, since it is clear and precise and consistent with common usage. The first requirement is that the thing satisfy a human need:

> Things that can be placed in a causal connection with the satisfaction of human needs we term *useful things*. If, however, we both recognize this causal connection, and have the power actually to direct the useful things to the satisfaction of our needs, we call them *goods*.
>
> If a thing is to become a good, or in other words, if it is to acquire goods-character, all four of the following prerequisites must be simultaneously present:
>
> 1. A human need.
>
> 2. Such properties as render the thing capable of being brought into causal connection with the satisfaction of this need.
>
> 3. Human knowledge of this causal connection.
>
> 4. Command of the thing sufficient to direct it to the satisfaction of the need. (p. 52)

Here is Menger's introductory paragraph to his second chapter, "Economy and Economic Goods"; Menger is in complete agreement with Clark Hull and the stress physiologists that we are driven to satisfy our needs and if we don't we will suffer or be destroyed, but if we satisfy them we will live and prosper. In Menger's view, this is the most important of human endeavors:

> Needs arise from our drives and the drives are imbedded in our nature. An imperfect satisfaction of needs leads to the stunting of our nature. Failure to satisfy them brings about our destruction. But to satisfy our needs is to live and prosper. Thus the attempt to provide for the satisfaction of our needs is synonymous with the attempt to provide for our lives and

well-being. It is the most important of all human endeavors, since it is the prerequisite and foundation of all others. (p. 77)

He continues:

> In practice, the concern of men for the satisfaction of their needs is expressed as an attempt to attain command of all the things on which the satisfaction of their needs depends. If a person has command of all the consumption goods necessary to satisfy his needs, their actual satisfaction depends only on his will. We may thus consider his objective as having been obtained when he is in possession of these goods, since his life and wellbeing are then in his own hands. The quantities of consumption goods a person must have to satisfy his needs may be termed his *requirements*. The concern of men for the maintenance of their lives and well-being becomes, therefore, an attempt to provide themselves with their requirements. (p. 77-78)

Menger notes the importance of providing not only for immediate needs but for future needs as well, since if people only provided for present needs they would not be able to save themselves from destruction at some future time of dire need.

A bit later on in the book Menger says that the fact that not everyone within a society can obtain the goods to satisfy every one of his needs has determined the form that social life has taken: it led to competition as each person within a society tries to meet his needs at the expense of all others, which led to the creation of the law to restrain this competition, including the institution of private property to secure individuals in what they possess.

Menger states explicitly that goods have value because they satisfy needs:

If the requirements for a good are larger than the quantity of it available, and some part of the needs involved must remain unsatisfied in any case, the available quantity of the good can be diminished by no part of the whole amount, in any way practically worthy of notice, without causing some need, previously provided for, to be satisfied either not at all or only less completely than would otherwise have been the case. The satisfaction of some one human need is therefore dependent on the availability of each concrete, practically significant, quantity of all goods subject to this quantitative relationship. If economizing men become aware of this circumstance (that is, if they perceive that the satisfaction of one of their needs, or the greater or less completeness of its satisfaction, is dependent on their command of each portion of a quantity of goods or on each individual good subject to the above quantitative relationship) these goods attain for them the significance we call value. Value is thus the importance that individual goods or quantities of goods attain for us because we are conscious of being dependent on command of them for the satisfaction of our needs.[1] (p. 114-115)

Menger is clear to emphasize that value is fundamentally a matter of human psychology, and is not inherent in any particular object. A thing has value because we perceive it to be able to satisfy our needs:

The value of goods, accordingly, is a phenomenon that springs from the same source as the economic character of goods—that is, from the relationship, explained earlier, between requirements for and available quantities of goods.[2] But there is a difference between the two phenomena. On the one hand, perception of this quantitative relationship stimulates our provident activity, thus causing goods subject to this relationship to become objects of our economizing (i.e., economic goods). On the other hand, perception of the same relationship makes us aware of the significance that command of each concrete unit[3] of the available quantities of these goods has for our lives and well-being, thus causing it to attain value for us.[4] Just as a penetrating investigation of mental processes makes the cognition of external things appear to be merely our consciousness of the impressions made by the external things upon our persons, and thus, in the final analysis, merely the cognition of states of our own persons, so too, in the final analysis, is the importance that we attribute to things of the external world only an outflow of the importance to us of our continued existence and development (life and well-being). Value is therefore nothing inherent in goods, no property of them, but merely the importance that we first attribute to the satisfaction of our needs, that is, to our lives and well-being, and in consequence carry over to economic goods as the exclusive causes of the satisfaction of our needs. (p. 115-116)

A Theory of the Arts

There can't be a complete theory of human nature without accounting for the arts. Some of the writers I've cited talk about the arts a bit, and a partial theory can be constructed from the aggregate of these views. However, I don't think they explain them fully. I'd like to incorporate the mythologist Joseph Campbell's work to fill in the gaps. Campbell's work is erudite and he does his best to be consistent with the best of what is known in the natural sciences. Also, his work is used by real artists to create real art. Most people have probably not heard of Campbell but they will likely have heard of *Star Wars* and *the Lion King*, which were heavily influenced by his work, particularly *the Hero with a Thousand Faces*. A popular book for screen writers, *the Writer's Journey* by Christopher Vogler, talks about how to use Campbell's theory to write excellent screen plays. I should note that Campbell was heavily influenced by the work of the psychologist Carl Jung, and Jung is popular in his own right with professional writers of fiction. Jung was a student of Sigmund Freud and though he differed from Freud on many things, nevertheless the subconscious mind plays a central role in his theory. The subconscious mind also plays a central role in the theories of the crowd psychologists, which will make it easier to unify the two fields.

What is interesting to me is that the unconscious Campbell is working with in his theories isn't, for the most part, the subconscious mind which most of us are familiar with, but the collective unconscious of Jung's theory. The individual subconscious organizes the experience of the individual in a species. However, Jung thought that the members of each species had subconscious experiences which they all shared. That might sound at first sight to most of today's scientists like wacky New Age nonsense, but Campbell shows in *the Masks of God* that it can be convincingly explained in terms of commonly accepted principles of animal behavior.

Campbell talks in *the Masks of God: Primitive Mythology*, the first volume of the four-volume series, about innate releasing mechanisms and the inherited images in our subconscious minds. Other animals have these, too. This is how baby turtles know to head for the sea after hatching from their eggs. They don't have to learn how to swim or where to swim to; they are born knowing these things.

Innate releasing mechanisms are structures in the nervous system that allow an animal to respond to circumstances which it has never encountered before. The sign stimulus or releaser is an inherited image in the subconscious mind of an organism; when an object observed in nature matches it closely enough, a corresponding instinctive reaction is triggered. Newborn chicks will dart for cover when a hawk flies overhead but not when the bird is a gull, duck, heron, or pigeon. Also, if the wooden model of a hawk is drawn over their coop on a wire, they react as though it were real, unless it is drawn backward, in which case there is no response. So the action of taking cover is the innate action linked to the sign stimulus of the moving hawk image which was recognized by the chicks.

Campbell says that even if all of the hawks in the world were to vanish, their image would still sleep in the soul of the chick, never to be aroused unless by some accident of art. The clever experiment with the wooden hawk is an example of this, he says. With such art the obsolete reaction could still recur, at least for a certain number of generations, and it would be difficult to explain the reaction unless something were known about the earlier danger of hawks to chicks. It would strike us as surprising that living gulls, herons, and pigeons had little effect on chicks, but that a work of art struck some very deep chord.

Campbell thinks that the sign stimuli or releasers correspond to the archetypes which, according to C.G. Jung, exist in the collective unconscious of a species. Campbell says that Jung's theory is a development of the earlier theory of Adolf Bastian. Bastian hypothesized that there were certain elementary ideas that were fundamental to all mankind, but that these ideas were articulated and elaborated in different ways in different cultures; these latter ideas he called ethnic ideas. Campbell cites the ethologist Niko Tinbergen's book, *the Study of Instinct*, as his source on innate releasing mechanisms. Tinbergen was one of the twentieth century's best ethologists, so the information is reliable and the theory ought to be sound.

Campbell talks next about the ethology of play. He thinks a lot of our behaviors are forms of play. He thinks that humans are actually immature apes, which is why we retain our habit of play into adulthood—or at least many of us do. He thinks that our ability to learn new things into adulthood is also due to our immaturity. This is what makes us less under the control of instinct than other species are. It's what makes our behaviors more varied, and makes us more adaptable. We can control and even inhibit our own responses. Campbell quotes the animal psychologist Konrad Lorenz as saying that every study of man was undertaken as a result of our capacity for play.

Campbell thinks that art is also a form of play. When we create art we're creating sign stimuli for us to react to. In not only poetry and love but in religion and patriotism, when art is effective it provokes actual physical responses, like tears, sighs, interior aches, spontaneous groans, cries, bursts of laughter, wrath, and impulsive deeds. He says that the biology, psychology, sociology, and history of these sign stimuli may be said to constitute the field of his subject, the science of comparative mythology. He says that mythology is the mother of the arts, although it's also the daughter of her own birth.

Campbell then talks some more about sign stimuli. He thinks that super-normal stimuli may play a large role in mythology and the arts. Super-normal stimuli are artificial stimuli which we show a stronger response to than we show to their ordinary analogues. He gives as an example of this in nature. There is a species of butterfly in which the male prefers females of a darker hue to ones with lighter hues, and if the male is exposed to a model darker than any female found in nature it will prefer it to the darkest females of its species. The same sort of thing happens with our own species. Campbell thinks that the use of makeup in the human female creates super-normal sign stimuli for the human male. He explains ritualization, hieratic art, masks, gladiatorial vestments, kingly robes, and every other human improvement on nature as products of super-normal sign stimuli and man's predisposition to play into adulthood. With regard to religion and mythology, the gods themselves are super-normal sign stimuli.

Campbell distinguishes between literary metaphor, which is addressed to the intellect, and mythology, which is aimed primarily at the central excitatory mechanisms and innate releasing mechanisms of the whole person. A functioning mythology can be defined, he says, as a corpus of culturally maintained sign stimuli fostering the development and activation of a specific type, or constellation of types, of human life. Campbell doesn't distinguish between what is "culturally conditioned" and "instinctive" since, he says, all human behavior is culturally conditioned, and what is culturally conditioned in us is all instinct. He says that there are two kinds of innate releasing mechanisms: images which are stereotyped and those which are open. In some species the animal responds to very specific images—these are the stereotyped images—but according to Campbell there are none of these in our own species. Rather, in our species, the images are very general, or open; the specific images are determined by common experience. This is what he means when he says that human behavior is simultaneously "culturally conditioned" and "instinctive."

Campbell thinks that children may fear the witches in fairy tales because the witches correspond to some sign stimulus. He suggests that in the distant past cannibalism was not uncommon; he thinks there were older women who ate children, too. We just don't remember why the witches in these stories have strong effects on children. So if we come across something in fiction that appeals strongly to us, but we are unable to explain our reactions, there is probably some sign stimulus at work.

Some of the other authors I've cited have talked about art as well. Lippmann believed that art influences our stereotypes, the categories of thought through which we perceive and think about the world. The censors want to censor art because they understand this intuitively and don't want people to be influenced in what they regard as the wrong directions. I've talked in detail about how these categories are created.

John Boyd's theory of learning can apply to art as well as anything else. It seems to me that artists are also destroying and creating categories of ideas, only they work with fiction as well as with fact, and they portray fictional, not real, worlds, although even fictional worlds can convey important truths about the human experience. Because artists work with fiction they can make use of super-normal stimuli, whereas someone who sticks strictly with the facts is confined to using normal stimuli in his models of the world. So one possible way to differentiate artists from scientists is to say that artists use super-normal sign stimuli in creating models of the world while scientists use only normal stimuli.

Ross talked about how artists often rebel against authority and convention and are therefore frequently unsociable. He said that advocating "art for art's sake" was really an attempt by artists to avoid being constrained by any kind of moral obligation to the community. He said that art can shape behavior by means of subconscious suggestion: it can, for example, encourage high, if unrealistic, expectations in people, and people will nevertheless strive to emulate the models presented to them. A perfectly accurate rendering of the facts might not have the best effects on people. So there is an agreement between Ross and Campbell that art influences people through the medium of the subconscious mind. They also agree that fiction has a powerful influence on human conduct.

I also talked about Kay Jamison's work on the relationship between creativity and mental illness. An astonishing number of famous artists, novelists, poets, and composers displayed symptoms commonly associated with bipolar or unipolar depression. My position on creativity is that it works like Boyd said it did. Recall that according to Trotter, the herd suppresses original thoughts and behaviors and those who part with the herd in these respects experience psychological distress. Trotter's theory also presupposes that ideas and behaviors are transmitted by means of the subconscious mind. So I think we're getting close to having a comprehensive, coherent view of what art is about.

What if what we respond to in art is sign stimuli which are instinctive in their general forms, but in their specific forms they are culturally conditioned? Campbell explains the instinctive aspect of it well enough, but how are the culturally-conditioned aspects determined? I think crowd psychology is what is responsible for that part.

A Discourse on Winning and Losing

Boyd's (1987) name for his *magnum opus* is a *Discourse on Winning and Losing*. "Destruction and Creation" is one part out of the seven parts that make it up. That part is a monograph; then there are four briefings, which were in Boyd's lifetime delivered as such. There are two other parts in addition to these called "Conceptual Spiral" and "the Essence of Winning and Losing," but Boyd doesn't talk about these explicitly in the abstract. "Conceptual Spiral" is part of the introduction. "Patterns of Conflict" is a compendium of ideas and actions for winning in a competitive world. "Organic Design for Command and Control" contains Boyd's theory of management; it's how to get groups of people to cooperate and win in a fast-changing, imperfectly-understood environment. "The Strategic Game of ? and ?" is about the mental twists and turns that one may take in developing schemes to achieve one's purposes. "Destruction and Creation" is about how we evolve concepts for understanding and coping with our environment. "Revelation" is a brief summary of the work. "The Essence of Winning and Losing" is a dense summary of Boyd's OODA Loop concept. I say "dense" because his entire system is condensed into just six slides, or four if you don't include the ones for the front and back matter.

In "Conceptual Spiral," Boyd redefines science and technology in terms of his theory. Recall what he says in "Destruction and Creation" about the analysis and synthesis of ideas; this is what he's talking about below:

> **Science** can be viewed as a self-correcting process of observations, analyses/synthesis, hypothesis, and test

> whereas

> **Engineering** can be viewed as a self-correcting process of observations, analyses/synthesis, design, and test.

Boyd was both a scientist and an engineer, by the way. He developed the theory behind the F-15 and F-16 planes and he led the teams that created them. So he speaks from experience as well as from his reflections upon these matters.

Notice how there are four parts to each definition: observation, analysis/synthesis, hypothesis/design, and test. These form a cycle which is repeated over and over again in order to develop newer and better theories or designs. And the cycles for the two are very similar, the only difference being that in science you develop hypotheses and in engineering you develop designs. The same concept can be extended to other fields, like warfare for example, or any other competitive situation. The general form of this theory, independent of any particular endeavor, is called the OODA loop. The OODA in the OODA loop stands for Observe, Orient, Decide, Act. This is the cycle that must be repeated whenever you are developing new concepts, which you must continually do if you are to succeed in any competitive endeavor.

Boyd actually does not get into his OODA loop theory just yet, but I thought I should mention where he is heading. Most of "Conceptual Spiral" is about Boyd's fallibilist philosophy, though he doesn't call it that. Fallibilism is the doctrine that we can never have a perfect understanding of the world, although there is a truth about the world which can be approached, even if it can never be reached. Boyd argues in addition to this that our understanding of the world approximates less and less toward the truth unless we make active efforts to learn more about it and adapt to it. This is truer in war than almost anywhere else. Armies are always moving about, trying to outmaneuver one another, trying to deceive each other about their intentions and actions; the truth a short time ago may have been that the enemy was in front of you; the truth right now may be that they are on your flanks; the truth a short time from now may be that they have you surrounded. So I am thinking that military theorists are inclined more than theorists in other fields to view the world as dynamic and our understanding of that world as uncertain. In the natural sciences the laws of the universe are assumed to be static. A creative theorist might posit universes with different laws, but the background assumption is that natural laws are constant.

Boyd argues that in order to understand and adapt to a rapidly changing environment, it is necessary to get accurate, up-to-date information about it, and to constantly develop new concepts that correspond to it, and to constantly test and apply them. This cycle never ends, as the environment never stops changing, and if you stop, you'll be overwhelmed.

The next part is "Patterns of Conflict." Here he talks about the moral, mental, and physical levels of war, and he introduces the OODA loop.

Boyd says that a good fighter plane is able to pick and choose engagement opportunities, yet has fast transient characteristics that allow it to either force an overshoot by an attacker or else stay inside a hard-turning defender. He applies these specific air-to-air combat ideas to warfare generally. He says that in order to win, we should operate at a faster tempo or rhythm than our adversaries, or, better yet, get inside the adversary's observation-orientation-decision-action time cycle or loop (OODA loop). This will allow us to appear ambiguous and thereby generate confusion and disorder among our adversaries, since our adversaries will be unable to generate mental images or pictures that agree with the rapid, menacing patterns they are competing against.

Boyd says that we should exploit weapons and operations that generate a rapidly changing environment, and which inhibit an adversary's capacity to adapt to such an environment. Quick and accurate observations, orientation, and decisions help accomplish this. This could entail maintaining a fast tempo, engaging in fast transient maneuvers, and making quick kills. The adversary's ability to adapt is impaired by deliberate attempts to cloud or distort his observations, orientation, and decisions, and by impeding his actions.

So Boyd's key idea here is to compress the time which it takes for us to cycle through the OODA loop while expanding the time it takes the adversary to cycle through it. This gives us a decisive advantage in adapting to rapidly changing conditions.

Boyd talks about the different theories of war that have been developed over the years. The first one he talks about is Sun Tzu's theory, which the ancient general formulated in his famous treatise *the Art of War*. This work was apparently Boyd's favorite of the bunch. Sun Tzu's themes were harmony and trust, justice and well-being, inscrutability and enigma, deception and subversion, rapidity and fluidity, dispersion and concentration, surprise and shock. His strategy was to gather the best intelligence possible while impairing the enemy's ability to grasp the situation at hand; to attack the enemy's plans as the best policy, and to disrupt his alliances failing that, and to attack his army failing that, and to attack his cities only when all else fails; and to employ cheng and ch'i maneuvers to quickly and unexpectedly hurl strength against weaknesses. Sun Tzu's goals were to subdue the enemy without fighting and to avoid protracted war.

Boyd thinks that the commanders of antiquity acted more along these lines than modern commanders have. Modern strategists in the West are more concerned with winning battles and taking cities than with grand strategy, mobility, and deception. Boyd says that his discussion so far has not delved into moral factors like doubt, fear, and anxiety, but these are all important factors in war. The Mongols exploited them to great effect.

The Mongols had a number of advantages over their enemies: they were superior in terms of mobility, communications, intelligence, and leadership. They used widely separated strategic maneuvers, with appropriate stratagems, baited retreats, hard-hitting tactical thrusts, and swirling envelopments to uncover and exploit the vulnerabilities and weaknesses of their adversaries. At the same time they made clever and calculated use of propaganda, including terror, to play upon the adversary's doubts, fears, and superstitions so as to undermine his resolve and destroy his will to resist. Their aim was conquest as a basis to create, preserve, and expand the Mongol nation, and in this they were extraordinarily successful.

Boyd notes that the Mongols were able to outmaneuver and defeat enemies far more numerous than themselves without being defeated separately or in detail. He thinks they were able to do it by using the advantages mentioned above to get inside the decision cycles of their adversaries. The Mongols created impressions of terrifying strength by seeming to come out of nowhere and yet be everywhere.

Next Boyd talks about the eighteenth century theorists Saxe, Bourcet, Guibert, and Du Teil. These men emphasized plans with several branches, mobility of force, cohesion, dispersion and concentration, operating on a line to threaten alternative objectives, and concentrating direct artillery fire on key points.

Napoleon was influenced by these thinkers and applied their ideas early on in his career as a general. So ambiguity, deception, and rapid, easy movement enabled Napoleon to surprise and successively defeat fractions of superior forces. However, in later campaigns, as emperor, he relied increasingly on massed direct artillery fire, dense infantry columns, and heavy cavalry going against regions of strong resistance, at the cost, in time, of crippling casualties. The Spanish and Russian guerrillas acted in unexpected ways; they combined their knowledge of the terrain with mobility, and used it to disperse and concentrate their forces, allowing them to harass, confuse, and eventually defeat the French.

Boyd thinks that the ideas of these eighteenth century theorists, along with Sun Tzu's, are effective both in regular and guerrilla warfare.

Boyd talks about the advantages of France's revolutionary army. The revolution generated high morale in the new leaders and citizen-soldiers, and this was magnified by their successes against invading armies. Another advantage was the subdivision of the army into smaller self-contained but mutually supporting units— that is, divisions. The army had the ability to travel light and live off the countryside without extensive baggage, many supply wagons, and slow-moving resupply efforts. They marched rapidly because they moved at 120 steps a minute instead of the standard 70 steps a minute. They also stopped adhering to the 1791 Drill Regulations which forced the army into the well-regulated and stereotyped use of column and line formations for movement and fighting. These factors combined to make the French army far more mobile than their adversaries.

After this Boyd talks a bit more about the difference between Napoleon's early tactics and his late tactics. Boyd thinks Napoleon became predictable in the end, matching strength against strength with stereotyped tactics.

Next Boyd talks about Clausewitz's theory of war. Boyd says that Clausewitz overemphasized decisive battle and underemphasized strategic maneuver. Clausewitz also overemphasized method and routine at the tactical level. The likely result of the regulated stereotyped tactics and unimaginative battles of attrition he advocated is a bloodbath. Boyd criticizes Jomini's theory as well; he thinks that if Jomini's advice were followed it would lead to stereotyped operations unless the commanders grasped the subtleties of the theory.

Boyd says that the problem with Clausewitz and Jomini is that they didn't appreciate how effective loose, irregular tactical arrangements could be, nor did they appreciate the value of stealth and deception in disordering the enemy's operations. Boyd thinks that the major flaw in the approaches of Clausewitz, Jomini, and Napoleon was an emphasis on adaptability at the top and regularity at the bottom.

Next Boyd talks about the warfare of the nineteenth century, which emphasized mass formations and stereotyped tactics and so on even more than these strategists did. Mobility and deception were further deemphasized.

Boyd talks about the infiltration and guerrilla tactics that developed during World War I. Then he talks about the Blitzkrieg tactics that were used in World War II. So mobility and surprise were coming back into fashion after the old methods had proved futile.

"Patterns of Conflict" has more to say about the history of military thought, but just know that he favors increasing the initiative in subordinates because he thinks that makes them more adaptable to changing circumstances. He admires something the German military did: they allowed subordinate officers considerable initiative as to how to carry out orders, but the senior officers determined what they were to do; however, the orders remained fairly general so that there was room to adapt to changing circumstances. Boyd says that the Germans favored implicit over explicit communication. So they had a lot of common understandings which enabled them to coordinate their activities without having to talk to each other about them.

In "Organic Design for Command and Control," Boyd constructs a new command and control model. He argues against the prevailing model of concentrating decision-making at the top and relying as much as possible on technology to make decisions. He thinks that more attention should be paid to human beings and the way they can best make decisions.

Boyd talks about the importance of a group having similar mental patterns of the world because this is what allows them to coordinate their activities without explicit communication. These are the same mental patterns that he talks about in "Destruction and Creation." The part of the OODA loop this corresponds to is Orientation. With shared orientations the subordinates in a group can be allowed greater discretion about the means to the ends decided by the leaders. Without shared mental pictures of the world, the group can't act as an organic whole when confronting the external environment.

Boyd says that it's important not to allow a bureaucracy to hinder the group's ability to interact with the external world. Instead, arrange things that leaders and subordinates alike can interact continuously with the external world and with each other. This allows them to develop impressions of the outside world that are both commonly held and consistent with reality, which allows them to cooperate more effectively to achieve their goals.

A similar implicit orientation for commanders and subordinates alike allows them to diminish their friction and reduce time. This allows them to exploit variety and rapidity while maintaining harmony and initiative, which thereby enables them to get inside the adversary's OODA loops, which thereby magnifies the adversary's friction and stretches out his time; this denies the adversary the opportunity to cope with events as they unfold.

Orientation is, according to Boyd, the most important part of the OODA loop because it decides the ways we observe, decide, and act. Orientation is the repository of our genetic heritage, cultural tradition, and previous experiences. The OODA loop describes what is going on in the command and control process, so it might with reason be called the C&C loop. Operating inside of an adversary's OODA loop means operating inside his command and control loop.

Boyd prefers to have a system where the leaders lead more than they manage. They should give subordinates enough freedom to do their best work, and they should monitor them and show proper appreciation when they do well. I would imagine that some degree of coercion would still be necessary, though. He notes that given what he just said the title "Organic Design for Command and Control" might not be an appropriate title, and he suggests that "Appreciation and Leadership" makes a better one.

Boyd gives a concrete example in "the Strategic Game of ? and ?" of what he talks about in "Destruction and Creation":

Illustration

• Imagine that you are on a ski slope with other skiers—retain this image.

• Imagine that you are in Florida riding in an outboard motorboat—maybe even towing water-skiers retain this image.

• Imagine that you are riding a bicycle on a nice spring day—retain this image.

• Imagine that you are a parent taking your son to a department store and that you notice he is fascinated by the tractors or tanks with rubber caterpillar treads—retain this image.

Now imagine that you:

• Pull skis off ski slope; discard and forget rest of image.

• Pull outboard motor out of motorboat; discard and forget rest of image.

• Pull handlebars off bicycle; discard and forget rest of image.

• Pull rubber treads off toy tractors or tanks; discard and forget rest of image.

This leaves us with

Skis, outboard motor, handlebars, rubber treads

Pulling all this together

What do we have?

Snowmobile

Boyd says that it's important to remain open to a wide variety of ideas and experiences in order to obtain the raw material for this process. It's this method of generating new ideas that allows us to adapt to changing environments. If we close ourselves off from new ideas and experiences then we will have trouble adapting.

Boyd says that it's important to remain open to the environment in other respects as well; isolation, whether it be from ideas or allies, rarely bodes well for an organism. This being the case, in order to win in a competition with others, we should expand our interactions with the environment as much as possible while limiting the adversary's interactions with the environment as much as possible.

In war, there are three main areas where this principle applies—to physical, mental, and moral factors. The physical factors are those pertaining to the world of matter, energy, and information which we live in and feed upon. The mental factors are the emotional or intellectual activity we generate to adjust to or cope with the physical world. The moral factors are the cultural codes of conduct or standards of behavior that constrain, as well as sustain and focus, our emotional and intellectual responses.

Boyd talks about physical, mental, and moral isolation. Physical isolation occurs when we fail to gain support in the form of matter, energy, and information from others outside ourselves. Mental isolation occurs when we fail to discern, perceive, or make sense out of what's going on around us. Moral isolation occurs when we fail to abide by the ethical norms which others expect us to follow.

Then he talks about physical, mental, and moral interaction. Physical interaction occurs when we freely exchange matter, energy, and information with others outside ourselves. Mental interaction occurs when we generate images or impressions that match up with the events or happenings that unfold around ourselves. Moral interaction occurs when we live by the ethical norms that we profess and which others expect us to uphold.

Boyd talks next about how to isolate adversaries. They can be isolated physically by severing their communications with the outside world as well as by severing their communications with each other. They should be cut off from their allies and from the uncommitted through diplomatic, psychological, and other efforts. To cut them off from one another we should penetrate their system by being unpredictable, otherwise they can counter our efforts. The enemy can be isolated mentally by presenting them with ambiguous, deceptive, or novel situations, as well as by operating at a tempo or rhythm they can neither make out nor keep up with. Operating inside their OODA loops will accomplish this by disorienting or twisting their mental images so that they can neither appreciate nor cope with what is really going on. Adversaries isolate themselves morally when they visibly improve their well-being to the detriment of others. This is often done by violating ethical norms which they profess to uphold or which others expect them to uphold.

Then Boyd talks about how to interact more effectively with the environment. We can interact more effectively with the physical environment by opening up and maintaining many channels of communication with the outside world—with people we depend upon for sustenance or support. We can interact better mentally by learning from a variety of sources; this will allow us to generate mental images that match up with the world we are have to interact with. We can interact more effectively at the moral level by adhering to the ethical norms that others expect us to adhere to.

The last part of Boyd's treatise is "Revelation." There is only one slide, and it summarizes everything he has been saying:

Revelation

A loser is someone is someone—individual or group—who cannot build snowmobiles when facing uncertainty and unpredictable change;

Whereas,

A winner is someone—individual or group—who can build snowmobiles, and employ them in an appropriate fashion, when facing uncertainty and unpredictable change.

Bibliography

Bernays, E.L. (1923). *Crystallizing Public Opinion*. New York: Liveright Publishing Corporation.

Bernays, E.L. (1928) *Propaganda*. New York: H. Liveright.

Bion, W. R. (1961). *Experiences in Groups*. London: Tavistock.

Le Bon, G. (1896). *The Crowd, a Study of the Popular Mind*. London: Macmillan and Co. (Original work published in 1895)

Boyd, J.R. (1987) *A Discourse on Winning and Losing*.

Burnham, J. (1941) *The Managerial Revolution: What is Happening in the World*. New York: John Day Co.

Campbell, J. (2008) *The Hero with a Thousand Faces*. Novato: New World Library. Original work published in 1949.

Campbell, J. (1991) *The Masks of God, Vol. 1: Primitive Mythology*. New York: Penguin Books. Originally published in 1959.

Conway, W.H. (1915). *The Crowd in Peace and War*. London: Longmans, Green and Company.

Coram, R. (2002). *Boyd: The Fighter Pilot Who Changed the Art of War*. New York: Little, Brown and Company.

Dawkins, R. (1976). *The Selfish Gene*. New York City: Oxford University Press

Lippmann, W. (1922). *Public Opinion*. New York, Harcourt, Brace and Company

Lopreato, J., & Crippen, T.A. (2001). *Crisis in Sociology: The Need for Darwin*. New Brunswick: Transaction Publishers.

Plato, & Jowett, B. (1908). *The Republic of Plato*. Oxford: the Clarendon Press.

Hill, K. 'Sexism' Public-Shaming Via Twitter Leads To Two People Getting Fired (Including The Shamer) (2013, March 21), *Forbes*. Retrieved from www.forbes.com.

Hull, C.L. (1943). *Principles of Behavior, an Introduction to Behavior Theory*. New York, London: D. Appleton-Century, Incorporated.

James, W. (1890). *The Principles of Psychology*. New York: Henry Holt and Company.

Jamison, K.R. (1999). *Night Falls Fast: Understanding Suicide*. New York: Knopf.

Jamison, K.R. (1993): *Touched with Fire: Manic-Depressive Illness and the Artistic Temperament*. New York: The Free Press.

Jevons, W.S. (1871). *The Theory of Political Economy*. London: Macmillan and Co.

Kuhn, T.S. (1996). *The Structure of Scientific Revolutions* (3rd ed.). University of Chicago Press. (Original work published in 1962)

Mackay, C. (1852). *Memoirs of Extraordinary Popular Delusions and the Madness of Crowds*. London: Office of the National Illustrated Library (Original work published in 1841)

Mallock, W. H. (1918). *The Limits of Pure Democracy*. London: Chapman and Hall.

Martin, E.D. (1920). *The Behavior of Crowds; a Psychological Study*. New York and London: Harper & Brothers.

Maslow, A.H. (1943). "A Theory of Human Motivation." Psychological Review, 50(4), 370–96.

Menger, C. (2011). *Principles of Economics*. Auburn: the Ludwig von Mises Institute. (Original work published in 1871)

Michels, R. (1915). *Political Parties: a Sociological Study of the Oligarchical Tendencies of Modern Democracy*. New York: Hearst's International Library Co. (Original work published in 1911)

Mosca, G. (1939) *The Ruling Class* [*Elementi Di Scienza Politica*]. New York: McGraw-Hill Book. (Original work published in 1896)

Pareto, V. (1935). *The Mind and Society* [*Trattato Di Sociologia Generale*]. New York: Harcourt, Brace, and Company. (Original work published in 1916)

Pareto, V. (1991). *The Rise and Fall of Elites: An Application of Theoretical Sociology*. New Brunswick: Transaction Publishers. (Original work published in 1901)

Ross, E. (1901). *Social Control: A Survey of the Foundations of Order*. New York, The Macmillan Company; London, Macmillan & Co., ltd.

Sidis, B. (1898). *The Psychology of Suggestion: a Research into the Subconscious Nature of Man and Society*. New York: D. Appleton and Company.

Smiles, S. (1859). *Self-Help; with Illustrations of Character and Conduct*. London: S. W. Partridge & co.

Smolin, L. (2006). *The Trouble with Physics*. Boston: Houghton Mifflin.

Surowiecki, J. (2004) *The Wisdom of Crowds: Why the Many Are Smarter Than the Few and How Collective Wisdom Shapes Business, Economies, Societies and Nation*. New York: Little, Brown.

Tarde, G. (1903). *The Laws of Imitation*. New York: Henry Holt and Company. (Original work published in 1890)

Trivers, R. L. (1971). "The Evolution of Reciprocal Altruism". *The Quarterly Review of Biology* **46** (1): 35–57

Trotter, W. (1919). *Instincts of the Herd in Peace and War.* London: T. F. Unwin. Originally published in 1916.

Von Uexküll, J. (2010). *A Foray into the Worlds of Animals and Humans: With A Theory of Meaning.* Minneapolis: University of Minnesota.

Vogler, C. (2007) *The Writers Journey: Mythic Structure for Writers, 3rd Edition.* Studio City: Michael Wiese Productions. Original work published in 1992.

Whyte, W.H. (1957). *The Organization Man.* New York: Doubleday Anchor Books

Wilson, D.S., and Wilson, E.O. (2007). Rethinking the Theoretical Foundation of Sociobiology. *Quarterly Review of Biology, 82*(4), *327-348*

Wilson, E.O. (1998). *Consilience: the Unity of Knowledge.* New York: Knopf.

Made in the USA
San Bernardino, CA
19 June 2020